Pressures and Protests

The Kennedy Farm Program

and the Wheat Referendum of 1963

Chandler Publications in

POLITICAL SCIENCE

Victor Jones, Editor

Pressures and Protests

The Kennedy Farm Program and the Wheat Referendum of 1963

A Case Study by

DON F. HADWIGER & ROSS B. TALBOT

Iowa State University: *Ames, Iowa*

Chandler Publishing Company / San Francisco 94105
124 Spear Street

Library of Congress Catalog Card No. 64-8160

Printed in the United States of America

To Edith and Claude Hadwiger

Contents

Illustrations and Documents

Preface: THE CASE-STUDY APPROACH

Pressures and Protests is a case study of the Kennedy farm program during the nearly three years that John F. Kennedy was President of the United States. Our original intentions were to place the Food and Agricultural Act of 1962 as the center of discussion and use earlier and later legislative actions as foreground and follow up to that act. The tragic assassination of President Kennedy placed all his legislative proposals and actions in the highlight of his time in office.

As now written, *Pressures and Protests* should enable the reader to understand how the 1961 Emergency Feed Grains program, the Agriculture Act of 1961, the Food and Agriculture Act of 1962, and the extension of the Emergency Feed Grains program in 1963 came to be laws of the land. Also, we shall describe the campaign which preceded the 1963 wheat referendum, offer an explanation for the defeat of the Administration's proposal in that referendum, and give a synopsis of the passage of the voluntary farm bill of 1964.

Case studies of legislative process are hardly novel. The method has been used considerably in recent years because the modern fashion in political science is that of realism. Political scientists, quite generally, are of the opinion that students need to be brought face-to-face with the real world of politics. They need to see the instruments of political power—pressures and protests—in action.

Controversy exists, however, as to whether the emphasis should be on the historical study of ideas and institutions, or on the ongoing process of decisionmaking. We think the case method can reconcile these opposing views. Traditionalists and behavioralists can both be accommodated within the framework of the method and we hope that our study may be at least a slight contribution toward such rapprochement.

The farmer presents us with a political success story which is worthy of serious study. What does this story offer to the student and other readers?

First, we hope it gives him pleasure. We set out to write a story which would be lively and instructive for the reader who relishes the zest and inspiration of American politics.

Second, the study should bring new insights into our understanding of human behavior. Harold Lasswell's proposition has been considered throughout, and the reader hopefully will gain new insights into who wanted what farm policies; why certain individuals desired such policies; and how they went about seeking their particular objectives.

Third, the reader might logically move from knowledge to reflection. The good life is the life of contemplation, or so Aristotle contends in his *Ethics*. We have intended to leave the selection of values to the reader, but perhaps our value judgments slip out on occasion. If so, we offer no special apology. Politics is the study of power, but the ultimate question is still: power for what? The operative ideals which constitute the core of the American creed are more important than a recounting of how men behaved in certain political situations. At different points in the study, we have compared the ideal with the action. For the most part, however, the reader is asked to climb to a peak on his own Mount Olympus and to sit there and contemplate whether what did happen was what he believed ought to have happened.

Fourth, we are of the belief that the Greek concept of the active and involved citizen, ruling and being ruled, is still the goal for the American citizen. The concept is admittedly more difficult for a citizen living in a mass society, but the ideal remains the same. Our study is not of the "how to do it" variety, but throughout our intention has been to relate "what happened." If our intention has been achieved then the reader might desire to move from reflection to involvement in the great game of politics. If so, we honor him with the proud title of "Mr. Citizen."

Finally, it is our position that case studies cannot be replicated. The structure and dynamics of power which came forth in these legislative struggles will never recur in quite the same way again. Yet, much is learned from the study of contemporary politics. And the gradual development of the case study approach may prove that replication, at least of method, is quite possible.

Our first task, however, is to look backwards. The first chapter is based upon the simple and basic assumption that the past is prologue. Political science without history, said Sir John Seeley, has no roots. To uncover the manifold roots of American farm policy would carry this study too far afield; still we feel we must first refer to the main threads from the past if only to make clear that farm policy under President Kennedy is but one recent chapter of an old, fascinating story.

DON HADWIGER
ROSS TALBOT

Iowa State University
Ames, Iowa
June, 1964

Acknowledgments

INFORMATION for this case study was gathered in interviews—more than 200 in all—with legislators, Kennedy (and later Johnson) administration officials, farm leaders, and others who were farm-policy participants. These interviews, as well as surveys of voters and other participants in the 1963 wheat referendum, were made possible by a grant from the Edgar Stern Family Foundation. One of the authors (Don Hadwiger) was able to gain firsthand experience in agricultural politics in 1959, by virtue of an American Political Science Association Congressional Fellowship which enabled him to serve as a temporary staff member for the Committee on Agriculture of the U.S. House of Representatives, and for then-Senator John F. Kennedy.

We also relied on accounts in *Wayne Darrow's Farmletter*, *Kiplinger Agricultural Letter*, the *Wall Street Journal*, the *New York Times*, the *Washington Post*, the *Des Moines Register*, in farm-organization publications, and in general and specialized farm periodicals.

Several leading participants in farm policy read the manuscript and noted errors of fact and interpretation. These included John A. Baker, Assistant Secretary of Agriculture; W. E. Hamilton, Director of Research for the American Farm Bureau Federation; Edwin A. Jaenke, Associate Administrator of the Agricultural Stabilization and Conservation Service, U.S. Department of Agriculture; Reuben Johnson, Acting Director of the Washington office of the National Farmers Union; Willard H. Lamphere, Associate Director of Information, Agricultural Stabilization and Conservation Service, USDA; Hyde H. Murray, Minority Clerk of the Committee on Agriculture, House of Representatives; John A. Schnittker, Director of Agricultural Economics, USDA; and

Jane Taylor of the National Association of Wheat Growers. Errors of fact were discovered and corrected by Dr. Gladys L. Baker, Vivian Wiser, and Jane M. Porter of the Agricultural History Branch, Economics Research Service, USDA.

To all these busy but generous persons, to our interviewees and farmer respondents, to Mrs. Helen Hill Miller, and to the Stern Family Foundation, we wish to express our deep appreciation. We are grateful to our typist, Mrs. Edna Henry, for her fine work.

Far from having relieved us of responsibility for errors, however, our manuscript readers have reminded us that the reality was more complex than a contained version of it can easily accommodate. In time, no doubt, other accounts of what happened will complement and also challenge ours.

Published material from numerous sources has been made available by copyright holders and reproduced with their kind and cordial permission: The American Farm Bureau Federation and *AFBF Newsletter*, cartoons in Illustrations 11, 27, 28, and 34, and other materials. The *Chicago Tribune*, a cartoon in Illustration 34. The *Congressional Quarterly*, Illustration 25. The *Denver Post*, cartoons in Illustrations 23 and 26. The Farmers Union and the *Farmers Union Herald*, cartoons in Illustrations 4, 10, 31, 34, and other materials. The Kansas Farm Bureau and *KFB Newsletter*, a cartoon in Illustration 34. The National Grange, Illustration 30. The *North Dakota Union Farmer*, Illustration 35. The *Omaha World Herald*, a cartoon in Illustration 23. The *St. Louis Post-Dispatch*, cartoons by Mauldin in Illustrations 4 and 12. The *Tuscola County Advertiser*, Illustration 32. The United States Department of Agriculture and individual members of its staff—some of whom preferred not to be identified—furnished valuable documentary information and statistics.

Don Hadwiger, who had major responsibility for this volume, wishes to express his appreciation for the guidance of Edith and Claude Hadwiger, who with the sole assistance of "Grandpa Bill" still produce enough wheat annually on their Northwest Oklahoma farm to fill the bread and other flour needs of more than 3,000 Americans. To them, his parents, this book is dedicated.

Pressures and Protests

The Kennedy Farm Program

and the Wheat Referendum of 1963

Abbreviations

ASCS	Agricultural Stabilization and Conservation Service
CEA	Council of Economic Advisers
ORRRC	Outdoor Recreation Resources Review Commission
REA	Rural Electrification Administration
USDA	United States Department of Agriculture

All of the above are departments or agencies of the United States Government.

AFBF	American Farm Bureau Federation
GTA	Grain Terminal Association
MFA	Missouri Farmers Association
NAWG	National Association of Wheat Growers
NFO	National Farmers Organization
NFU	National Farmers Union
CED	Committee for Economic Development

1. *Where Did the Kennedy Farm Program Come From?*

On May 21, 1963, the wheat farmers of America (some who had grown no wheat the preceding year, and some who had grown very little, and thousands who had grown thousands of bushels) went to polling booths and rejected the latest government program of production controls and guaranteed prices.

Farm organizations and officials in favor of the program said growers would receive $2 a bushel for their wheat, if they accepted the program, whereas the price might fall to only $1 a bushel without it.

The Farm Bureau, and some congressmen, said that not only was the projection of $2 wheat nonsense, but that if the farmers rejected the program the government would provide a better one. Wheat farmers could not be, and would not be, left to the poverty of $1 wheat.

So the farmers drove to the polls. As they left their farms to go to the booths some of them knew that storage bins, ships, sheds, and granaries were already stuffed with millions of bushels of surplus wheat—and other grains. Some of them realized that the cost of storage to the taxpayers was $1 billion a year. And a few, perhaps, wondered how less than 8 percent of the population could be involved in a way of life costing the government $6 billion a year in round figures. Agriculture was the third largest item in the federal budget, exceeded only by the interest on the debt, and the Department of Defense.

They knew, many of them, that the votes they were casting concerned one phase of a new comprehensive program to help the farm families of the land—a program involving rural renewal, recreation areas, industrial development. The New Frontier did not want the old method of legislating commodity-by-commodity. The new group of young men in office wanted to think in terms of rural America *and* urban America. The new program might not be visionary, but it was still to be experienced on any widespread scale.

Meantime wheat farmers wanted no part of the one phase on which they were entitled to vote. And opponents of the measure were right. A new bill was passed. The pressures and protests of three years resolved themselves in compromise.

Sources in the Past

Where did the Kennedy farm program come from? Some opponents of Kennedy administration farm measures said its proposals originated in the long-gone, desperate, depression years and therefore did not fit the relatively prosperous present. In truth, ideas such as were proposed to deal with the farm problem in 1961 and 1962 could be traced even to the Old Testament, could be found in the voluminous writings of 19th-century American reformers, and in the literature and the laws of other countries. The roots of policy are certainly long and tangled; and we cannot take for granted that the present generation of policymakers always knows and appreciates what an earlier generation did and thought, or what another country has experienced.

Still, if we are to give due credit to the men involved, and if we are to understand what happened after 1960, we must review the great farm depression of the 1920's and 1930's. Beginning with an implement company executive named George Peek, we must refer to a string of vigorous men who were intrigued by the problems of agriculture, found a partial answer, and peddled it in Washington. Invariably these men were regarded as crackpots—though they were often first-rate farm economists—and they never became quite respectable. They were persistent and articulate, however, and their ideas often became law.

Seeking to remedy low farm prices in the 1920's, Peek tramped in and out of Washington offices pushing his two-price plan which became the basis for the famous McNary-Haugen bill, twice passed by the congressional farm bloc with the help of the new American Farm Bureau Federation. But supporters of this bill learned, because they could not override President Coolidge's vetoes, that they must also have access to the executive branch of the government to achieve their aims. Peek, Farm Bureau officials, and other agricultural leaders sparked an effort in 1928 to get rural votes for Alfred E. Smith, and Smith received surprising farmer support. But he lost to Herbert Hoover, who was reluctant to involve government deeply in the problems of agriculture, even after the economic collapse of 1929.

In the 1932 presidential election year the national depression was three years old, and the farm depression was twelve years old. Dakota farmers were killing their cattle for lack of feed or markets, while Iowa farmers rioted, and thousands of bankrupted farmers all over the country—some called Okies, and some called Arkies and some called by no name—loaded their old cars and headed for the dismal migrant camps of California. Hard times were everywhere and smothering clouds out of the dust bowl were indicative of a massive drought.

Peek knew this was the year to be selling a farm program, and so did M. L. Wilson, a Montana professor who was in Washington to urge congressional action on the voluntary domestic allotment plan. Like other leading idea men, Wilson got an appointment to see the front-running Democratic candidate, New York Governor Franklin D. Roosevelt.

A summary of Wilson's interview with Roosevelt is instructive as to how policy is initiated, and because it reveals that, in a sense, all the main proposals for dealing with the 1962 farm program were already crudely formulated in 1932. Here is the substance of what took place in a half-hour interview in the summer of 1932, in the anteroom of the New York Governor's office:

ROOSEVELT: What's wrong with the McNary-Haugen bill?
WILSON: It would increase production.
ROOSEVELT: That's right. What's your plan?
WILSON: Governor, I would lay a tax on processors—make processors pay a tax on each bushel of wheat they use, which would go to the farmer who produced that wheat. But farmers would be required to leave some of their cropland idle. To do this, we would have to educate the farmers and get their approval. Otherwise, like prohibition, such a farm program just wouldn't work. My plan has three advantages: (1) It would raise farm income without increasing production. (2) It would be administered by farmers, and therefore there would be no government bureaucracy. (3) It wouldn't cost the federal government any money.
ROOSEVELT: How did this plan go in the Congress?
WILSON: The Democrats wouldn't buy it, but I did get Congressmen Clifford Hope of Kansas and Senator Peter Norbeck to introduce it late in the 1932 session.
ROOSEVELT: What would you do about submarginal land?
WILSON: Get some land and retire it.
ROOSEVELT: Is there anything else?
WILSON: Yes. Governor, I was attracted by your speech to the Conference of Governors, in which you talked of attracting industry to rural areas.
ROOSEVELT: Do you think we can get support for this proposition?
WILSON: Yes.

As he wheeled out of the room, Roosevelt told his aides—Raymond Moley and Rexford Tugwell—to keep in touch with Wilson, because Roosevelt's first campaign speech, if he were nominated, would likely be on agriculture.

The processing tax, which was made law in 1933 and struck down by the Supreme Court in 1936, is in principle like the Kennedy administration's *Wheat Certificate Plan.* The acreage retirement scheme suggests the *Cropland Retirement Plan* which the Farm Bureau put forward in 1961 as the alternative to the Kennedy farm program. Roosevelt's proposal to bring industry to rural areas was a precursor of the Rural Areas Development program which was begun under Secretary of Agriculture Ezra Benson in the 1950's and was an integral part of the comprehensive farm program that President Kennedy sent to Congress in 1962.

Yet to compare the hasty depression laws with recent program proposals might be somewhat like comparing Wilbur Wright's first airplane with today's aircraft. Though some said in 1962 that we had yet to find a farm program that would work, new tools had by then been fashioned with which to analyze the agricultural economy and its political environment, both of which were much more complex than was once assumed.

The Farm Economists' Contribution

To a considerable extent new understanding had been brought about by individuals and groups within the profession of farm economics, a discipline derived from the field of general economics by the land-grant-college system. Many farm economists devoted themselves originally to the more pedestrian microeconomics (study of a single relationship or unit of production) rather than to the study of economic systems. By fixing on ways to improve farm management, for example, farm economists contributed much to the efficiency of American agriculture.

At the same time they developed a flair for quantitative analysis. Partly at the urging of farm economists, the rural-oriented Congress favored them with an abundance of data-gathering services, which these scholars put to use to construct imaginative models of the farm economy. Farm economics produced not only first-rate technicians but excellent theorists as well.

But the emphasis on theory brought criticism: some of the best scholars had not bothered to mesh their theories with political reality, with the result that the economists' airy propositions exasperated the policymakers who occasionally were obliged to listen to them. Farm economists and politicians often revealed a lack of respect for one another, as illustrated by a congressional farm leader's refusal to add a farm economist to his staff. "They lie too much," he said. "I prefer a lawyer any time."

Some economists, on the other hand, have felt it would be futile to strive for workable programs which Congress could accept. Professor Theodore Schultz said Congress was not much swayed by economic considerations.

> Congress now legislates on farm policy as it enacted tariffs prior to the reciprocal trade agreement approach. We need to remind ourselves that the passage of the lamentable Smoot-Hawley tariffs was in no way deterred or tempered by the mass protest of economists. Economic considerations are not given a high priority in such political logrolling.[1]

Even the farm organizations formerly paid little attention to the advice of professional economists.

Although most prominent economists (even in 1962) passed up such opportunities as existed to be active in the process of making government policy, a breed of economists did emerge which wanted not only to understand the problems, but to find acceptable solutions and sell them.[2]

Men so dedicated found places in the Roosevelt Administration, where they built career staffs of men like themselves, and through these agents they accumulated a body of data which became a precious aid to rationality. Although their most ambitious agency, the Bureau of Agricultural Economics, was reorganized by hostile Congressmen in the mid-1940's, some economists meanwhile were moving into congressional offices, and into the congressional re-

[1] T. W. Schultz, "Omission of Variables, Weak Aggregates and Fragmentation in Policy and Adjustment Studies," *Problems and Policies in American Agriculture.* (Ames: Iowa State University Press, 1959.)

[2] The creed of this minority was restated by Secretary Freeman in a speech to the American Political Science Association in 1962: "Leaders and experts must do more than find solutions. They must sell those solutions to the people of the United States. Perhaps the job of building public understanding of the problems at hand and the choices we face in solving them will be even more difficult than it will be to arrive at the solutions themselves . . . I would urge that, in the words of Jefferson, you seek 'not merely to say things that have never been said before; but to place before mankind the common sense of the subject in terms so plain and firm as to command their assent.' "

search arm—the Legislative Reference Service—and into staff positions within the farm organizations. In addition, university and interuniversity teams studied public policy for agriculture, and state extension education services introduced local farm leaders to relevant new economic data.

The weight of economics in political decisionmaking was affirmed in 1960 and 1961, when four different economist teams undertook to predict what would happen if government ceased to support prices and control production of certain commodities.[3] After all four teams had concluded that a return to the free market would cause prices to fall drastically, politicians ceased to advocate an immediate return to free prices, even though the theme was still popular with some constituents.

Framers of the Kennedy farm program also relied on such sophisticated projections, and congressional committees ordinarily consulted economists before they made major changes in the bills. By the 1960's, solid economic data and new economic techniques had become a part of the process of making decisions on farm policy.

A New Crisis in the 1950's

In the 1950's, however, economic realities were obscured. Agriculture was in a crisis, but without dust clouds and mortgage foreclosures to dramatize it.

The statistics were dramatic enough. The converging trends of the catapulting technological revolution had signaled an explo-

[3] Geoffrey Shepherd *et al.*, *Production, Prices and Income Estimates and Projections for the Feed-Livestock Economy*, Iowa Agricultural Experiment Station Special Report 27, Ames, Iowa, August 1960; U.S. Department of Agriculture, *Projections of Production and Prices of Farm Products for 1960–1965, According to Specified Assumptions*, in U.S. Senate Document 77, 86th Congress, 2d Session; and "Possible Effects of Eliminating Direct Price Support and Acreage Control Programs," *Farm Economics* No. 218 (October 1960) pp. 5813–5820; and *Economic Policies for Agriculture in the 1960's*, prepared for the Joint Economic Committee, 86th Congress, 2d Session.

sion in agricultural productivity. Yet, even some economists seemed to underestimate its impact.

The French political scientist Raymond Aron has said there are two kinds of history: technological history and traditional history. Technological history is the pacesetter which is often overlooked: the steam engine, the cotton gin, the farm-to-market road, and the cotton picker have all conditioned our lives in ways which the traditional history of political affairs has tardily acknowledged.

In the 1950's—traditional history would report—there was a mess in agriculture for which the Democratic Congress blamed Secretary Benson and for which Secretary Benson blamed the Congress and past administrations. But neither the Congress nor Secretary Benson (though he spoke in favor of radical changes in farm legislation) were prepared to propose a change in government policy severe enough to meet this new challenge of abundance.

To illustrate the magnitude of the myriad improvements in all processes of agriculture: an Iowa acre grew half again as much corn in 1960 as it did in 1950. A Great Plains acre grew twice as much wheat in the 1950's as it did in the 1920's. Between 1950 and 1960, 33,000 cotton-picking machines replaced one million men. One farmer could produce in 1960 almost three times as much as he could 25 years earlier. In 1962 the average farmer fed about 28 people. Even the milk cow managed to boost her average output by one-third during the 1950's.

Suddenly the means were at hand, technically, to feed more than twice the existing population of the world, using only the world's existing cultivated land, and to do it with a very small percentage of the world labor force. These techniques—applied in the United States—had produced an abundance of food and fiber. This was our farm problem. (See Illustration 1.)

In a way this abundance was a unique blessing, since many in the United States and in the world did not have adequate diets. Policymakers pooled their imaginative schemes to use our extra food.

Yet, there did seem a limit to what the most humanitarian

administrators could give away through school lunches, food packages, missionaries, and foreign governments without disrupting normal food markets and having other disturbing results. It was true that our population was increasing as well as our national income, but by no means fast enough to use the increased farm production. Diets improved qualitatively as meat consumption soared, but per capita consumption declined from World War II levels.

Desperately, a search was made for industrial uses for farm products. Wheat, for example, had always been used to make glue and could also be converted into very expensive auto fuel, but it became clear that industrial uses would absorb a relatively small portion of the total farm production. Surpluses accumulated rapidly in the 1950's, after the Korean War had provided a temporary respite. Since the American people were reluctant to destroy these surpluses, they had to be stored—in huge refrigerated caves, in spectacular mile-long granaries built on the flat plains, in old Liberty ships wallowing in our harbors, and in bins and granaries everywhere in rural America.

Some farm spokesmen painted a bright future, saying that ways would be found to use the surpluses: they might be needed (though perhaps inaccessible) in the event of nuclear war. These surpluses, some said, were monuments to free enterprise. At first they were monuments also to the farmer's political power, but as storage got to be very big business, the builders and operators of storage facilities—big private firms, crossroads grain dealers, and even farmer cooperatives—seemed to be as influential as the farmers. The huge annual storage subsidy had created a political interest, though it masqueraded behind such slogans as "protect the family farm," "freedom for farmers," and "keep the Secretary of Agriculture from becoming a dictator."

Economists agreed there was excess production caused by too many resources in agriculture. Few suggested curtailment of the governmental research and education programs which had spurred the technological revolution, but economists did argue as to which

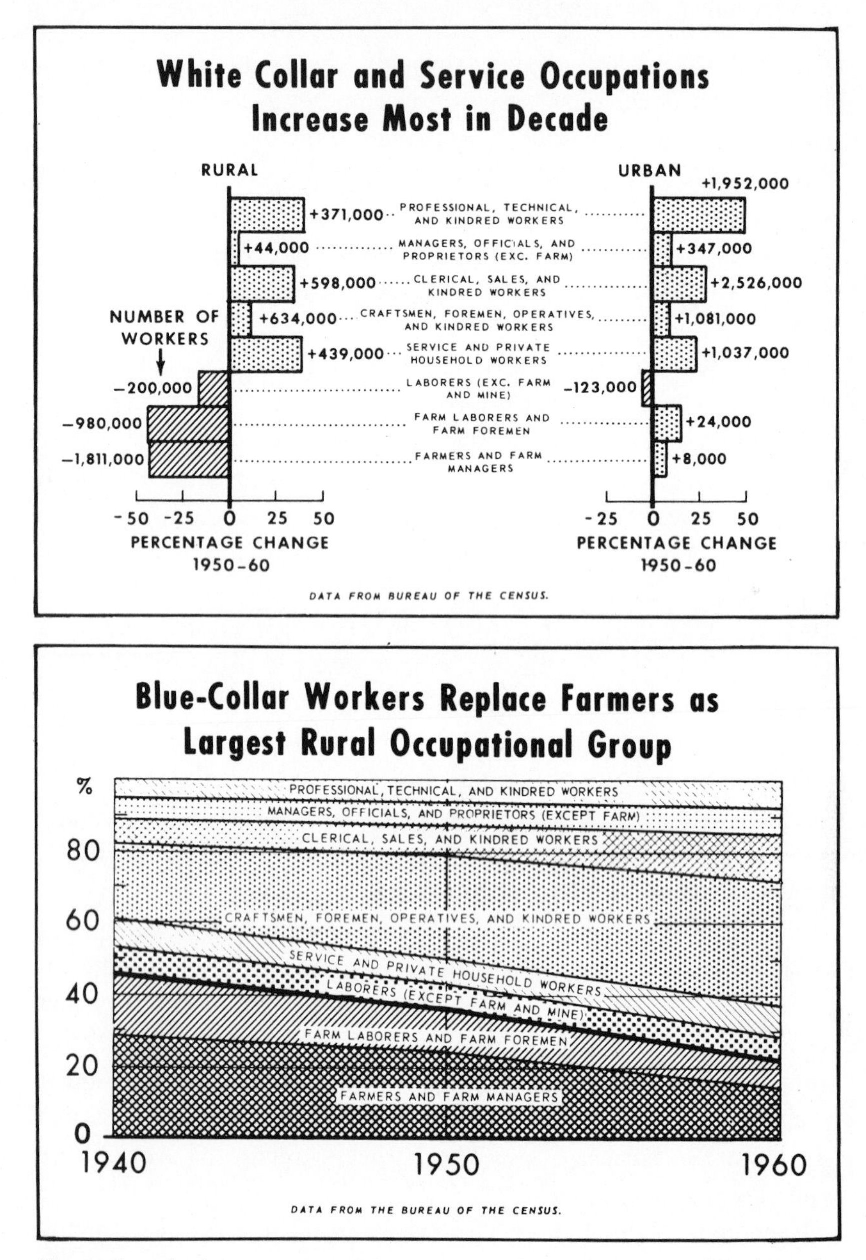

Illustration 1. AGRICULTURE'S TECHNOLOGICAL REVOLUTION. Although the average American citizen cannot remember the time we didn't have a farm problem, few citizens realized how enormously complicated the problem became in the short space of 10 years, the years from 1950 to 1960.

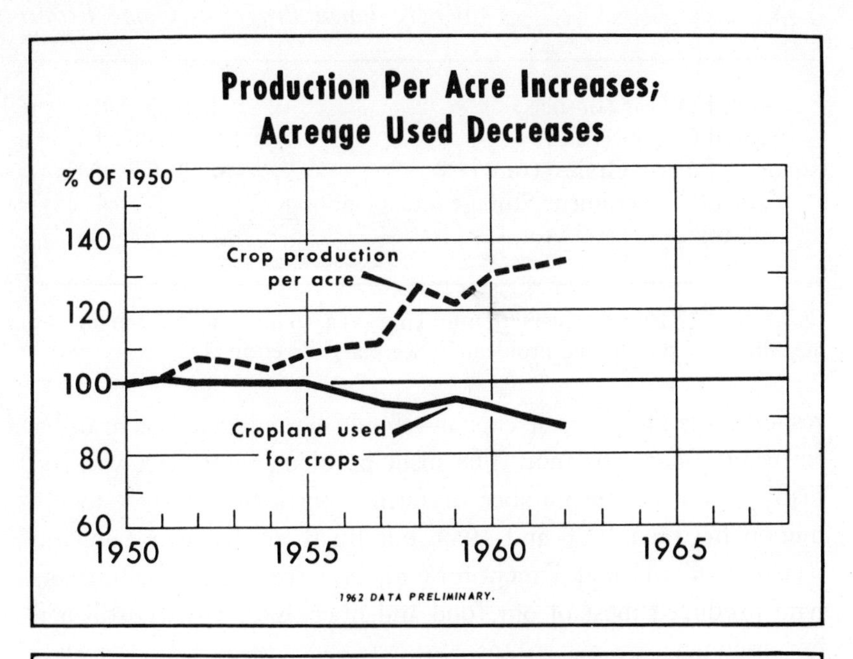

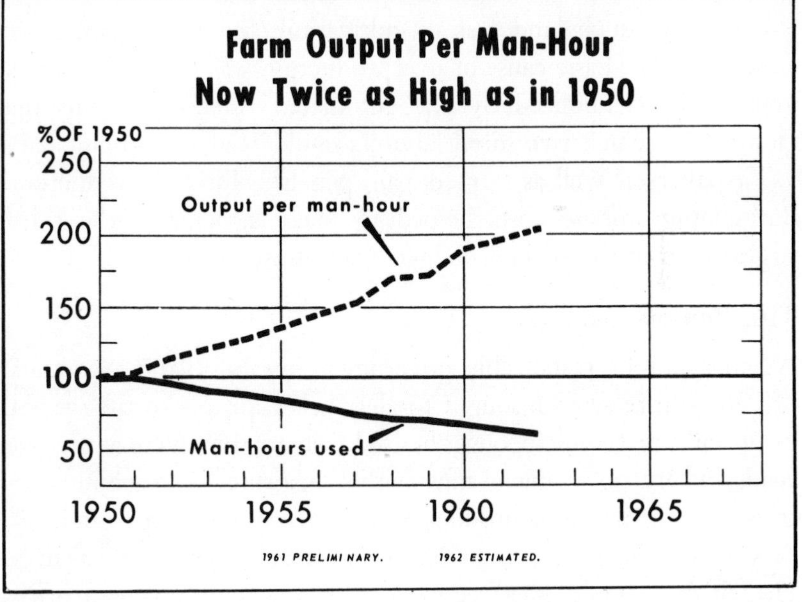

As these four charts show, a dramatically reduced number of farmers produced a fantastically increased amount of crops. (Source: *Agricultural Yearbook* 1963, USDA)

Stored Wheat (bushels)	1,500,000,000
Stored Cotton (bales)	7,500,000
Stored Feed Grains (tons)	84,000,000
Cost of Government Storage and Handling, for 1961 fiscal year	$1,000,000,000

Illustration 2. STORAGE COSTS TO THE TAXPAYER. "How can we convey the magnitude of the storage problem?"–Secretary Freeman, 1961.

resource—land, labor, or capital—should be reduced first in order to bring about a balance. The main problem, some said, was too many farmers. The number of farms decreased from 5.4 to 3.7 million between 1950 and 1960, but by then less than 2 million were actually needed. Except for a top layer of commercial farmers who produced most of our food and fiber, most farmers still had low incomes.

Also, too much land was in cultivation. But some economists argued that the basic cause of overproduction was too much capital investment, symbolized by the automated three-story "chicken factory" in which two hired laborers could feed 10,000 chickens.

Taxpayers as well as farmers paid penalties for overproduction. Burgeoning storage costs helped to make agriculture the third largest item in the federal budget. (See Illustration 2.)

THE BENSON PROGRAM

As an agent of responsible government in the 1950's, Secretary of Agriculture Benson sought to alert urban people to the scandal in agriculture. Simultaneously he told farmers they were at a crossroads, where government must either institute far-reaching controls over agricultural production or government must gradually cease to support farm prices. Benson preferred the latter alternative. He felt that—under the free market—as oversupply caused prices to fall, less land, labor, and capital would go into agriculture. As a result, production and consumption would come into balance.

Although the Democratic Congresses after 1954 were hostile

to Benson's scheme, he did get some changes that were in the direction he wanted to go. But he fell short in his predictions as to future yields, and surpluses piled up faster. It began to look as if the Eisenhower administration had underestimated the problem. For production to be balanced prices would have to fall lower than Secretary Benson had anticipated—perhaps lower than most farmers would find tolerable.

Congressional Democrats did not feel obliged to present an alternative to meet the challenge of technology. As the opposition party seeking victory in future elections, they passed high-price-support bills which President Eisenhower vetoed and they made the most of Secretary Benson's embarrassing failure to control surpluses or to maintain farm income. Campaigning against the unpopular Benson program in the 1954, 1956, and 1958 elections, farm-state Democrats won many congressional seats, state governorships, and control of some ordinarily Republican legislatures.

Yet a search went on for a workable alternative to Secretary Benson's program—in the National Democratic Advisory Committee, in the offices of Democratic congressional farm leaders, in the sympathetic National Farmers Union, and among farm economists. Besides being workable, such a program would have to be acceptable to groups within the Democratic Party, to the next Democratic presidential candidate, to the Congress, and ultimately even to farmers.

2. *Senator Kennedy — Candidate Kennedy*

As SENATOR from Massachusetts during most of the 1950's, John F. Kennedy had little reason to be interested in agriculture. Like many other urban-based Northeastern legislators, he at first supported Secretary Benson, explaining later that he felt Bensen deserved a chance to try his programs. But at the 1956 Democratic convention, Kennedy learned, while barely missing the vice presidential nomination, that Midwestern delegates were cool toward him because of his pro-Benson farm votes.

On subsequent farm issues Kennedy tended to be guided by the vote pattern of Midwestern Democratic Senator Hubert Humphrey, as both he and Humphrey became serious presidential hopefuls.

After 1958, Kennedy constantly received advice on agriculture from economists, farm congressmen, and farm-group lobbyists who hoped Kennedy would go on record in his speeches or votes as being sympathetic to their particular views. Kennedy in turn hoped to gain the confidence of these farm spokesmen who would have influence at the 1960 Democratic convention, though he was careful to stay free of commitment to any particular farm program, just as his callers tended to remain uncommitted to any particular candidate for the presidency.

As one ritual to demonstrate this sympathy without commitment, Kennedy's senatorial office surveyed and made some changes in a bill prepared mainly by Professor Willard Cochrane of the University of Minnesota, former President of the American Farm Economics Association. Cochrane was prominent among those who sought agreement on a Democratic farm program. His bill had been presented to all the Democratic presidential aspirants by John Baker, Washington representative of the National Farmers

Union. Instead of introducing his revised bill in the Senate, Kennedy mailed copies of it to state-level Farmers Union presidents, and to others who might agree with its basic provisions, seeking their comments.[1]

Senator Kennedy's Farm-Policy Advisers

Meanwhile, Senator Kennedy looked for a farm policy adviser, at first passing over Cochrane because of his long association with rival candidate Hubert Humphrey. Farmers Union former publicist Robert Lewis was hired in late 1959.

Informally, others began to serve as advisers. One of these was John Schnittker, then ending service as a staff member of President Eisenhower's Council of Economic Advisers. In that capacity, and earlier as a professor at Kansas State College, Schnittker had carefully studied the economics of wheat production. In a joint research effort with other wheat-state economists, Schnittker had conceived a range of technically feasible alternatives, and combinations of alternatives, for stabilizing wheat production. The problem, as he saw it, was to work toward a political context in which one of these alternatives would be made politically feasible. Like George Peek, M. L. Wilson, and Willard Cochrane, Schnittker was a policy salesman, though a pragmatist rather than an advocate of a particular plan. He felt Kennedy was also pragmatic, and that only a Democratic administration could enact an effective farm program. He placed himself in the Kennedy camp late in 1959.

In June of 1960, Willard Cochrane indicated at a conference that he would like to help Senator Kennedy in any way possible. In response, Kennedy's office sought his advice on several matters, and then asked him to serve on the Kennedy team at the Democratic convention. Cochrane asked that Kennedy call him personally because he did not want to be a "fifth wheel" in the campaign. Kennedy did call him, and Cochrane became his principal farm policy adviser.

[1] One of the authors, Don Hadwiger, was a participant at this time as a member of Senator Kennedy's legislative staff.

Acknowledgments in a book like this one are difficult. The ideas and the integrating point of view presented have grown with me over at least a decade, and have benefited from the work and writing of many people. Perhaps the men who contributed most to the key ideas and integrating point of view of this book were the author's colleagues in the old, old Bureau of Agricultural Economics: H. R. Tolley, Bushrod W. Allin, James G. Maddox, John M. Brewster, Howard L. Parsons, John A. Baker, and James P. Cavin. The development and sharpening of the conceptual parts have resulted in large measure from the criticisms of, and discussions with, such men as George E. Brandow, Robert L. Clodius, W. W. Wilcox, T. W. Schultz, Roger W. Gray, and J. K. Galbraith.

Illustration 3. THE MYRIAD SOURCES OF POLICY. A paragraph from Willard Cochrane's book *Farm Prices: Myth and Reality* (University of Minnesota, 1958). The list given by Cochrane is a distinguished one. Tolley is deceased. Later assignments of others on the list are as follows:

Allin: Former president of the American Farm Economics Association. In 1961, Outlook situations board in the office of Administration, Economics Research Service, which Cochrane headed under Secretary Freeman.

Maddox: In 1961, professor of Agricultural Economics, North Carolina State University.

Brewster: In 1961, special projects economist, USDA, an authority on the structure of production units in agriculture, whose tenants favoring the family farm dovetailed with Cochrane's program aims.

Parsons: In 1961, professor of Agricultural Economics, University of Wisconsin.

Baker: In 1961, Assistant Secretary of Agriculture, in charge of credit, forestry, world development, soil conservation service, and other projects. His USDA office was two doors from Cochrane's.

Cavin: In 1961, director of a Division of the Economics Research Service.

Brandow: In 1961, professor of Economics, Pennsylvania State University.

Clodius: In 1961, chairman, Department of Agricultural Economics, University of Wisconsin.

Wilcox: Coauthor of a text with Cochrane, and also with Cochrane, coauthor of the 1961 temporary feed-grains legislation. In 1961 Wilcox was a senior analyst in the legislative reference service. His function, as in many prior years, was to provide advice generally to those who did not choose to seek it from the experts in the USDA, and therefore the system often put him at odds with Cochrane and the Kennedy administration.

Schultz: Economic theorist at the University of Chicago, who in 1961 again offered a radical alternative to Cochrane's supply-management pro-

Shortly before the Democratic convention when it became quite likely that Kennedy would win the nomination, Kennedy was able to announce that the Farmers Union Washington Director, John Baker, was also helping him to frame a program. In accepting the assistance of Baker, Cochrane, Lewis, and Schnittker, the candidate was by the same token beginning to commit himself to a farm program.

Willard Cochrane

One of the oldest among those who became new frontiersman of agriculture in the Kennedy administration, Cochrane had been a theorist for the dedicated, uniquely liberal Democratic-Farmer-Labor party in Minnesota, which was headed by Minnesota Governor Orville Freeman and the two U.S. Senators from Minnesota, Hubert Humphrey and Eugene McCarthy. He had also been part of the earlier mentioned New Deal Bureau of Agricultural Economics, one of those magic small-group relationships which had stimulated new insights in its members and also forged friendships, loyalties, and ambitions which would last a lifetime. (See Illustration 3.)

So Cochrane's commitment, and his program for agriculture had many sources, some of which were decades in the past. Cochrane had advanced his hypotheses at many scholarly meetings, and following the meetings, he had been obliged to defend and reform them in intimate hotel room sessions with other top farm economists.

---

gram, who in the past left a wake of fresh—often unwelcome—ideas, and students fired with scholarly and political ambitions.

Gray: In 1961, professor at the Food and Research Institute, Stanford University.

Galbraith: In 1961, helped guide the administration's efforts from an office within the White House, and later as ambassador to India. Left a big mark on the 1962 legislation.

Cochrane's Program

As one way to disseminate his views, Cochrane had summed them up in a small book for laymen, *Farm Prices: Myth and Reality,*[2] which served as a rationale for those who advised Democratic governors and congressmen, those who staffed Democratic-oriented organizations, and those who ultimately framed the farm plank in the 1960 Democratic platform.

Cochrane agreed with Secretary Benson that farmers were at a crossroads. Overproduction threatened the farm economy. Unlike Benson, who felt government could and should retreat from the price support field, Cochrane felt governmental discipline was more needed than ever.

"We've got a bull by the horns," he often said. "Either we hold on tighter or it will run all over us."

Cochrane was himself a sort of bull, who insisted to fellow economists that remedies must be politically acceptable, but some of his associates felt his lack of diplomacy ultimately decreased his effectiveness both in the Congress and in the White House.

Cochrane feared that slovenly contrived, surplus-accumulating farm programs would fall of their own weight. Once this happened and the farm economy was obliged to take Benson's free-market route, Cochrane predicted that a burgeoning agricultural production would bring chronically low prices and force out wave after wave of efficient commercial farmers. So the final result would be destruction of the "family farm," which Cochrane prized as a way of life, and which he felt was most efficient.

Cochrane conceded it would take stiff measures to bring production in line. Additional mandatory controls would immediately have to be imposed on producers of surplus commodities. Ultimately government management of supply and demand for agricultural commodities would extend directly or indirectly to most other major commodities, because resources idled by controls on some commodities would flee to the production of the commodities that were not controlled.

[2] St. Paul: University of Minnesota Press, 1958.

"Frankly," Cochrane said, "regulation would have to be as thorough as that of a public utility."

Cochrane was not at all sure that commercial family farmers would accept such comprehensive regulation. But he believed they should be given the opportunity to choose this route to survival. He thought also that another obstacle to the enactment of a workable farm program was the logrolling process in Congress, which was responsible for the existing inadequate patchwork of farm laws.

As a way around this obstacle, Cochrane and others wrote a legislative bill in 1959, in which it was assumed Congress would recognize its inability to enact production controls, and would restrict itself to setting the broad guidelines within which the executive branch would actually write the farm programs. Cochrane later felt that this procedural change, which became the heart of the 1961 farm bill, was his principal legislative innovation.

Cochrane's book reviewed various mechanisms through which government could balance production, and also noted mechanisms to keep up farm income which would act as incentives for farmers to support the program. Each mechanism had its limitations, but Cochrane felt that if the Secretary of Agriculture were allowed to use all of them in intricate combinations, then government could in fact stabilize the farm economy.

Production-Control Mechanisms

The mechanisms Cochrane suggested had all been used or suggested for use in previous years, and one or another would be emphasized in all of the alternatives which Congress considered or enacted during 1961 and 1962:

1. *Controlling the number of acres planted.* Since 1938 this had been the principal mechanism applied to certain basic commodities. All producers of some commodities had to comply with marketing quotas (expressed in terms of acres) or else face stiff financial penalties. But farmers applied new technology to raise more and more on their allotted acres. Another problem was that, over time, the quotas themselves became valuable and thus raised the price

of the land to which they were attached. Also many bureaucrats were needed to explain programs, measure acres, and enforce rules.

Before marketing quotas could be applied, it was the law and the custom to submit the question to affected producers voting in a referendum. If two-thirds of the voters favored controls, then all producers would have to comply, since all would benefit from the higher market prices that would result from the program.

(The dissenters often protested vigorously, as did Stanley Yankus, who was bankrupted by government penalties and all but imprisoned because he ignored the restrictions in raising wheat for his chickens. Appearing before a congressional committee, Yankus cited the Declaration of Independence, waved a copy of the U.S. Constitution, and charged tyranny, dictatorship, and totalitarianism. Having so characterized his government, Yankus sought refuge in Australia, where the chickens as well as the grain were produced under quota.)

2. *Regulating the amount of produce sold off a farm.* In the case of sugar, for example, the federal government divided a domestic quota among regions, then subdivided it again among individual farmers, based on their past production.

It was objected that production controls of either type froze production patterns, and gave a monopoly to those who happened to have a history of past production entitling them to a share of the market. To regulate the amount sold might also require destruction of some commodities produced in excess of the quota. And the Secretary of Agriculture would have to make so many important decisions that he might ultimately become a czar for all of agriculture, favoring political friends and destroying political enemies.

Farm-Income Mechanisms

In return for accepting controls, farmers would be guaranteed higher income—through higher, stable prices, and through subsidies of various types. These rewards did not in fact have to be accompanied by controls binding on all producers. Instead, bargains could be made with individual farmers to limit the acres planted or the amount sold in return for a substantial subsidy. But such voluntary programs were presumed to cost a great deal more money than the mandatory programs—in Cochrane's opinion much more because excessive overproduction would bring higher treasury costs than the taxpayer was willing to tolerate.

Here is a list of six mechanisms by which the farmer has been rewarded for reduced production under either a *voluntary* or a *mandatory* controls program:

1. Price supports. The federal government would set a price value for each unit of a commodity, and would lend that amount to the farmer who would put up his commodities as collateral. If the market price of the product did not go above the loan rate, the farmer ordinarily would keep his loan money and the government would take over his commodities, which it then stored, or sold on the domestic or foreign market, or disposed of in some other way. Price supports were a traditional means of maintaining farmer income, and were the device under which government surpluses had been accumulated.

2. The processing tax. The government could require the processor (as for example, flour millers) who purchased a commodity to pay a tax on it, or to buy a certificate from the government before using the commodity. The proceeds from this certificate would then be returned to the farmer. In this way, the actual price of the product might go down, while payments from the processing tax would keep the farmer's income high.

This processing tax might be paid in connection with only one use of the produce, as the miller whose flour is for human consumption might pay a processing tax, but not the company that converted wheat into cattle feed or glue. The processing tax might permit more of the product to be sold abroad because prices would move more freely. It would remove the need for a taxpayer's subsidy to the farmers. However, the processing tax might indirectly raise consumer food prices.

3. The two-price plan. This was an old favorite, championed in the McNary-Haugen plan of the 1920's. It assumed that government could require a high price for the primary use of a product in the United States, while permitting the surplus to be sold abroad, or for secondary uses, at whatever price it would bring. But in international parlance this was called "dumping," a reprehensible practice against which foreign countries were likely to retaliate. The two-price scheme posed difficulties also because there could be but one price for identical grain in the grain (futures) market.

Since wheat farmers were presumed to favor the two-price plan, however, the designation "two-price program" was used to describe the 1962 wheat-certificate program which actually employed the processing tax as a means to reward farmers.

4. Compensatory payments. Government might boost farm income by direct cash payments to farmers. As featured in the program of Truman's Secretary of Agriculture, Charles Brannan, compensatory payments were not linked with total productivity, so that the small family farm could receive an income supplement which the huge corporation did not need. With farm income maintained through government grant, lower farm prices could then help discourage overproduction and fewer controls would be needed. Brannan's plan precipitated a prolonged fight between Secretary Brannan and Alan Kline, then President of the American Farm Bureau Federation. As a result the words *compensatory payments* or *direct payments* came to have a high emotional content in the 1950's. Few farm congressmen voted for the Brannan plan because influential bigger farmers opposed it: farmers did not want to be on the government dole; and it seemed more vulnerable to the impulses of future budget-cutting policymakers than did the price-supports programs.

The Brannan Plan did attract support from organized labor, because it promised to keep food costs low and to slow down the movement of farmers to the cities where they competed on the labor market.

A Brannan Plan was finally enacted for wool producers in 1954 and compensatory payments were introduced into the feed-grains and wheat legislation in the 1962 Act.

5. *Government could rent and thus retire excess land.* One farm program after another had been based on the principle that it is better to reduce production by paying the farmer to leave some land idle than by removing farmers, or reducing the profits and thus the capital invested in farming. Some thought government might in time actually have to purchase a great deal of land to be used for parks, freeways, or public institutions, but government had already rented much cropland. Through the 1956 short-term soil bank acreage-reserve program as much as 22 million acres were retired for short periods, and under the subsequent conservation-reserve program, as of 1960, about 29 million acres had been rented by government for five- or ten-year periods, during which the government paid part of the cost for converting this cropland to grass, water reservoirs, game preserves, and other uses.

6. *Diverted acres.* Another scheme for voluntary reduction in acreage was to induce a farmer to idle a percentage of his cropland for a year, by offering him higher prices or a compensatory payment on the smaller crop he did produce, plus a substantial rental payment for the diverted acres. These rental payments might be payments in kind—that is, the government gave the farmer grain from government stocks equivalent to a percentage of what the farmer probably would have raised on the diverted acres. The farmer usually would accept a cash payment rather than take delivery on the government grain, in which case the government could sell that grain on the market and thus reduce surplus stocks a little. This was the surplus-cutting feature of the Kennedy feed-grains program of 1961.

The above list does not include all the major government mechanisms used in adjusting production or in raising prices and farm income. But hopefully, we have introduced a vocubulary adequate to deal with commodity legislation in the three years of the Kennedy administration. Now we may pick up the strings of the 1960 campaign during which President Kennedy became firmly committed to the principles of the Cochrane supply-management program.

To win an impressive number of Midwestern delegates at the Democratic convention, candidate Kennedy promised to produce a program to raise farm income. He emphasized at the convention that the farm problem was the most important domestic issue. And in accepting the Democratic nomination, he assumed leadership of an existing coalition of men and groups presumed to be in agreement on a set of statements called the party platform.

Farm Policy in the Campaign

The 1960 Democratic party platform was in the ordinary propagandistic style. Yet a careful interpreter of its ambiguous phrases could find the outlines of the Democratic farm program. Its key provision on agriculture definitely committed the party to "work for full parity of income" and to control production through such mechanisms as Willard Cochrane had suggested:

> The Democratic Administration will work to bring about full parity income for farmers in all segments of agriculture by helping them to balance farm production with the expanding needs of the nation and the world. Measures to this end include production and marketing quotas measured in terms of barrels, bushels, and bales, loans on basic commodities at not less than 90% of parity, production payments, commodity purchases, marketing orders and agreements.[3]

As was the custom in accepting the Democratic nomination, Kennedy stated that he supported the Democratic platform. More

[3] Daniel M. Ogden, Jr., and Arthur L. Peterson, in their book *Electing the President 1964* (Chandler Publishing Co., San Francisco, 1964) wrote: ". . . the complete 1960 Democratic platform was a fairly typical major-party platform. It indicated the direction in which the Democratic Party hoped to go without making specific promises to reach the destination. It reflected the objectives of the groups having significant power within the Party. And, by 'glittering generalities' it also reflected the issues upon which the Party was so divided that no firm position could be taken. Yet, overall, it was a platform with a strong liberal tone." (p. 68)

specific commitments, however, were to be found in his subsequent campaign statements.

The Campaign Speechs

Kennedy's basic farm program was stated in a campaign "white paper" first written by Willard Cochrane and then revised by John Baker, and also in three campaign speeches drafted mainly by Cochrane.

In these speeches were two key points:

1. Farmers had a hard choice to make. They could not expect to find a market at a fair price for all they could produce nor could government absorb their surplus production. They must either accept controls on production, or be forced out of farming by low prices. At Sioux Falls, South Dakota, on August 21, 1960, Kennedy stated this position:

I give you no assurance that you can have high income and unlimited production and no controls with no regard to the taxpayers. Rather [mine] is a program which will take work and sacrifice and discipline.

2. Candidate Kennedy offered to guarantee fair income by preventing overproduction of farm commodities. This was Cochrane's supply-management program, spelled out in Kennedy's speech at Sioux Falls:

First, we pledge ourselves to securing full parity of income for the American farmer.

Secondly, we intend to assure this parity of income primarily through supply management, the adjustment of supply to demand at parity income prices.

Purchases and loans will be necessary on some commodities at certain times to supplement supply management. But a basic instrument assuring parity of income will be supply management controls, including the use of marketing quotas, land retirement with conservation practices, marketing orders and agreements and other devices to be used either together or separately.

In his Sioux Falls speech, Senator Kennedy also went on record in favor of Cochrane's proposal that Congress delegate program-writing authority to the Secretary of Agriculture—who would, however, consult with appointed farmer committees before acting.

The Campaign for the Farm Vote

In the campaign, many men and women bent their energies to organizing and propagandizing farmers, under Cochrane's general supervision. Kennedy's farm aide, Robert Lewis, ran a "Farmers for Kennedy" operation from Washington which solicited independent and Republican support for the candidate and his program.[4] A "resources" group headed by liberal Mississippi Congressman Frank Smith prepared propaganda and press releases on farm issues. A research committee operating under Kennedy's legislative assistant Myer Feldman tapped liberal writers and staff people for policy statements and for material used in briefing Kennedy for the television debates with Vice President Richard Nixon.

Meanwhile, in expectation of victory at the polls, Kennedy named several advisory committees to prepare legislation for 1961. A group authorized to survey the whole farm problem was the Soth-Giannini committee, which included J. N. Efferson, Louisiana State professor, Lauren Soth, respected author and editorial-page editor of the *Des Moines Register*, and Jess Tapp, board chairman of the gigantic California Bank of America. In its report this committee emphasized a massive government rental of productive land rather than controls on production. Its proposals found some support within the administration, but were anathema to many Democratic farm leaders, and in any case were not considered acceptable to farm communities. A committee on wheat was headed by John Schnittker, who subsequently joined the New

[4] *Electing the President 1964* (see note 3) reported: "Farmers for Kennedy-Johnson set up units in as many states as possible and used an elaborate system of regional directors to coordinate activities and to provide special advice in particular commodity areas. . . . Local groups also inserted paid advertising in weekly newspapers, distributed Farmers for Kennedy-Johnson literature, supplied speakers before local groups, raised funds, and talked up Kennedy for President—a very important technique in rural areas."

Frontier administration in order to implement his committee's proposals. A cotton advisory committee headed by Alexander Nunn of Alabama decided to make no long-range recommendations, but a corn advisory committee headed by Iowa Governor Herschel Loveless did suggest a program similar to that soon enacted in the temporary feed-grains bill.

Mandate of the Voters

In the presidential election Kennedy carried the rural areas of the South, where there were relatively more farmers than in any other section of the country. He also apparently got well over 40% of the farmer votes elsewhere, even though Vice President Nixon was said to have more personal appeal for Midwestern farmers and small-town people.[5] The farm issue undoubtedly won votes for the Democrats—"victory margins" in such crucial states as Minnesota, Illinois, Missouri, and Wisconsin.

But for what program did farmers vote, if any? Relatively few voters paid attention to campaign speeches and party platforms, despite the valiant efforts of the propagandists. Many rural Kennedy voters—perhaps most of them—were obviously taking the opportunity to protest against Benson, without realizing that Kennedy was also offering them a hard choice. Many voters remembered that Democratic administrations did more than Republicans to raise farm prices, perhaps forgetting for the moment that Democrats also advocated more controls. Polls of Iowa farmers invariably revealed a majority of farmers in favor of high price supports, and a large majority opposed to controls on production. It is exceedingly doubtful that many farmers voted for the hard choice. Yet the President was committed. The men who advised him would be running the Department of Agriculture or wielding influence from within a farm organization, or from a congressional office. After the votes came in, some of the Kennedy farm team would scuffle with one another momentarily in a contest for

[5] Theodore White, *The Making of the President,* 1960 (New York: Pocket Books, Inc., 1961), p. 333.

the highest offices. Most would soon find themselves in comfortable offices with wall-to-wall carpeting and stately leather furniture, with a glossy walnut desk—and a sobering amount of responsibility. They would be called New Frontiersmen, though a few had once been Fair Dealers, and even New Dealers.

Like the Republicans whose desks they took over, most New Frontier administrators were convinced that there was a hard choice to make and it was in the farmers' interest to make it as soon as possible. They would frame this choice as attractively as they could, and attempt to sell it to Congress. They would keep the President's picture on the wall, and hope he would continue to support their cause. Opponents would call them eggheads, bureaucrats, smart alecks, and Washington farmers—this was part of the game. They would, for a few years, also be big shots, though at lower salaries than had they joined an organization that sold cattle feed instead of farm programs. They were the substance of the agriculture arm of the presidential Democratic party and, it is fair to say, agents of responsible government.

3. *The U.S. Department of Agriculture (USDA)*

Secretary Orville Freeman

Why did President Kennedy, in late November of 1960, choose Orville Freeman to be his Secretary of Agriculture, instead of Willard Cochrane, or John Baker, or Missouri Farmers Organization President Fred Heinkel, or some other qualified person?

Freeman had lost his bid for a fourth term as Minnesota governor. He also lacked a farm background, although he had learned to milk a cow during summertime farm experience. To his credit, Freeman had nominated Kennedy at the Democratic Convention. Freeman was young, tough, a practical liberal, a proven administrator. He fit the New Frontier image, and his personality must have appealed to the President. He looked more like a farmer—even in street clothes—than did his predecessor Benson pictured in plaid shirt, muddy high-top shoes, and ten-gallon hat.

Freeman must also have had Minnesota Senator Hubert Humphrey's strong support, though some of Freeman's other close friends warned him that to take the job would be political suicide.

As Secretary of Agriculture, Freeman soon endeared himself as a person to leading Democratic farm leaders. After a year in action, he received a rare standing ovation from the House Agriculture Committee. City congressmen remarked that while Secretary Benson was the wrong man with the right program (an end to agricultural subsidies), Freeman was a fine person with the wrong program. Freeman's honesty and his background as a professional politician were rated highly. When asked whether he should begin

"IF IT WEREN'T FOR THE HONOR I'D JUST AS SOON WALK."

Illustration 4. THREE VIEWS OF A CONFRONTATION. Secretary Freeman and his Department were watched by farm-country newspapers. Here is what Mauldin foresaw before the inauguration. From the *St. Louis Post-Dispatch*, December 19th, 1960.

Hope He Doesn't Catch His Pants on It

Illustration 4. From the *Farmers Union Herald,* January 23rd, 1961–Jim Zilverberg.

to cut down production by shooing powerful cattlemen off the grazing lands, Freeman earned esteem and affection with the quick reply: "My views on that are very practical. I do not think it makes much difference what I think about it." [1] Freeman proved

[1] *Hearings on the Food and Agriculture Act of 1962.* House Committee on Agriculture, p. 186.

Illustration 4. From the *Farmers Union Herald*, March 20th, 1961–Jim Zilverberg.

able to communicate with Congress, as Secretaries Benson and Brannan before him had not.

As Governor of Minnesota, Freeman had been a leading Midwestern Democrat, active on the farm issue. In 1958 he had authorized a study of Minnesota agriculture, completed by a technical staff of five headed by Willard Cochrane, then a professor at the University of Minnesota. Their scholarly 200-page report covered such subjects as the history of agriculture in Minnesota, land values, marginal farmers, agriculture-related industries, dairy problems, and the level of farm income, especially as it was related to supply and demand.[2] The latter discussion reflected Cochrane's thesis that supply of agricultural commodities would inevitably exceed demand in a free market, which would create severe financial pressures jeopardizing the family farm.

Decisionmakers

Though Freeman had done much to spark the farm issue in the Midwest, when named Secretary he was still not well acquainted in national agricultural policy circles. To have some trusted people around him, Freeman brought to Washington a number of talented associates from his Minnesota administration, and he relied more heavily on this "Minnesota crowd" in the early weeks than he or they preferred. This group moved into empty U.S. Department of Agriculture (USDA) offices late in December, and began organizing to run the USDA, while Willard Cochrane took charge of work on the legislative program.

Some in the Minnesota group stayed on to become advisers or helpers to the Secretary. Freeman's principal adviser and political confidant—in addition to his knowledgeable wife—was Mrs. Dorothy Jacobson, a businesslike former professor of political science and an associate during Freeman's six-year governorship. Mrs. Jacobson was overseer of sundry projects, and she coordinated speechwriting. In a phrase with awesome significance to those in administrative hierarchies, she was "closest to the Secretary."

Thomas R. Hughes, also a political scientist, was Freeman's assistant who coordinated the work of Freeman's other seven assistants. Among other duties, Hughes communicated with the

[2] *Report of the Governor's Study Commission*, State of Minnesota, 1958.

White House on routine matters, and cleared patronage appointments with the National Democratic Committee. Also prominent among the Minnesota group was Joseph Robertson,—a third political scientist and former tax commissioner of Minnesota, and Rodney Leonard, Secretary Freeman's press secretary.

In scouting for other staff members, Secretary Freeman and President Kennedy's brother-in-law Sargent Shriver thumbed through the card file which Kennedy's aides had built over the years just in case they suddenly needed to hire several thousand men to run the government. In selecting assistants, Freeman got advice, too, from would-be employees: whatever the cause-and-effect relationship, most of the political appointees were not wall flowers.

In late January Freeman announced those who would hold top offices. (See Illustration 5.)

1. His Undersecretary would be Charles Murphy, North Carolinian, for years a bill drafter for the Senate, and a former assistant to President Truman, an 18-hour-a-day man whose job inevitably would be to run the Department while Freeman made speeches, testified before committees, and worried about high policy. Murphy's assistant later explained how Freeman and Murphy divided the work of the Secretaryship: "Charlie mostly sits; Secretary Freeman mostly moves."

2. James T. Ralph, as Assistant Secretary for Marketing and Stabilization, was given suzerainty over the highly political *Agricultural Stabilization and Conservation Service* (ASCS) (at that time called the Commodity Stabilization Service) that administered the price supports programs. In this position, Ralph was able to plug hard for new authority to issue national marketing orders. A Tennessean who was briefly California Governor Brown's Secretary of Agriculture, Ralph was later dismissed by Freeman for involvement in the Billie Sol Estes scandal.

3. John Duncan, Jr., Assistant Secretary for Marketing and Foreign Agriculture, who later added Ralph's duties to his own, was president of the Georgia unit of the American Farm Bureau

Federation, the nation's largest farm organization. Duncan had been one of the leaders in a 15-year-long rebellion by several Southeastern state groups against the national Farm Bureau's move away from price supports. Duncan's peanut, cotton, and tobacco producers had stayed in the Farm Bureau, despite their differences, on the understanding that the national organization would not oppose controls on Southern commodities. Duncan was the Administration's "Farm Bureau representative," unacceptable though he was to Farm Bureau's national bureaucracy. Duncan also provided one of the much-needed links with powerful senior Southern congressmen. (Secretary Freeman himself even prized a personal tie with the Southland, resulting from his marriage to a North Carolinian.)

4. Horace Godfrey, a North Carolinian, was named Administrator of the ASCS (at that time Commodity Stabilization Service). Godfrey had worked his way up through the ASCS farmer committee system (discussed on pages 55).

5. Several Farmers Union men gained important places in the USDA. Kennedy campaign aide John Baker had been head of the Washington NFU office. At first as Director of Agricultural Credit and then as Assistant Secretary of Agriculture, Baker promoted farm credit, and later also supervised forestry, soil conservation, and rural redevelopment activities. Robert Lewis became an important Freeman adviser on dairy policy though officially he was made only a Deputy Administrator in the ASCS.

6. Director of Agricultural Economics Willard Cochrane was authorized to hire an elite team of economists (Staff Economics Group) who, with other economists in the USDA's Economic Research Service, helped Cochrane develop farm programs. One of these, Linley Juers, was depended upon for dairy legislation. Another, John Schnittker, played the central role in developing and selling a legislative wheat program.

Additional policy assistance was obtained from some other second-rank political appointees. Ed Jaenke, named Associate Administrator of the ASCS, was called in for conferences on legislative strategy because of his experience as former assistant to Senator Stuart Symington (D., Mo.). Jaenke and Schnittker later served as USDA witnesses and then as lobbyists in various congressional subcommittees. Freeman sought good advice and expert legislative help wherever he could find it, keen as he was otherwise for efficient administrative organization and formal observance of hierarchy.

The Organization of the Department

The remainder of this chapter consists of Illustrations 5 and 6.

Illustration 5 is a selection of materials from the 1961–1962 *U.S. Government Organization Manual.* These show the structure of the Department, the principal personnel (many mentioned in this book and especially in this chapter), and functions and services of some of the divisions within the department.

Illustration 6 shows the number of employees in the various executive departments. The Department of Agriculture is third in number of employees, exceeded by the Post Office Department and the Department of Defense.

Illustration 5. The U.S. Department of Agriculture. Relations of officers and divisions. Numbers, added for this book, indicate persons holding offices: (1) Orville L. Freeman; (2) Charles S. Murphy; (3) Thomas R. Hughes, Mrs. Dorothy H. Jacobson, Rodney E. Leonard; (4) Joseph H. Robertson; (5) John Duncan, Jr.; (6) James T. Ralph; (7) Willard W. Cochrane; (8) John Baker; (9) Horace Godfrey, Edward Jaenke, Robert G. Lewis. Hughes, Leonard, Robertson, and Mrs. Jacobson were associates of Secretary Freeman when he was Governor of Minnesota. The Commodity Stabilization Service (9) became the Agricultural Stabilization and Conservation Service on June 14, 1961. (Modified from p. 625 of *U.S. Government Organization Manual,* 1961–1962)

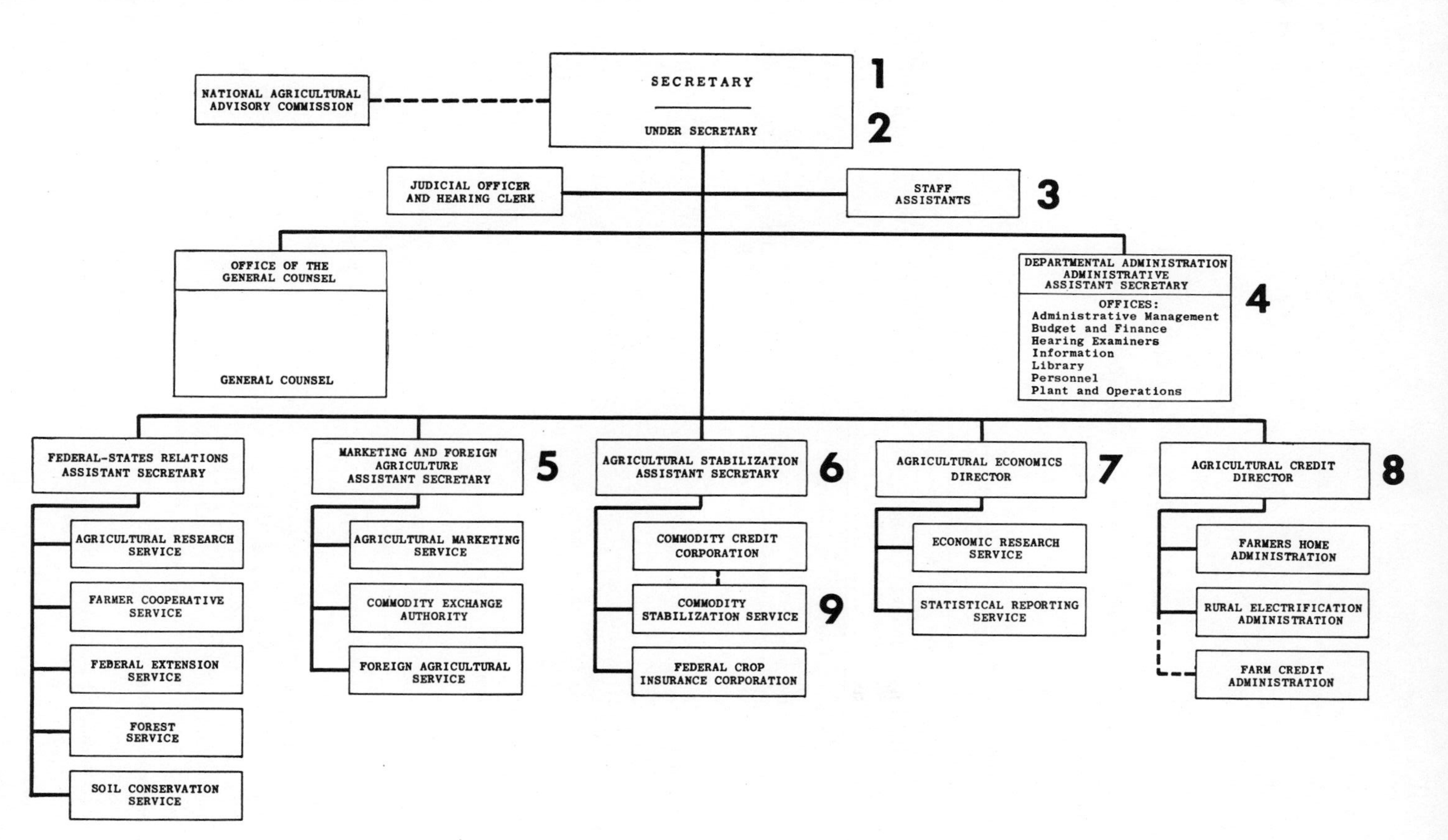

SECRETARY
UNDER SECRETARY
1
2
NATIONAL AGRICULTURAL ADVISORY COMMISSION
JUDICIAL OFFICER AND HEARING CLERK
STAFF ASSISTANTS
3
OFFICE OF THE GENERAL COUNSEL
GENERAL COUNSEL
DEPARTMENTAL ADMINISTRATION ADMINISTRATIVE ASSISTANT SECRETARY
OFFICES:
Administrative Management
Budget and Finance
Hearing Examiners
Information
Library
Personnel
Plant and Operations
4
FEDERAL-STATES RELATIONS ASSISTANT SECRETARY
AGRICULTURAL RESEARCH SERVICE
FARMER COOPERATIVE SERVICE
FEBERAL EXTENSION SERVICE
FOREST SERVICE
SOIL CONSERVATION SERVICE
MARKETING AND FOREIGN AGRICULTURE ASSISTANT SECRETARY
5
AGRICULTURAL MARKETING SERVICE
COMMODITY EXCHANGE AUTHORITY
FOREIGN AGRICULTURAL SERVICE
AGRICULTURAL STABILIZATION ASSISTANT SECRETARY
6
COMMODITY CREDIT CORPORATION
COMMODITY STABILIZATION SERVICE
9
FEDERAL CROP INSURANCE CORPORATION
AGRICULTURAL ECONOMICS DIRECTOR
7
ECONOMIC RESEARCH SERVICE
STATISTICAL REPORTING SERVICE
AGRICULTURAL CREDIT DIRECTOR
8
FARMERS HOME ADMINISTRATION
RURAL ELECTRIFICATION ADMINISTRATION
FARM CREDIT ADMINISTRATION

DEPARTMENT OF AGRICULTURE [1]

Fourteenth Street and Independence Avenue SW.
REpublic 7–4142

OFFICIALS

Secretary of Agriculture	ORVILLE L. FREEMAN.
Under Secretary	CHARLES S. MURPHY.
Assistant Secretary	FRANK J. WELCH.
Assistant Secretary	JOHN P. DUNCAN, JR.
Assistant Secretary	JAMES T. RALPH.
Director, Agricultural Credit Services	JOHN A. BAKER.
Director, Agricultural Economics	WILLARD W. COCHRANE.
Administrative Assistant Secretary	JOSEPH M. ROBERTSON.
General Counsel	JOHN C. BAGWELL.
Deputy General Counsel	EDWARD M. SHULMAN.
Executive Assistant to the Secretary	THOMAS R. HUGHES.
Assistant to the Secretary	GEORGE A. BARNES.
Assistant to the Secretary	RODNEY E. LEONARD.
Assistant to the Secretary	MRS. DOROTHY H. JACOBSON.
Assistant to the Secretary	KENNETH M. BIRKHEAD.
Correspondence Review Officer	A. SYDNEY SKOGLUND.
Judicial Officer	THOMAS J. FLAVIN.
Federal-States Relations, Assistant Secretary	FRANK J. WELCH.
Agricultural Research Service:	
Administrator	B. T. SHAW.
Associate Administrator	M. R. CLARKSON.
Deputy Administrator, Utilization Research and Development	GEORGE W. IRVING, JR.
Deputy Administrator, Farm Research	T. C. BYERLY.
Deputy Administrator, Regulatory Programs	W. L. POPHAM.
Deputy Administrator, Experiment Stations	E. C. ELTING.
Director, Institute of Home Economics	HAZEL K. STIEBELING.
Executive Assistant Administrator, Management	F. H. SPENCER.
Farmer Cooperative Service, Administrator	JOSEPH G. KNAPP.
Federal Extension Service:	
Administrator	E. T. YORK, JR.
Deputy Administrator	GERALD H. HUFFMAN.
Assistant Administrator	LUKE M. SCHRUBEN.
Assistant Administrator	EWARD W. AITON.
Forest Service:	
Chief	RICHARD E. MCARDLE.
Assistant Chief, Program Planning and Legislation	EDWARD C. CRAFTS.
Assistant Chief, National Forest Resource Management	EDWARD P. CLIFF.
Assistant Chief, National Forest Protection and Development	ARTHUR W. GREELEY.
Assistant Chief, State and Private Forestry	W. S. SWINGLER.
Assistant Chief, Forest Research	V. L. HARPER.
Assistant Chief, Administrative Divisions	CLARE W. HENDEE.

[1] Organization chart on page 37

DEPARTMENT OF AGRICULTURE

Federal-States Relations, Assistant Secretary—Continued	
Soil Conservation Service:	
Administrator	DONALD A. WILLIAMS.
Deputy Administrator	GLADWIN E. YOUNG.
Assistant Administrator, Field Services	JEFFERSON C. DYKES.
Assistant Administrator, Soil Survey	CHARLES E. KELLOGG.
Assistant Administrator, Management	WILLIAM R. VAN DERSAL.
Assistant Administrator, Watersheds	HOLLIS R. WILLIAMS.
Marketing and Foreign Agriculture, Assistant Secretary	JOHN P. DUNCAN, JR.
Agricultural Marketing Service:	
Administrator	O. V. WELLS.
Deputy Administrator, Marketing Services	ROY W. LENNARTSON.
Deputy Administrator, Marketing Research	OMER W. HERRMANN.
Assistant Administrator, Management	HENRY G. HERRELL.
Commodity Exchange Authority:	
Administrator	ALEX C. CALDWELL.
Deputy Administrator	ARTHUR R. GROSSTEPHAN.
Foreign Agricultural Service:	
Administrator	ROBERT C. TETRO.
Deputy Administrator	RAYMOND A. IOANES.
Assistant Administrator, Agricultural Attaches	GERALD E. TICHENOR.
Assistant Administrator, Market Development and Programs	PATRICK M. O'LEARY.
Assistant Administrator, Agricultural Trade Policy and Analysis	GUSTAVE BURMEISTER.
Assistant Administrator, Management	W. A. MINOR.
General Sales Manager	FRANK M. LEROUX.
Agricultural Stabilization, Assistant Secretary	JAMES T. RALPH.
Commodity Credit Corporation:	
President	CHARLES S. MURPHY.
Executive Vice President	HORACE D. GODFREY.
Secretary	LIONEL C. HOLM.
Controller	JAMES J. SOMERS.
Treasurer	RULON GIBB.
Chief Accountant	J. W. VAUGHAN.
* Commodity Stabilization Service:	
Administrator	HORACE D. GODFREY.
Associate Administrator	EDWARD A. JAENKE.
Deputy Administrator, Price Support	ROBERT G. LEWIS.
Deputy Administrator, Production Adjustment	EMERY E. JACOBS.
Deputy Administrator, Operations	FRANK W. HUSSEY.
Federal Crop Insurance Corporation:	
Manager	JOHN N. LUFT.
Agricultural Credit, Director, Agricultural Credit Services	JOHN A. BAKER.
Farmers Home Administration:	
Administrator	HOWARD BERTSCH.
Deputy Administrator	FLOYD F. HIGBEE.
Assistant Administrator (Insured Loan Funds)	LAWRENCE BROCK.
Assistant Administrator (Program)	J. V. HIGHFILL.
Assistant Administrator (Operations)	(VACANCY).
Rural Electrification Administration:	
Administrator	NORMAN M. CLAPP.
Deputy Administrator	RICHARD A. DELL.
Assistant Administrator (Electric)	RICHARD H. WOOD, Acting.
Assistant Administrator (Telephone)	(VACANCY).
Assistant Administrator for Administration	JOHN W. SCOTT.

* Agricultural Stabilization and Conservation Service.

Agricultural Economics, Director — WILLARD W. COCHRANE.
Economic Research Service:
Administrator — NATHAN M. KOFFSKY.
Statistical Reporting Service:
Administrator — HARRY C. TRELOGAN.
Departmental Administration, Administrative Assistant Secretary — JOSEPH M. ROBERTSON.
Office of Administrative Management, Director — JOSEPH P. LOFTUS.
Office of Budget and Finance, Director — CHARLES L. GRANT.
Office of Hearing Examiners, Chief Hearing Examiner — G. OSMOND HYDE.
Office of Information, Director — R. LYLE WEBSTER.
Library, Director — FOSTER E. MOHRHARDT.
Office of Personnel, Director — ERNEST C. BETTS, Jr.
Office of Plant and Operations, Director — F. R. MANGHAM.
Office of the General Counsel, General Counsel — JOHN C. BAGWELL.
Deputy General Counsel — EDWARD M. SHULMAN.

Federal-States Relations

Agricultural Research Service

The Service conducts research relating to the production and utilization of agricultural products. It also conducts regulatory programs that involve enforcement of plant and animal quarantines, meat inspection, control of diseases and insect pests of animals and plants, and related work. Both the research and the regulatory activities are carried on at numerous locations in all of the States, Puerto Rico, the Virgin Islands, and a number of foreign countries. Most of the research is in cooperation with State agricultural experiment stations and other public and private agencies.

Special pioneering laboratories conduct basic research to advance the present limits of knowledge in specific areas of the agricultural sciences.

Regulatory programs conducted by ARS include (1) meat inspection activities, (2) animal disease eradication programs, (3) animal inspection and quarantine activities, (4) plant pest control work, and (5) plant quarantine work.

Farmer Cooperative Service

The Service performs research, educational, and advisory service work to assist the 4 out of 5 farmers of this country who now belong to marketing, farm supply and related service cooperatives. It conducts these research studies and service activities on problems of management, financing, organization, policies, merchandising, product quality, costs, efficiency, and membership. It publishes the results of such studies, confers and advises with officials of farmer cooperatives, and works with educational agencies, cooperatives, and others to disseminate information on cooperative principles and practices.

Federal Extension Service

Cooperative extension work derives its name from the fact that the Department, the land-grant colleges of the States and Puerto Rico, and the county governments share in the financial, administration, and subject-matter responsibilities. Extension agents work with farmers, homemakers, youth through 4–H Clubs, and with others engaged in marketing agricultural products. The departmental office is composed of administrative and professional personnel serving as the liaison between departmental research and action agencies and the administrative and extension subject-matter staffs at the respective land-grant colleges. County extension agents are located in nearly all the counties of the United States. These agents make available to farmers, farm homemakers, and rural youth the results of research conducted by the Department of Agriculture, the land-grant institutions, and other research agencies, adapted to local farm, home, and market conditions. Extension work is also conducted with rural nonfarm and, to some extent, with urban families.

Forest Service

The Forest Service is charged with the responsibility for promoting the conservation and best use of the Nation's forest lands, aggregating approximately a third of the total land area of the United States.

NATIONAL FORESTS.—The Service administers 154 national forests, together with national grasslands, land utilization project lands, experimental forests, and other lands aggregating about 186,000,000 acres.

Soil Conservation Service

The Soil Conservation Service was established under authority of the Soil Conservation Act of 1935 (49 Stat. 163; 16 U. S. C. 590 a–f), and charged with the responsibility of developing and carrying out a permanent national soil and water conservation program. The principal duty of this agency is to assist farmers and ranchers in locally organized, farmer-directed soil conservation districts, through its planning technicians and other soil and water conservation specialists who live and work in the districts. By January 1, 1961, there were 2,879 such districts, covering 1,677,612,000 acres and including 4,608,000 farms and ranches in the States, Puerto Rico, and the Virgin Islands.

The Service also is responsible for administering the flood control and watershed and river investigations activities of the Department of Agriculture.

Marketing and Foreign Agriculture

Agricultural Marketing Service

The Agricultural Marketing Service administers broad marketing, distribution, and related programs and activities of the Department, including assigned defense production and mobilization activities.

MARKETING RESEARCH.—Marketing research, authorized by the Research and Marketing Act of 1946, as amended, is directed toward increasing the efficiency of marketing of agricultural commodities by means of better marketing practices, methods, facilities, and equipment in such areas as assembling, handling, packing, packaging, transporting, storing, processing, wholesaling, and retailing agricultural products.

MARKET NEWS.—This service provides current, unbiased information to producers, processors, distributors, and others to assist them in the orderly marketing and distribution of farm commodities.

The grading and inspection programs are designed to certify to producers, shippers, processors, distributors, dealers, and consumers the quality and condition of agricultural commodities and food products.

FREIGHT RATE SERVICES.—AMS, acting for the Secretary of Agriculture, has the responsibility for obtaining fair and reasonable rates and essential services necessary to efficient transportation of agricultural commodities and farm supplies.

MARKETING AGREEMENTS AND ORDERS.—Marketing agreement and order programs, carried on under authority of the Agricultural Marketing Agreement Act of 1937, help to establish and maintain orderly marketing conditions for certain commodities and their products.

AMS makes payments to commercial exporters and others to encourage exports of surplus commodities, and makes payments to encourage diversion of surplus commodities from normal channels of trade to new markets and new uses.

NATIONAL SCHOOL LUNCH PROGRAM.—AMS administers this program under authority of the National School Lunch Act of 1946. Through grants-in-aid to States, AMS provides financial assistance to public and private schools, of high school grade or under, operating nonprofit school lunch programs. These funds are provided to schools on the basis of their need for assistance and the number of meals served. The Federal funds must be matched by funds from sources within the States.

Commodity Exchange Authority

The Commodity Exchange Administration was established pursuant to an order of the Secretary of Agriculture of June 30, 1936, to administer the Commodity Exchange Act. From 1923 to 1936 it had been known as the Grain Futures Administration. Consolidated in 1942 with other agencies of the Department of Agriculture, it was reestablished February 1, 1947, pursuant to Secretary's Memorandum 1185, as a separate agency of the Department and designated as the Commodity Exchange Authority.

The major functions of the Commodity Exchange Authority are to maintain fair and competitive pricing in the commodity futures markets.

Foreign Agricultural Service

The Foreign Agricultural Service represents the United States Department of Agriculture in foreign matters.

The office has primary responsibility for developing foreign markets for United States farm products.

Agricultural Stabilization

Commodity Credit Corporation

The CCC is managed by a board of directors, subject to the general supervision and direction of the Secretary of Agriculture, who is an ex officio director and chairman of the board. The board consists of six members (in addition to the Secretary of Agriculture), who are appointed by the President of the United States by and with the advice and consent of the Senate.

In addition to the board of directors, the CCC has a five-member advisory board, the members of which are appointed by the President of the United States. Not more than three of the members may belong to the same political party. The advisory board meets at least every 90 days to survey the general policies of the CCC.

The CCC is capitalized at $100,000,000. CCC also has authority to borrow not to exceed $14,500,000,000 for use in carrying out its programs.

In carrying on its operations, the CCC utilizes the personnel and facilities of the Commodity Stabilization Service.

One of the major programs of the CCC is price support.

Commodities acquired under the price support program are disposed of through domestic and export sales, transfers to other Government agencies, and donations for welfare use. The CCC is also authorized to exchange surplus agricultural commodities acquired by the CCC for strategic and critical materials produced abroad.

Administration of American operations under the International Wheat Agreement is a responsibility of the CCC.

Under its storage facilities program, CCC (1) purchases and maintains granaries and equipment for care and storage of CCC owned or controlled grain in areas where commercial storage facilities are inadequate, (2) makes loans for the construction or expansion of farm storage facilities, and (3) undertakes such other operations as may be necessary to provide storage adequate to carry out efficiently and effectively CCC's programs.

Commodity Stabilization Service

[Renamed Agricultural Stabilization and Conservation Service]

The Commodity Stabilization Service is responsible for operations falling into the following categories: (1) acreage allotments and marketing quotas; (2) milk and tobacco marketing agreements and orders; (3) price support, inventory management, procurement, domestic disposal, and other programs of the CCC; (4) emergency feed assistance programs for the relief of agriculture from the effects of any major disaster; (5) agricultural conservation programs and practices assigned CSS under the Soil Conservation and Domestic Allotment Act; (6) conservation reserve of the Soil Bank; (7) International Wheat Agreement Act; (8) storage, shipping, and related service activities; (9) administration of the Sugar Act; and (10) assigned mobilization and defense activities.

Personnel and facilities of CSS are utilized in the administration of Commodity Credit Corporation programs.

Federal Crop Insurance Corporation

The basic purpose of Federal Crop Insurance is to promote the general welfare by providing farmers the opportunity to strengthen their financial position through insurance of money spent to produce crops against loss from causes beyond their control such as weather, insects, and disease.

Agricultural Credit

Farmers Home Administration

The Farmers Home Administration was established under the authority of the Farmers Home Administration Act, approved August 14, 1946 (7 U. S. C. 1001, note).

The agency provides credit for specific types of farmers who cannot get the financing they need elsewhere at reasonable rates and terms.

Rural Electrification Administration

The Rural Electrification Administration was created by Executive Order 7037 of May 11, 1935, under authority of the Emergency Relief Appropriation Act of 1935, approved April 8, 1935 (49 Stat. 115). Statutory provision for the agency was made in the Rural Electrification Act of May 20, 1936 (49 Stat. 1363; 7 U. S. C.

901 et seq.). This law authorized loans for facilities to bring central station electric service to persons in rural areas who did not have it. REA became a part of the Department of Agriculture under Reorganization Plan II, effective July 1, 1939. An act approved September 21, 1944 (58 Stat. 739; 7 U.S.C. 903), liberalized the terms of REA loans and removed the time limitation from its lending program. REA was authorized by act approved October 28, 1949 (63 Stat. 948; 7 U.S.C. 901), to make loans for the purpose of furnishing and improving rural telephone service.

LOAN TERMS.—The act of September 21, 1944, established the interest rate on all REA loans at 2 percent, and fixed the permissible loan period at a maximum of 35 years.

Agricultural Economics

Economic Research Service

AGRICULTURAL ECONOMICS RESEARCH.—Agricultural economics research includes broad economic and analysis programs on factors affecting agricultural prices and income, commodity outlook and situation, food demand, consumption, and supply.

MARKETING RESEARCH.—Marketing research is concerned with market costs, structure, and development, market potentials, and the distribution and merchandising of agricultural products. Studies are conducted to determine the potentials for market expansion of agricultural products. The movement of agricultural products through marketing channels and the economic aspects of public distribution programs are studied to obtain information to aid agricultural industries in improving the merchandising of their products. Cost analysis research is conducted on the marketing of crops and animal products to determine ways of increasing efficiency and reducing costs, increasing returns to growers and providing consumers with the choices they desire. Emphasis in marketing research is placed on products in abundant supply requiring additional outlets. The research results are widely disseminated.

FARM ECONOMICS RESEARCH.—ERS administers a national program of economic and statistical research on farm problems involving the efficient use of labor, land, buildings, and equipment in farm production, and adjustment in farming to technological development and changing market outlets.

FOREIGN AGRICULTURAL ANALYSIS.—ERS analyzes and interprets world conditions and developments affecting foreign markets for U.S. farm products.

Statistical Reporting Service

The Statistical Reporting Service, created by Secretary's Memorandum 1446, Supplement 1, dated April 3, 1961, administers (1) a program concerned with the review, coordination, and improvement of statistics in the Department, and (2) crop and livestock estimates and reporting programs.

TABLE 7.—*Organization and personnel summary, Jan. 1, 1947, to Jan. 1, 1964*[1]

Organization	Jan. 1—					
	1947	1952	1957	1962	1963	1964
Executive Office of the President	1,027	1,252	1,217	1,609	1,538	1,550
Executive departments	1,790,264	2,124,156	2,075,807	2,050,529	2,082,871	2,080,141
Department of State	22,704	30,194	33,595	39,718	40,928	42,357
Department of Defense:						
Office of the Secretary of Defense	----------	2,157	1,690	3,146	27,367	34,441
Department of the Army	629,194	530,883	430,212	397,499	387,048	371,636
Department of the Navy	377,284	462,835	393,332	352,927	345,098	338,069
Department of the Air Force	----------	281,052	350,681	305,488	306,877	299,215
Department of the Treasury	102,447	89,409	78,424	80,191	83,648	84,779
Department of Justice	24,280	31,306	30,520	30,861	31,813	31,682
Post Office Department	458,988	511,609	523,416	586,235	588,826	595,571
Department of the Interior	49,693	54,964	48,578	53,946	58,442	61,963
Department of Agriculture	80,325	66,162	82,421	91,644	96,753	98,412
Department of Commerce	37,600	55,747	47,065	28,334	29,501	30,707
Department of Labor	7,749	7,638	5,927	7,669	8,820	9,269
Department of Health, Education, and Welfare	----------	----------	49,946	72,871	77,750	82,040

Illustration 6. EXECUTIVE PERSONNEL GROWTH. The number of workers in the Department of Agriculture increased by about 18,000 between the years of 1947 and 1964, although the number of farms in the United States declined in roughly the same period–1950–1960–from 5.4 million to 3.7 million. (Organization of Federal Executive Departments, Report of the U.S. Senate Committee on Government Operations, Report No. 24, 88th Congress, 2nd Session.)

4. *From Temporary to Permanent Legislation*

FREEMAN WAS expected to come forth with a new farm program in 1961 since President Kennedy had promised it. But despite the advance work of the Kennedy-appointed advisory committees, it would take time for the new Secretary to decide on a full-blown program, and to sell it to Congress and the country. In the meantime, it was decided, emergency legislation should be passed to stop the buildup of wheat and corn surplus stocks. Most wheat had already been planted when Freeman took office in midwinter, but there might be time for a quick temporary corn bill to be passed and to be implemented before the corn was planted in the spring.

The emergency feed-grains bill, drafted by the USDA under Freeman before he took formal command there, was thrown in the hopper on February 16th, and cleared the Congress for the President's signature March 22. This bill was a product of many minds which had focused on the feed-grains problem especially after the failure of the Benson corn legislation of 1958. The bill's public authors were members of a special feed-grains advisory committee, chaired then by Missouri Farmers Association President Fred Heinkel, and included notables from around the country. The Committee was advised by Willard Cochrane who, with congressional reference specialist Walter Wilcox, drafted the bill and then polished a final draft.

TERMS OF THE FEED-GRAINS BILL

Under the voluntary-participation approach taken in the feed-grains legislation, subsidies and higher price supports were offered

Year	*Government investment in feed grains program*	*Size of surplus, millions of tons*	*Change in amount of surplus, millions of tons*
1953	$ 816	27	
1954	1,340	32	+ 5
1955	1,691	39	+ 7
1956	2,020	43	+ 4
1957	2,201	49	+ 6
1958	2,633	59	+10
1959	2,880	68	+ 9
1960	3,121	75	+ 7
1961	3,360	85	+10
1962	2,594	72	—13
est. 1963	2,366	61	—11

Illustration 7. THE FIGURES ON A FARM BILL THAT WORKED: What happened to feed grains during a ten-year period. (Source: Testimony of Secretary Freeman, *Hearings on the Feed Grains Bill of 1963*, Senate Committee on Agriculture and Forestry, p. 9.)

to those producers of corn and grain sorghums who would reduce their production by 20% or more. Farmers were paid an amount equal to half the normal yield on the diverted acres (those they agreed not to plant), and in addition, those who complied with the program got price supports at $1.20 a bushel for corn. After some controversy, and for the first time, the government was given power to drive down the market price by selling corn surpluses on the open market. This would keep noncompliers from enjoying price benefits without making any sacrifices. The market price of corn which noncompliers received would be kept twenty cents below the support price given to compliers—the difference between profit and loss for many farmers. Under this program the federal government would be taking over much $1.20 corn and selling even larger quantities of $1.00 corn. Farm income would go up; the surplus would go down. The cost of the program would be high but less than it cost the government to store bigger and bigger surpluses.

Offered while the new President and Congress were still in their honeymoon period, the bill got adequate support from Democrats and a scattering of rural Republicans.

By the time the bill cleared the Senate the USDA had already completed the tedious work of translating the legislative guidelines into detailed administrative regulations. The administration was elated at passage of the first major New Frontier legislation.

The bill was most significant, as it turned out, because it worked so well over the short-run period: despite a per acre increase in corn production, total feed-grains production dropped 10% in 1961. (See Illustration 7.) Republican leaders had charged that it would be too expensive, make the Secretary a czar, disrupt the grain trade, farmers would not like it, and that it simply would not work. If they had been right, the subsequent, tougher schemes of the Kennedy administration might have had a better chance of passage. Instead, in the following year, leading Midwestern Republicans were urging renewal of this successful, even if expensive "temporary" legislation, as an attractive alternative to the stiffer, cheaper legislation that Freeman was then ready to prescribe.

Choosing the Approach to Permanent Legislation

What kind of permanent program should the Administration put forward? And what form should the legislation take? These were related questions.

One alternative was the Cochrane bill, which assumed that a comprehensive program was needed—a complex system of controls for all of agriculture. Based on past legislative failures it also assumed that such a program could not emerge through the ordinary legislative procedure: (a) the administration framed bills (b) which were introduced by a congressman and (c) then sent to a standing (Agriculture) committee, (d) where public hearings and private sessions were held, (e) after which the revised bill was sent to the floor, (f) voted on, (g) then dispatched to the other House where the process was repeated before the bill went to the President for approval, or veto.

The Cochrane bill proposed a new procedure: Congress would delegate the power to write farm programs to the Secretary of Agriculture. Under Cochrane's plan, the Secretary of Agriculture would choose a farmer advisory committee for each commodity. Two-thirds of the members on each committee would have to be selected from nominees elected by the ASCS farmer committees which administered the commodity programs in areas where the particular commodity was raised. The Secretary (Freeman) would be free to choose the other third of the membership from among appropriate farm organizations. Having called members of such a commodity committee to Washington, and having consulted with them as to whether or not a program was needed and what it should be, the Secretary could then draft a program and submit it to the President for approval.

In Cochrane's proposal, Congress would be involved only in that it could veto a commodity program within sixty days after it was submitted, but if it did so there would be no program at all for that commodity during the next year. Farmers, too, were given a chance to reject mandatory control programs in annual producer referendums.

The alternative to Cochrane's comprehensive, procedural bill was the commodity-by-commodity approach under which new supply-management programs for each commodity would be framed by the USDA, and sent one by one to the Congress to be handled in the regular manner. This approach was favored by those on Freeman's new staff who had previously served on the Hill (in congressional offices) including Undersecretary Murphy, Edwin Jaenke, and Robert Lewis. These men did not think a comprehensive program was needed, since only a few commodities were then in surplus. Furthermore, they were certain that Congress could not be persuaded to pass the Cochrane bill, though it might well approve supply-management programs for the troublesome commodities if bills for each were introduced by friendly congressmen, without overt administration sponsorship. The administration could wait until these bills had gained support, from Republicans as well as Democrats, before throwing its own weight behind them to assure passage.

After weeks of discussions, the choice was made between the Cochrane bill and the commodity-by-commodity approach, at a Saturday afternoon showdown session held in Secretary Freeman's spacious office. Present besides Freeman and Murphy were economist John Galbraith, presidential assistant Myer Feldman, Kermit Gordon of the President's Council of Economic Advisers, and three Budget Bureau experts. At this session in early March, Freeman tentatively decided to recommend the commodity-by-commodity approach.

Later in the same weekend, however, President Kennedy and his elite group of White House advisers reversed the judgment in favor of the Cochrane bill.

On March 16th, the President sent down his agricultural message, followed a month later by a comprehensive bill which embodied the Kennedy farm program. At the heart of it was Cochrane's procedural change.

Why the Cochrane Bill?

President Kennedy and his advisers hoped that a dramatic attack on the farm problem would contribute substance to the recently proclaimed New Frontier. Moreover, the Cochrane bill would serve as a vehicle for education, which Freeman felt had to precede legislation. The first step, in Freeman's judgment, was to convince farmers that overproduction was about to ruin them, to convince urban America that it was in their interest to save the efficient family farm, and to persuade Congress that the watered-down commodity programs which ordinarily emerged from the logrolling process would not do the job. Indeed, this was an emergency, Freeman later argued, which justified the delegation of power to the Executive. The Cochrane bill expressed what the administration thought was needed to deal with the crisis in agriculture.

Difficult as it might be to secure procedural change, it could be argued that such change was the only way to secure effective supply-management programs.

Farm policy had once been made by a coalition of rural leaders, and some of them still looked wistfully for a new rural coalition which might gather the strings of common purpose as did a senate-centered farm bloc during the twenties, or for a farm organization leader like former Farm Bureau President Edward O'Neal. During the Roosevelt years O'Neal had bridged party lines, had reached understandings with urban labor, and had joined the hands of corn, cotton, and wheat representatives.

Since then, however, cooperation within agriculture had given way to various interpenetrating conflicts. Farm regions had become jealous and competitive as commodities had begun to move from one area to another: cotton to the Southwest and West, feed grains to the Plains and South, beef to the South, and poultry to the South. Even among producers of the same commodity there was often conflict. Milk producers near Eastern and Southern metropolitan centers wished to exclude Midwestern producers from these markets. Producers of each kind of wheat argued they should be given distinctive treatment. Big wheat producers accused growers of small acreage of having "stolen" wheat acreage by means of a provision which exempted acreages of less than fifteen acres from controls.

In recent years the farm problem had become a good election issue for the party out of power, so that Democratic legislators rarely consulted and almost never voted with Republicans, and vice versa. It seemed every bitter party fight during the 1950's had widened the breach.

Though Congressional parties were eager critics, neither party was anxious when in power to legislate solutions. With Benson as Secretary of Agriculture, forty Democratic congressmen vied for one vacant seat on the House Agriculture Committee in 1958. But in 1961, and again in 1963, leaders had to draft reluctant Democrats to the Committee, where they would then be frontline defenders of controls rather than carefree opponents of low prices.

Republicans, likewise, could unite in opposition to Democratic proposals but were split when it came to suggesting alternatives.

The Congressional Agriculture Committees

These many conflicts were exposed in the Agriculture Committees of the House and the Senate. Ordinarily, work was done and decisions were made in Congress by these standing committees, whose members had expert knowledge of the subjects dealt with by their committee, and also had a constituency interest in these subjects. But given the divisive elements in agricultural policy, it was to be expected that neither the House nor the Senate Agriculture Committees would be strong.

Partly because most rural Democrats have been from the South, Southerners held the powerful chairmanships and senior positions on both Senate and House Committees. In a way this was fortunate for the Kennedy administration, in that the Southern representatives had already legislated mandatory controls for their cotton, tobacco, peanuts, and rice (see Illustration 8), and were insistent that other commodities be similarly disciplined.

Freeman sought advice from the chairman of the Senate Agriculture Committee, Allen Ellender, almost as soon as he was appointed Secretary of Agriculture. Subsequently he and the Louisiana senator became mutual admirers working closely together.

House Agriculture chairman, Harold Cooley of North Carolina, shared his power and function, in unique fashion, with Vice-Chairman W. R. Poage of Texas. Poage, even more than Cooley, was fond of jousting with the opposition although this did not

---

Illustration 8. The Commodities and the Committee Members. Most members of the Agriculture Committee speak for the one or two commodities which are produced in their constituencies. Legislators from the wheat and feed grains areas were mostly Republicans, while the Democrats happened to come from cotton, tobacco or rice constituencies. Information was obtained from correspondence and from Charles O. Jones, "Representation in Congress: House Agriculture Committee" American Political Science Review, June 1961, 358–367.

House Democrats	*Principal commodities represented*
Harold Cooley (North Carolina) Chairman	Tobacco
W. R. Poage (Texas) Vice Chairman	Cotton and Rice
George Grant (Alabama)	Cotton and Rice
E. C. Gathings (Arkansas)	Cotton and Rice
John L. McMillan (South Carolina)	Tobacco
Thomas G. Abernethy (Mississippi)	Cotton and Rice
Watkins M. Abbitt (Virginia)	Tobacco
Paul C. Jones (Missouri)	Cotton and Rice
Harlan Hagen (California)	Diversified
Lester R. Johnson (Wisconsin)	Dairy, Livestock, Small Grains
Ross Bass (Tennessee)	Tobacco
W. Pat Jennings (Virginia)	Tobacco
D. R. Matthews (Florida)	Tobacco
Merwin Coad (Iowa)	Corn and Livestock
J. Floyd Breeding (Kansas)	Wheat
Frank A. Stubblefield (Kentucky)	Tobacco
Harold B. McSween (Louisiana)	Rice and Cotton
Daniel K. Inouye (Hawaii)	Diversified
Ralph Harding (Idaho)	Beef, Cotton, Wheat
G. Elliot Hagan (Georgia)	Cotton
Graham Purcell (Texas)	Wheat and Beef
Senate Democrats	
Allen J. Ellender (Louisiana) Chairman	Rice and Cotton
Spessard L. Holland (Florida)	Fresh fruits and Vegetables Diversified
James O. Eastland (Mississippi)	Cotton and Rice
Herman E. Talmadge (Georgia)	Peanuts, Cotton, Rice and Tobacco
William Proxmire (Wisconsin)	Dairy, Livestock, Small Grains
B. Everett Jordan (North Carolina)	Tobacco and Cotton
Stephen M. Young (Ohio)	Corn and Livestock
Philip A. Hart (Michigan)	Diversified
Eugene J. McCarthy (Minnesota)	Dairy, Livestock, Small Grains
Maurine B. Neuberger (Oregon)	Diversified

always win harmony in Committee, or votes in the House of Representatives. Twelve of the other sixteen House committee Democrats were interested primarily in rice, cotton, peanuts, or tobacco. Yet not all Southern representatives would follow Cooley and Poage in their vigorous championship of supply management, and not all Southern senators supported Senator Ellender, because traditional Southern commodities were giving way to nonsupported beef and poultry, and to growing industrial production. Further, the civil-rights issue was placing some Southerners on both committees in a position of total opposition to the Kennedy administration.

In the House Agriculture Committee, virtually the only Democratic spokesmen for the commodities most in trouble were J. Floyd Breeding who represented half of the western Kansas wheat producers, Lester Johnson, dairy legislator from Wisconsin, and the Reverend Merwin Coad from Iowa's corn belt. On the Senate Agriculture Committee were four northern liberals, including Freeman's Minnesota friend Senator Eugene McCarthy.

In contrast, most legislators from the corn, wheat, and dairy areas were Republicans. Republicans on the House committee included uncompromisingly conservative senior figures and skillful, aggressive young men whose effective opposition was taken for granted, even though divisive commodity interests and the dogmatic pressures of farm organizations would keep this minority from uniting around an alternative legislative proposal.

Republicans on the Senate committee were respected men, and some where moderates. The ranking member, George Aiken of Vermont, was leader of a group of Senate Republican liberals who often voted with the Democrats—except on farm policy! Liberal Republican Senator John Sherman Cooper of Kentucky had voted for supply management for tobacco, and Republican Milton Young of North Dakota (nicknamed "Mr. Wheat" because of his long-standing interest in and influence over wheat legislation) had often been willing to cross party lines for a wheat program that would keep up North Dakota incomes. These Republican moderates, however, tried to be responsive to their party leaders.

That the politically and philosophically divided Agriculture committees could pilot administration commodity bills through the cross currents of many differences seemed most unlikely.[1] In subsequent hearings on the Cochrane bill, Vice-Chairman Poage joked about the congressional impasse on farm policy: "My colleague from Iowa [Republican leader Hoeven] convinced me that a bill ought to be passed . . . when he said it [the Cochrane bill] was a radical departure from our present system. (Laughter) If there is any thing we need it is a radical departure from our present system."[2]

The Farmer Committee System vs. Farm Organizations

Another reason for the Cochrane bill was to raise the status of the USDA-affiliated ASCS farmer-committee system. Beginning in 1933, the USDA had organized and used farmer committees at the state, county, and community levels to administer production-control programs, and also as a mechanism to bring farmers into the decision process. Through the committee system, farmers could become informed about farm policy, and other issues, and also could find a voice in political affairs, where local lawyers and businessmen might otherwise be dominant.

State committeemen were selected by the Secretary of Agriculture, though generally from the ranks of the 10,000 county committeemen, and 80,000 community committeemen. It was this structure, presumed to have a vested interest in production-control programs, which would nominate a majority of the members of Secretary Freeman's policy advisory committees.

But why should the government sponsor new channels for democratic action, as the Cochrane procedure endeavored to do, when farmer organizations already existed which could make their views known in our nation's capital? This important question requires an explanation.

One could not assume that existing organizations in 1961 were

[1] See John Heinz, "The Impasse in Agricultural Legislation," *Yale Law Journal* (April, 1962), pp. 952–978.

[2] *Hearings on the Agriculture Act of 1961*, House Committee on Agriculture, pp. 52–53.

neutral mechanisms to mirror farmer views. These organizations often seemed less interested in learning what grass roots farmers wanted than they were in strengthening certain rural attitudes which would generate support for their own long-established policies, and then in capitalizing on this support in their lobbying activities. Some farm organizations seemed to give highest priority to an effort to weaken or destroy competitor groups.

Most farm groups were called commodity organizations because they were composed of the more active producers of a particular commodity, and they devoted themselves to improving the position of producers of that commodity.

Some commodity groups, such as those representing sugar producers, had been able through their own lobbying efforts to get what they desired, but others had failed, in part because of conflicts between different commodities and even among the producers of the same commodity.

In addition there were four general farm organizations, each of which presumed to represent and harmonize the economic interests of all types of producers, and to speak for the other interests of rural America.

The oldest of the general farm organizations was a fraternal society, the Grange, once the vehicle of vigorous agrarian protest. With slackened political interest and an aging membership in recent years, the Grange had assumed a slightly conservative policy position until—fearful for the future of the rural community in a laissez-faire farm economy—the Grange leadership decided to back most of the Kennedy programs. The membership of the Grange was small, located mainly in the Northeast, Middle Atlantic and the Pacific Northwest.

The youngest general farm organization was the National Farmers Organization, which had sprung from Midwestern farm discontent of the 1950's. NFO, whose membership was secret and presumed to be relatively small, was most interested in serving as a vehicle for strengthening farmer bargaining power in the marketplace, in the manner of labor unions, but NFO did work for federal supply-management programs as a helpmate to its private efforts.

The National Farmers Union was an old organization, smaller than the Grange, active in the Plains area and to a lesser extent, in the Midwest and South. This organization ran farm cooperative businesses in these areas, and received some financial assistance from a huge separately controlled cooperative grain marketing and storage association (The Farmers Union Grain Terminal Association) which Farmers Union had initiated years ago.

The Farmers Union, headed by a dynamic President—James Patton—had become functional and influential as a helpmate to Democratic farm congressmen, as a tenuous link in a chain of liberal interest groups, as a ceremonial voice of farmer liberalism, and as the farm policy arm of the Democratic Party. Cochrane's 1961 procedural bill had been earlier publicized by the group. When the bill was before the congressional committees, Farmers Union also produced thousands of farmer signatures on petitions favoring the bill, which were hauled from one congressional committee office to another as action on the bill proceeded. Farmers Union's big contribution in 1961, however, was in a supporting role to USDA in gathering a coalition of farm groups to support the new administration. (See Illustrations 9 and 10.) Following a courtship by USDA policymakers, and after preliminary conferences among themselves, the groups signed the following public treaty in late April, 1961, in which they joined hands in support of the Cochrane bill:

Farm organizations listed below met today at the Grange Building in Washington, D.C., and all agreed to support by either testifying for or filing a statement in behalf of the general objectives of the Agricultural Act of 1961, introduced this week by Senator Allen J. Ellender and Representative Harold D. Cooley:

American Cotton Producers Association, American Tung Oil Association, Association of Virginia Peanut and Hog Growers, Grain Sorghum Producers Association, Missouri Farmers Association, Na-

Illustration 9. Mail from the Constituency. In 1961, Farmers Union gathered thousands of farmers' signatures on behalf of supply-management programs, which lobbyist Reuben Johnson transported to committee hearings. Seen here looking at the signatures are left to right: Secretary of Agriculture Orville Freeman, Senate Agriculture Committee Chairman Allen J. Ellender, and Mr. Johnson. (National Farmers Union photo)

tional Association of Wheat Growers, National Corn Growers Association, National Farmers Organization, National Farmers Union, National Grange, and Plains Cotton Growers.

Everybody's Out of Step But . . . . .

— Drawn for Farmers Union Herald by Jim Zilverberg

Illustration 10. As the Farmers Union Herald Saw the Farm Bureau, May 8, 1961. Drawn by Jim Zilverberg.

Farmers Union, Grange, and some of the other small groups exercised political influence through the friendly ASCS committee system in areas where these farm organizations were strong, and they hoped to organize new memberships through the ASCS committees in other areas. Most important, perhaps, was the fact that these committees were organized in all rural counties. They were a means to rally support for supply-management programs at the grass roots throughout America.

The American Farm Bureau Federation

Younger than the Grange and the NFU, and by far the largest farm organization was the American Farm Bureau Federation, which had in an earlier day used another government bureaucracy —the Federal and State Extension Services—through which to organize across the nation. Now self-reliant with its own dynamic bureaucracy, and with farmer services such as low-cost insurance which attracted many members, the Farm Bureau had earlier declared war on the farmer committee system which it viewed as a powerful competitor. The Farm Bureau saw no virtue in supply-management programs, and ASCS farmer committees would have little role to play under the Farm Bureau program alternative.

Nor were ASCS committees necessary to represent farmers, in the opinion of Farm Bureau leaders. The Farm Bureau felt that the babble of farm voices could be best harmonized through its own organization, which had units in most counties throughout the U.S.

However, just as the Farm Bureau criticized the bias within the ASCS, others objected that the Farm Bureau had developed a conservative bias in its program and in its associations which had become extreme in recent years.

Since its origin as a helpmate of extension education agents, the Farm Bureau had always cooperated with business groups and in recent years had formed close links with such nonfarm groups as the U.S. Chamber of Commerce, the American Medical Association, and the National Association of Manufacturers. These organizations used a common vocabulary to express a common conservative ideology, each supporting the others' action programs, and all entering the electoral process through the mechanism of the Republican Party (except in the one-party Democratic South).

Some state Farm Bureaus turned to very conservative individuals and groups for assistance in conducting vigorous membership education programs. Under Farm Bureau sponsorship one such team, led by George S. Benson of Harding College, Searcy, Arkansas, operated one-day institutes for young people. These young people —and others who read Benson's articles in Farm Bureau news-

Illustration 11. THE FARM BUREAU'S ATTITUDE. Three cartoons object to controls from Washington. This one is from the *Kansas Farm Bureau News*, June, 1963.

papers—were warned that farm price programs, and other social and economic legislation passed since 1932, had set a dangerous trend which threatened our free society.

Resolutions passed at Farm Bureau conventions stressed a similar theme, which was given drumbeat repetition in Farm Bureau newspapers, in materials used to guide local policy development, in statistical tables, in cartoons, in pamphlets, in speeches, in movies and live dramatizations, and in books members were urged to read. (See Illustration 11.)

Illustration 11. A Farm Bureau cartoon as printed April 8, 1964, in the *AFBF Newsletter.*

But this vigorously promoted message, which harmonized nicely with some attitudes of rural and small-town people, was weakened wherever there were contradictory local voices which appealed to other strongly held farmer attitudes. To hold down the influence of these competing local voices, Farm Bureau leaders exerted every effort to defeat the Cochrane bill.

Illustration 11. A Farm Bureau cartoon from the *AFBF Newsletter* of April 13, 1963.

The Case against the Cochrane Bill

In testimony before the congressional committees, Farm Bureau's Shuman presented the case against the Cochrane bill. Since one purpose of the new procedure was to facilitate enactment of supply-management programs, Shuman attacked the programs themselves (discussed fully in Chapter VII) as well as the procedure.

On the latter point Shuman, and other opponents, particularly questioned the nature and adequacy of restraints on power under the Cochrane procedure. Shuman charged that the farmer committees would be "mere window-dressing" for a procedure in which the Secretary of Agriculture would actually write programs.[3] Two-thirds of the members of these advisory committees would be chosen from nominees elected by "per diem employees of the Department of Agriculture" [4] and the Secretary could select the other one-third of the members from the ranks of friendly farm organizations. Shuman pointed out that the Secretary might rig referendums too—by deciding who could vote, by offering unacceptable alternative choices, and by submitting programs in such order that one group after another would have to vote for controls or be flooded with refugees from other commodities.

Freeman denied that he would pack the advisory committees or rig referendums. He said any Secretary of Agriculture would regret it if he "did not follow in good faith the procedures called for in this bill." [5]

Proponents argued privately that the new procedure would increase farmer control over legislation, despite declining farmer representation in Congress. In particular, the farmer-dominated congressional agriculture committees would gain a stronger hand in that they would no longer have to induce urban-oriented Congresses to vote for producer-developed subsidies. To backstop producers the committees would have only to prevent unfavorable action in the Congress. Furthermore, relieved of program writing, the congressional committees would have more time to scrutinize administrative decisions, in the presence of new congressional authority to veto these decisions.

The congressional committees' adverse decision on the Cochrane

[3] *Hearings on the Agriculture Act of 1961*, House Committee on Agriculture, p. 254.

[4] *Ibid.*

[5] *Hearings on the Agriculture Act of 1961*, House Committee on Agriculture, p. 66.

procedure may well have turned on the committees' judgment as to its effect on their power and status. Apparently they were not convinced that they would become more influential as a result of delegating their legislative power to the Executive.

Neither did all congressmen accept the assumption that the Secretary of Agriculture was more capable than they of protecting farmers from the urban majority. Notwithstanding a perfunctory provision which charged the Secretary of Agriculture to see that farm programs served the general interest, the Cochrane procedure clearly rested on the belief that farm policy should be made by farm interests. Not only were programs to be written by farmer committees and sanctioned in farmer referendums, but they were also to be implemented by the farmers' patron, the Secretary of Agriculture. But farm legislators were not sure that the Secretary possessed enough autonomy—or enough influence—within the executive branch to protect and foster the considerable benefits which had been given to farmers, in the face of conflicting demands on federal resources. The next year, 1962, would provide considerable experience on this matter.

Results in 1961

By making a sincere effort to get Congress to approve the Cochrane procedure, Freeman satisfied budget-conscious individuals within the Kennedy administration who felt that the costs of agriculture programs could be reduced by use of this new procedure for devising and implementing the programs. He also satisfied many liberal farm spokesmen who, like Cochrane, felt this was the only feasible way to get comprehensive income protection for the family farmer.

The administration had submitted the Cochrane procedure to Congress as part of an omnibus bill which contained other provisions designed as sweeteners to attract votes for the Cochrane procedure. Freeman's group may have hoped, too, that the very large omnibus bill would so overload the congressional committee staffs that they would make fewer changes in the bill than if its

"YOU'RE NICE, AND I LIKE YOU, BUT I DON'T FEEL LIKE MOVING."

Illustration 12. Congress and the Kennedy Program. Mauldin in the *St. Louis Post Dispatch*. Used in *Post Dispatch* April 12, 1962, and in *National Farmers Union Newsletter*, June 23, 1962. Reproduced by permission.

various provisions were sent up one by one. Included in the omnibus bill was an extension of the National Wool Act that wool growers liked, and a provision to extend and expand the popular Food-for-Peace program under which billions of dollars of food surpluses were sold to underdeveloped countries, traded for strategic materials, and distributed to the needy by church organizations and other agencies including governments.

When it was evident that Title I of the omnibus bill—the Cochrane bill—would not be reported in 1961 from either standing committee of the Congress (see Illustration 12), the administration asked for renewal of the temporary feed-grains program for the next year (with some changes), and for passage of a temporary wheat bill which incorporated similar voluntary features. These programs, together with the Wool Bill, Food-For-Peace extensions, and other provisions, were in the omnibus bill which passed the Congress August 3rd.

When President Kennedy signed the bill a few days later, both he and Secretary Freeman hailed it as an administration victory.

The law did add authority to issue national marketing orders for a few additional commodities—cherries, turkeys, for example, and it gave more prestige to the advisory committees that candidate Kennedy had appointed in 1960, which had helped draft emergency legislation. The feed grains and wheat advisory committees were to be reappointed—with some membership change—in the fall of 1961.

But Willard Cochrane's procedural bill had not passed. Willard Cochrane's supply-management programs had yet to be submitted to the Congress.

5. *Framing Major Legislation*

IN LATE 1961, Willard Cochrane told a producer advisory committee, "you guys and the Budget Bureau have got me locked in a closet with no doors." Wayne Darrow, whose weekly farmletter kept bureaucratic, political, and farmer outposts informed about Washington events and let Washington farm politicians know what was cooking outside their respective bailiwicks, expressed the dilemma as it applied to Secretary Freeman in the following terms:

> [He's] caught between the Budget Bureau and public opinion, and the deep blue sea of parity desired by farmers and promised by President Kennedy in the 1960 campaign.[1]

To clarify, it should be said that the Budget Bureau was often seen as the "devil," by those who wanted a better shake for the farmer in 1962.

THE ROLE OF THE BUDGET BUREAU

In reality, the Budget Bureau was merely the servant of the President, though it did continually prompt him to save money. It worked in his line of vision, within the ornate Executive Office building across the lot from the White House, and Kennedy so regularly sought assistance from this collection of expert probers that it would have been difficult for them to become really removed, institutionalized, and tyrannical. When Budget men got really tough, as they did in late 1961, those willing to face the truth knew they did so at the direction of the President. In fact President Kennedy had made it clear to Secretary Freeman as well

[1] *Washington Farmletter*, December 2, 1961.

as to the Budget Bureau that he wanted to cut farm program costs substantially in future years.

Why single out agriculture for drastic reductions? The President wanted to achieve a balanced federal budget as a means to maintain stable prices and a sound currency; to do this, he had to make major cuts in one of the very large federal expenditures, such as allocations for agriculture or defense. But the President dared not withhold justifiable increases in the monstrous defense budget. (See Illustration 13.)

In addition, there were other serious new claims on federal resources. A decision had been made to "go for the moon" in order to benefit from the scientific breakthroughs sure to flow from this massive research effort, and to gain prestige. The President also foresaw new federal responsibilities in the field of education, and for some other social programs.

Decisions to cut existing programs were based, as usual, on both economics and politics.

The Council of Economic Advisers and the Farm Budget

Economic considerations would be expressed to the President by his Council of Economic Advisers. (The CEA was set up in 1946 to help the President maintain a healthy economy; each President appoints members for his term[s] of office.)

Though CEA chairman Walter Heller was Cochrane's friend and recent University of Minnesota colleague, the Council as a whole tended to be skeptical of production-control programs because they did not seem to promote national goals stressed by the CEA.[2] The CEA wanted full employment, and full utilization of all other economic resources, while the supply-management programs would intentionally idle some land and capital in agriculture, and would provide higher farm incomes which would slow migration of underemployed rural people into the

[2] Robert J. Lampman, CEA, "Goals for the American Economy," *Farm Goals in Conflict* (Ames, Iowa: Iowa State University Press, 1964), pp. 94–102.

	Est. amount spent in 1962 [a]	*Changes planned for 1963* [a]	*Actual changes in 1963* [b]
	(Billions of dollars)		
National defense	51.2	+1.5	+1.7
International affairs and finance	2.9	+0.1	−0.2
Space research and technology	1.3	+1.1	+1.3
Interest on national debt	9.0	+0.4	+0.8
AGRICULTURE AND AGRICULTURAL RESOURCES	6.3	−0.5	+1.1
Natural resources	2.1	+0.2	+0.3
Commerce and transportation	2.9	−0.4*	0.0
Housing and community development	0.5	+0.3	−0.5
Health, Labor, Welfare	4.7	+0.4	+0.3
Education	1.1	+0.4	+0.1
Veterans benefits and services	5.6	−0.3†	−0.2
General government	1.9	+0.1	+0.1
Total Budget Expenditures [c]	89.1	+3.4	+4.8

[a] *Budget in Brief for Fiscal 1963*, p. 8.
[b] Derived by subtracting the actual 1962 expenditures from actual 1963 expenditures, as listed in *Budget in Brief for Fiscal 1965*, pp. 78–79.
* To be saved by raising postal rates.
† A bookkeeping saving only.
[c] Figures are rounded, with the result that the sum of the columns may not be equal to the totals.

Illustration 13. PLAN TO BALANCE THE BUDGET BY CUTTING FARM-PROGRAM COSTS. Above is a comparison of the estimated amount spent in 1962, the changes planned for 1963, and the actual changes in 1963. *Budget in Brief* is issued annually by the Bureau of the Budget.

cities. CEA wanted to spend government funds where they would promote economic growth rather than, as in agriculture, where the intention was to curtail production.

The Council encouraged free competition as a way to promote efficiency, while supply-management programs assumed that uninhibited competition would bring ruin to the atomistic agricultural industry.

The CEA was not convinced that production-related farm programs contributed to an equitable distribution of economic rewards. CEA economists knew that supply-management programs were designed to help commercial farmers who were already much better-off than subsistence farmers.

The Farm Problem: Not the Only Political Issue

President Kennedy himself lacked sentimentalism for the family farm. Kennedy had praised it during the presidential campaign, and his administration had authorized research which indicated that the family farm would weather agriculture's technological revolution, and remain the most efficient, socially beneficial way to organize the production of food and fiber.

Still the President and his aides had become manifestly aware of the terrific budget outlays and mixed economic consequences of existing farm programs, particularly those for wheat, feed grains, and dairy. They knew tremendous budget reductions could be effected by reducing surplus stocks and also by reducing subsidies to farmers. Under the mandatory supply-management programs, subsidies could be replaced by higher supported prices, though higher farm prices might in turn cause somewhat higher food prices, and the administration was reluctant to do anything which might raise the cost of living.

At the same time President Kennedy did want to proceed toward the goal of "parity of farm income" promised in 1960. Total farm income had risen slightly in 1961, reversing an irregular but generally downward trend during much of the previous administration. The 1961 level was judged by Kennedy to be adequate, on the understanding that as many farmers retired each year (the average farmer was 57 years old), remaining farmers could each take a larger share of the pie. Thus individual farmer incomes would continue to inch up.

What if farmers and their spokesmen balked at ending some subsidies, and would not accept mandatory controls? To prevent this happening, the administration would try to help farmers understand that the preponderant urban voters (whose strength would increase with the congressional redistricting for 1963) with their backlog of justifiable, unfulfilled claims on the public treasury, would be demanding that costly farm programs end. Therefore, the farmer either had to choose an inexpensive program giving moderate income support, accompanied by controls, or government would have to cease supporting farm income.

Firm directions were handed down from the White House: the Secretary of Agriculture should come up with a program which would maintain farm income; the CEA should assure that it was not inflationary; the Budget Bureau should see that it promised very substantial savings. The President's advisers would mediate between the groups.

First Steps in Framing the Program

As a first step, teams of experts were put to work within the USDA, to explore alternative programs. Linley Juers was in charge of a dairy team consisting of one expert who knew estimating techniques, another expert to judge how the programs might be administered, still other experts whose job was to determine the cost, and the effects upon production and consumption, levels of surpluses, and so on. John Schnittker headed efforts to explore wheat alternatives; John Duncan worked on a cotton program; Willard Cochrane followed up on feed grains and took overall charge of the other developing commodity programs.

Meanwhile, through informal conversations, these USDA men exchanged thinking with representatives of the Budget Bureau and the Council of Economic Advisers.

(Had they confined themselves to the formal procedure for communication with these agencies, the USDA Budget-and-Finance Officer would have sent a legislative proposal to the Budget Bureau, where it would have been given to an examiner; there were three examiners whose specialty was the commodity programs. Next it would have been circulated to the Council of Economic Advisers, Treasury, and to other interested departments. When the examiner had stated his recommendations, and appended recommendations from CEA and other agencies, the legislative request would then be passed to the next higher level in the Budget Bureau —to the division chief, before whom the USDA would subsequently plead its case for the program. Following these formal hearings on the requests, the Budget Bureau's division chiefs would together make a decision on the legislative request, which could be appealed to a top Board whose members included a presidential assistant and the Director of the Budget Bureau. Department heads who were still dissatisfied might appeal a few big questions to the President himself.)

But only through continuous informal contacts among these agencies could all views be merged in the development of new agriculture legislation. The first informal meeting on the proposed legislation was in late August, 1961. The USDA's Murphy, Cochrane, and Schnittker sat down with people from the CEA and from all levels of the Budget Bureau, to discuss with them the programs they were considering for dairy, wheat, and feed grains. Basically, these were supply-management programs which would reflect all the goals: tighter controls and slightly higher farm prices, which could maintain farm income, reduce government costs, and not raise food prices much. This preliminary meeting was followed up during the fall with more meetings and telephone calls.

Most informal of all, and very useful, were comments scribbled in margins or sheets attached to draft proposals which circulated from one office to another. In these informal exchanges it became clear that some of the President's advisers wanted to reconsider the whole idea of supply management. James Tobin, member of the CEA, plainly preferred to drop supply management in favor of a

Schultz-type program which would allow farm prices to fall and under which the government would ease excess farmers and resources out of agriculture as quickly as possible. In addition, it was rumored that Secretary of the Treasury Douglas Dillon frowned on supply management. He had publicly expressed criticism of farm-program costs.

Even the President's chief assistant, Ted Sorensen, who would ultimately decide which road to take, was trying to get away from farm programs as such, and instead to put farmers and agriculture in the context of programs for the whole economy. Sorensen felt it was time for a reassessment. After a year in action there were new facts to consider. The mood of Congress could now be judged in terms of its reaction to the Administration's 1961 procedural bill. The costs of the Emergency Feed Grains program could be calculated. On August 30, 1961, voters in the wheat referendum had approved quotas sweetened by new voluntary features, but by a somewhat reduced margin from the previous year.

So the farm policy discussion was thrown wide open.

A Debate Over Supply Management

If there was to be a program other than supply management, it seemed there would have to be a Secretary of Agriculture other than Orville Freeman. Although other agencies—the CEA, the Budget Bureau—could criticize programs, and outline alternatives, only the Department of Agriculture was staffed to write a farm program. And since the alternatives to supply management involved a movement away from government support of farmers' incomes, it seemed clear that the USDA would stick to supply management so long as Freeman was Secretary.

Rumors began in mid-October that Secretary Freeman, who was visiting around the world, would soon resign to become Food-for-Peace Director. At about the same time, Farm Bureau President Charles Shuman was accorded an interview with the President, who was seeking Farm Bureau support for his high-priority trade bill which might allow the U.S. government to liberalize the new European Common Market trade walls. Shuman promised to help the President, adding pointedly that "Farm Bureau's efforts in behalf of reciprocal trade legislation would be impaired if the organization has to devote its major legislative efforts in 1962 to defeating unwise farm program proposals . . ." Shuman explained Farm Bureau's program to the President, and on emerging from the President's office to the floodlights and reporters outside, Shuman announced that Freeman's recently passed corn bill involved "a billion-dollar loss."

The big issue—whether to move away from supply management—was finally joined in the staff discussions. At a two-hour luncheon in the White House, CEA member Tobin presented an oral argument that commodity price programs were going nowhere, that there was no foreseeable termination point, and that perhaps the administration should move toward the free market, thereby moving resources out of agriculture. The group in attendance at the luncheon included Director of the Budget Bureau David Bell who took no sides, CEA member Kermit Gordon who shared Tobin's doubts about supply management, Dale Hathaway —a Professor of Agricultural Economics at Michigan State University called in for consultation by the CEA (Hathaway had also suggested new orientations)—and the USDA's articulate economists Cochrane and Schnittker. The Chairman of the CEA, Cochrane's Minnesota colleague, Walter Heller, was not present. The luncheon discussion was presumably for the benefit of President Kennedy's legislative assistant Myer Feldman, but it was also a warmup for another discussion the next day in the White House fish room where Sorensen listened and then decided to continue the supply-management approach.

Perhaps Sorensen never really had an alternative. By abandoning supply management the administration would have alienated most of its farm policy friends, including influential farm Democrats in the Congress. But by opening the question, Sorensen had certainly made it clear to the USDA that the President had reservations about supply management, unless the costs could be reduced.

As a result of Sorensen's decision, approved by the President, the rumors about Freeman's resignation could be squelched. After Freeman arrived home, he and Undersecretary Murphy emerged from a meeting with the President on Friday, November 17th, amid news leaks everywhere that the President was pleased that the temporary corn program had reduced costs (see table, p. 47), and that he had the fullest confidence in Secretary Freeman *because he had reduced costs.* As for the future: Freeman was apparently free to develop his own programs which would receive fullest White House support. But costs of the programs must be reduced far below the levels that the USDA group had wished. Such programs would be hard to sell to the Congress and to the farmers. So, even more than before, Freeman and his group were under the gun.

By mid-October Schnittker and Cochrane, working daily with other economists and with USDA lawyers, had come up with outlines of wheat and feed-grains programs, copies of which were sent to Murphy, to Godfrey, to Jaenke, and to other commodity people, who suggested revisions to Cochrane, Schnittker, and the repair crew. An amended version would again be sent to the policymakers, and to some departmental economists. The hope was that after many imaginations and minds had read, sifted, changed and decided on the words of the bill, most of the errors would have been spotted. The bill went through ten drafts and hundreds of hands before the eventual, final draft of late January, 1962. (See Illustration 14.)

Many People in the Policy Process

Meanwhile USDA policymakers were consulting with other groups —with staff from the congressional committees, with Washington representatives of the farm organizations, with spokesmen for "agribusiness," and grain traders. Freeman was happy to lunch with farm organization people who happened to visit Washington, and he spoke at the Farm Bureau Convention in mid-December. He told the Farm Bureau that their program (discussed, pp. 131–135) was too expensive, and indirectly Freeman made a case for supply management. Farm Bureau delegates applauded politely but then reaffirmed support for their own scheme.

Although USDA people were listening, they were also "educating" others as to the pressures on government for reduction in farm program costs, for a program that would not cause consumer reaction, and that would not stir regional antagonisms.

Telephone calls and memoranda were exchanged between program writers in the USDA and the Budget experts, and on a higher level between Undersecretary of Agriculture Murphy and Director David Bell and Legislative Reference Director Philip Hughes of the Budget Bureau, and also with Kermit Gordon of the Council of Economic Advisers. Since Agriculture was the item under which money was to be saved, top Budget Bureau officials gave much time to this 6% of the mammoth budget.

In the first two weeks of December, USDA program writers held an extended series of discussions with Budget Bureau and CEA people. By this time the supply-management approach had been settled on, as were the mechanisms to be employed in the bill. The fight was now over figures. How high should the price supports be? What percentage of normal yields should farmers get for diverted acres?

Most of these questions were loaded with intangibles. Budget Bureau people were warned that if figures were set too low, friendly farm organizations would not support the programs, Congress would not pass them, and farmers would not vote for them in the referendums. But how low was that?

USDA people were warned that their savings were projected with far too much optimism. Who was to know whether there would be rain or drought, bugs or hail? CEA people argued that the price of wheat should not be raised above $2 a bushel, so as

ADMINISTRATIVELY CONFIDENTIAL

FIRST DRAFT, REVISED PROGRAMS
11/13/61
Copy No. 1

A BILL

To improve and protect farm income, to reduce the carry-over and stabilize the supply of feed grains, to provide for an adequate and balanced flow of feed grains in interstate and foreign commerce, to amend the Agricultural Adjustment Act of 1938, as amended, by establishing a marketing program for feed grains and a marketing program for wheat, and for other purposes.

Be it enacted by the Senate and House of Representatives of the United States of America in Congress assembled, That this Act may be cited as the "Agricultural Act of 1962".

TITLE I - MARKETING PROGRAM FOR FEED GRAINS

Sec. 101. Subtitle B of title III of the Agricultural Adjustment Act of 1938, as amended, is further amended by inserting after part VI thereof a new part VII as follows:

"PART VII - MARKETING PROGRAM FOR FEED GRAINS

"DECLARATION OF POLICY

Too Blunt and too short

"Sec. 360a. It is declared to be the policy of Congress with respect to feed grains to reduce the annual carry-over of feed grains, to stabilize the supply of feed grains at a level consistent with any national policy with respect to strategic reserves, to provide for an adequate and balanced flow of feed grains so that the total supply of feed grains available for utilization for livestock feed is maintained at a level which is consistent with the production of the quantities of livestock and the products thereof that will be consumed and exported at fair prices, ?

Illustration 14. A CONFIDENTIAL MEMORANDUM AND H.R. 10010. The next eight pages present a comparison between the wording of sections of the *Food and Agricultural Act of 1962* as printed in H.R. 10010 (January, 1962) and the same sections as they appeared in a confidential USDA draft in November. The material was kindly released for use in *Pressures and Pro-*

87TH CONGRESS
2D SESSION

H. R. 10010

IN THE HOUSE OF REPRESENTATIVES

JANUARY 31, 1962

Mr. COOLEY introduced the following bill; which was referred to the Committee on Agriculture

A BILL

To improve and protect farm income, to reduce costs of farm programs to the Federal Government, to reduce the Federal Government's excessive stocks of agricultural commodities, to maintain reasonable and stable prices of agricultural commodities and products to consumers, to provide adequate supplies of agricultural commodities for domestic and foreign needs, to conserve natural resources, and for other purposes.

1 *Be it enacted by the Senate and House of Representa-*
2 *tives of the United States of America in Congress* ***assembled,***
3 That this Act may be cited as the "Food and Agriculture Act
4 of 1962".

I

tests by a USDA staff member. The marginal notations on the confidential draft were made by one of the persons involved in the many meetings and readings required for preparation of the bill.

The first thing to notice is the difference of emphasis between the description of H.R. 10010, and the description of the bill as it was stated in the

- 2 -

and to achieve the price goals for feed grains, livestock, and livestock products determined pursuant to section 105(c) (5) of the Agricultural Act of 1949, as amended.

"LEGISLATIVE FINDINGS

"Sec. 360b. The production of feed grains is a vital part of the agricultural production system of the United States, and feed grains move almost wholly in interstate and foreign commerce in the form of grains, livestock, and livestock products. Stable conditions therein are necessary to the general welfare.

"Excessive and deficient supplies of feed grains acutely and directly burden, obstruct, and affect interstate and foreign commerce in grains, livestock, and livestock products. When the available supply of feed grains is excessive, the prices of feed grains are unreasonably low and farmers over-expand livestock production in order to find outlets for feed grains. Excessive supplies of feed grains cause the marketing of excessive supplies of livestock in interstate and foreign commerce at sacrificial prices, endanger the financial stability of producers, and overtax the handling, processing, and transportation facilities through which the flow of interstate and foreign commerce in feed grains, livestock, and livestock products is directed. Deficient supplies of feed grains result in substantial decreases in livestock production and in an inadequate flow of livestock and livestock products in interstate and foreign commerce, with the consequence of unreasonably high prices to consumers. The livestock industry is one of the great basic industries of the United States with ~~ramifying~~ activities

Too long Check lawyers to see why so much justification needed

draft memorandum. H.R. 10010, after paying respect to the improving and protection of farm income, goes immediately to emphasis on reducing "costs of farm programs to the Federal Government," and reducing "the Federal Government's excessive stocks of agricultural commodities," and "to maintain reasonable and stable prices . . . to consumers." None of these items is in the description of the bill as it appears in the draft memorandum.

21

1 "PART VII—MARKETING QUOTAS—FEED GRAINS

2 "LEGISLATIVE FINDINGS

3 "SEC. 360a. The production of feed grains is a vital
4 part of the agricultural economy of the United States. Feed
5 grains move almost wholly in interstate and foreign com-
6 merce in the form of grains, livestock, and livestock products.
7 "Abnormally excessive and abnormally deficient sup-
8 plies of feed grains on the national market acutely and
9 directly burden, obstruct, and affect interstate and foreign
10 commerce. When the available supply of feed grains is
11 excessive, the prices of feed grains are unreasonably low and
12 farmers overexpand livestock production to find outlets for
13 feed grains. Excessive supplies of feed grains cause the
14 marketing of excessive supplies of livestock in interstate and
15 foreign commerce at sacrificial prices, endanger the financial
16 stability of producers, and overtax the handling, processing,
17 and transportation facilities through which the flow of inter-
18 state and foreign commerce in feed grains, livestock, and
19 livestock products is directed. Deficient supplies of feed
20 grains result in substantial decreases in livestock production
21 and in an inadequate flow of livestock and livestock products
22 in interstate and foreign commerce, with the consequence of
23 unreasonably high prices to consumers and loss of markets
24 for producers.
25 "The principal grains used for livestock feed are corn,

The next item of difference concerns Sec. 360a. A staff member had written in the margin: "Too Blunt and too short," as his comment on the

- 3 -

which are in interstate and foreign commerce or which directly affect interstate and foreign commerce at every point, and stable conditions therein are necessary to the general welfare.

"Recurring violent fluctuations from year to year in the available supply of feed grains disrupt the balance between the supply of livestock and livestock products moving in interstate and foreign commerce and the available supply of feed grains. Recurring [violent] fluctuations in the prices of feed grains resulting from corresponding [violent] fluctuations in the supply of feed grains directly affect the movement of livestock in interstate commerce from the range cattle regions to the regions where livestock is fed for market in interstate and foreign commerce, and also directly affect the movement in interstate commerce of feed grains, which are transported from the regions where produced to the regions where livestock is fed for market in interstate and foreign commerce.

"The principal grains used for livestock feed are corn, barley, grain sorghums, and oats. Although certain feed grains can be produced in some areas better than other feed grains, in general, one of several feed grains can be grown on the same land. A marketing program which provides for a single quota applicable to feed grains and which permits producers to determine, within the quota, which feed grains they shall produce will tend to effectuate the policy of the Act and will permit producers the maximum amount of freedom of choice consistent with the attainment of the policy of the Act.

"Feed grains which are allowed to mature, even though not harvested as feed grains, are an available source of livestock feed and have a

Declaration of Policy. In the final version presented to Congress, Sec. 360a was dropped, and Sec. 360b of the memorandum *Legislative Findings* became 360a of H.R. 10010. The staff member commented in the margin of the confidential draft that the section on *Legislative Findings* was "*Too long* check lawyers to see why so much justification needed."

From this point on a careful comparison of the texts indicates the manner

22

1 barley, grain sorghums, and oats. Although certain feed
2 grains are better suited for production in some areas than
3 other feed grains, in general, one of several feed grains can
4 be grown on the same land. A marketing program which
5 provides for a single quota applicable to feed grains and
6 which permits producers to determine, within the quota,
7 which feed grains they shall produce will tend to effectuate
8 the policy of the Act and will permit producers the maximum
9 amount of freedom of choice consistent with the attainment
10 of the policy of the Act.
11 "The conditions affecting the production and marketing
12 of feed grains are such that, without Federal assistance,
13 farmers, individually or in cooperation, cannot effectively
14 provide for a balanced supply of feed grains and the orderly
15 marketing of feed grains in interstate and foreign commerce
16 at prices which are fair and reasonable to farmers and
17 consumers.
18 "The national public interest and general welfare require
19 that the burdens on interstate and foreign commerce above
20 described be removed by the exercise of Federal power.
21 Feed grains which do not move in the form of feed grains
22 outside of the State where they are produced are so closely
23 and substantially related to feed grains which move in the
24 form of feed grains outside of the State where they are pro-
25 duced, and have such a close and substantial relation to the

in which the criticism was met (not entirely accepted), and at the same time shows that others were suggesting changes, as well. For example, a study of lines 11 to 17 on page 22, reproduced from H.R. 10010 in comparison

- 4 -

direct effect on the price of harvested feed grains, and such unharvested feed grains also affect the supply and price of livestock and livestock products. In the circumstances, such unharvested feed grains must be considered in the same manner as harvested feed grains in order to achieve the policy of the Act with respect to feed grains, livestock, and livestock products.

"The conditions affecting the production and marketing of feed grains, livestock, and livestock products are such that, without Federal assistance, farmers, individually or in cooperation, cannot effectively prevent the recurrence of disparities between the supplies of livestock and livestock products moving in interstate and foreign commerce and the supply of feed grains available for feeding, and provide for the orderly marketing of feed grains, livestock, and livestock products in interstate and foreign commerce at prices which are fair and reasonable to farmers and consumers.

"The national public interest and general welfare require that the burdens on interstate and foreign commerce above described be removed by the exercise of Federal power. By reason of the administrative and physical impracticability of regulating the movement of livestock and livestock products in interstate and foreign commerce and the inadequacy of any such regulation to remove such burdens, such power can be feasibly exercised only by reducing the annual carry-over of feed grains, and stabilizing the carry-over of feed grains at a level consistent with any national policy with respect to strategic reserves, in order that a stable and continuous flow of feed grains, livestock, and livestock products in interstate and foreign commerce at fair and reasonable prices may at all times be assured and maintained.

with 360a of the confidential memorandum shows that some substance of the *Declaration of Policy* was retained in the redraft of Sec. 360b of the confidential memorandum, which became Sec. 360a of H.R. 10010.

Other pages of H.R. 10010 are reproduced in Chapters VII and VIII, all marginal notes being those of a USDA staff member.

1 volume and price of livestock and livestock products in inter-
2 state and foreign commerce, that it is necessary to regulate
3 feed grains which do not move outside of the State where
4 they are produced to the extent set forth in this Act.
5 "The diversion of substantial acreages from feed grains
6 to the production of commodities which are in surplus supply
7 or which will be in surplus supply if they are permitted to be
8 grown on the diverted acreage would burden, obstruct, and
9 adversely affect interstate and foreign commerce in such
10 commodities, and would adversely affect the prices of such
11 commodities in interstate and foreign commerce. Small
12 changes in the supply of a commodity could create a sufficient
13 surplus to affect seriously the price of such commodity in
14 interstate and foreign commerce. Large changes in the
15 supply of such commodity could have a more acute effect on
16 the price of the commodity in interstate and foreign com-
17 merce and, also, could overtax the handling, processing, and
18 transportation facilities through which the flow of interstate
19 and foreign commerce in such commodity is directed. Such
20 adverse effects caused by overproduction in one year could
21 further result in a deficient supply of the commodity in the
22 succeeding year, causing excessive increases in the price of
23 the commodity in interstate and foreign commerce in such
24 year. It is, therefore, necessary to prevent acreage diverted
25 from the production of feed grains to be used to produce com-

1 modities which are in surplus supply or which will be in
2 surplus supply if they are permitted to be grown on the di-
3 verted acreage.

not to raise the price of bread even by a penny. (But as it turned out, the price of bread went up even after the price of wheat went down.)

Yet the things that could not be known were predicted as carefully as possible. Even political reactions were closely estimated by pooling the political knowledge of experienced men.

The Feed Grains and Wheat Advisory Committees

In judging political reactions the conferees got help in their closing sessions from meetings of the Feed Grains and Wheat Advisory Subcommittees, held December 14th and 15th. These subcommittees first met as a full committee to hear informative remarks by the official USDA representative, Willard Cochrane, and by the combined committee's official secretary, John Schnittker. Then discussions took place in the subcommittees.

Most members of these subcommittees had served on Kennedy advisory committees which met during the campaign and early in 1961. New members had been carefully picked (for example, there were no Farm Bureau officials) so that almost all would strive to reach accord with the administration. Even if one or two people did not like what the majority was doing they would likely not engage in futile opposition and thus jeopardize their seat on the committee.

Yet sharp controversey arose in these subcommittees, often between old acquaintances. Dominating the discussion in the Wheat Subcommittee were John Schnittker, for the USDA, and representatives of the Grange, Farmers Union, and the Wheat Growers, most of whom had served on Schnittker's 1960 campaign committee which roughed out the wheat certificate program that the administration was now about to introduce.

Much had happened since then. In February of 1961, the three groups had agreed on a specific certificate program which had been introduced in Congress by a bipartisan group of wheat state legislators. Meanwhile the USDA, too, had revised the original program, but in a form somewhat less attractive to farmers. The USDA version was cheaper, and it could be administered well.

At least the USDA and "friendly" farm groups were still in agreement that the existing wheat program would have to be changed, because it did not stop the pile-up of surpluses. Under the existing mandatory program, the farmers had to fallow over a third of their wheat acreage (though they were free to grow feed crops on it). There were stiff penalties on noncompliers. But since the Secretary could not make any further mandatory reductions under the law, Congress in 1961 had added a voluntary program under which farmers were paid to divert additional acres voluntarily.

Over the long run the key to reducing wheat surpluses, in the administration's view, was to break the legal barrier (the 55-million-acre minimum) so as to be able to make further acreage cuts under the mandatory program. On the other hand, some wheat producers still dreamed of a program without any acreage restrictions, but the wheat advisory subcommittee members knew that Midwestern and Southern congressmen would never let them release surplus wheat into the feed-grains market, nor could they hope to dump unlimited production abroad. Wheat growers on Freeman's advisory committee thus agreed that the alternative to some form of control was to let prices slide so low that many wheat farmers would be forced into bankruptcy. None wished that to happen.

These farm groups and the administration also agreed that the wheat certificate or two-price plan (see pp. 21–22), a long-time favorite scheme of the Wheat Growers and the Grange, would be a popular way to compensate farmers for further acreage cuts. But they did not agree as to how much of the wheat should be certificated or how certificates should be priced. Relative to the first problem, out of every ten bushels of wheat produced, roughly four bushels went for domestic food use, two for cash exports aided by a substantial federal subsidy, three for exports under food assistance programs, and the final bushel went for feed and other uses. Those farm groups represented in the advisory subcommittee wanted farmers to get bushel quotas—and certificates—for all domestic food wheat and for all wheat exports. On the other hand, the USDA planned to allow certificates only for domestic use and for as much of the cash exports as the Secretary saw fit to grant.

There was a dispute over how the certificates should be valued. Farm groups wanted their value to be based on scarcity. They expected that the Secretary would so regulate the supply of certificates that their price would be about a dollar. Added to $1.40—the world price of wheat—this would return farmers $2.40 for each bushel of certificated wheat. Furthermore, they wanted the certificates to be attached to the wheat, from the farm to the miller or exporter, so that wheat would be priced on the grain market with certificate (thus at $2.40) rather than without certificate (at $1.40).

But to raise the wheat price to $2.40 would add a penny to the price of each loaf of bread. The USDA was under orders not to raise the price of food. Schnittker and Cochrane had still other objections to the fluctuating-value certificate: such a program would be difficult to administer; fraud and manipulation might be possible; grain dealers, traders, and processors would rebel against it; urban congressmen might not vote for such a bread tax.

Instead, the Department favored letting the market price of wheat drop to world price levels. The federal government would then give farmers certificates the value of which was fixed at 70 cents per bushel. Farmers could cash these in whenever they wished, and whether or not they had a crop. These negotiable certificates would ultimately have to be bought by the millers and cash wheat exporters.

Wheat producers objected that consumers would be more alarmed if millers seemed obviously to be paying a "bread tax" of 70 cents per bushel than they would be because of any increase in the price of bread. Farmers had always preferred, too, to accept subsidized prices rather than to get a handout subsidy through the mail, as would occur under the USDA's plan. The complex administration program was also harder for farmers to understand, even if simpler to administer.

In addition to compensating wheat farmers with certificates, it was agreed that some additional payment should be made to farmers for the acres they would have to cut back. The USDA wanted the diversion payments to be relatively small—and for only a few years. The farm groups wanted them to be relatively larger, and for all future years.

For the feed-grains producers the issues were similar. To put mandatory controls on feed-grains producers—never before tried—would be like trying to saddle a wild stallion. Yet the voluntary program was very expensive. Arguments centered—with no conclusion reached—on the level of the price supports under such a controls program.

Thus, throughout the discussions with the farm groups, the main issue was money. During the two-day advisory committee meetings Cochrane and Schnittker shuttled back and forth, as mediators, between Budget Bureau-CEA meetings and the advisory committees, trying to find combinations of subsidies and costs that all could accept. But the farm group spokesmen on the advisory committees demanded increases in farm income even though this seemed impossible without increasing either food prices or government costs. Farm advisory committee members openly predicted that farmers would not vote for a program which involved more controls but no more income. On the other side the Budget Bureau was under orders to cut costs, and the CEA people would not tolerate inflationary prices.

As the meetings ended both groups understood the other's position though neither was free to come to terms. USDA people recognized that these farm leaders had to deal with a membership that was unready for harsh compromises as a means of gaining support from other regions, from urban legislators, and from any administration—farmers were unwilling to make the hard choice. Yet these friendly farm leaders would be asked to sell the program that the administration evolved. The farm leaders in turn were aware that USDA people had fought hard to raise subsidy levels within an administration that was more anxious to cut farm program costs than to raise farm income.

Both the wheat and feed-grains programs were complicated, involving questions which the advisory committees and even Congress could hardly come to grips with, but which might determine the agricultural future of regions, and states, and individual farmers. Many such important questions would clearly have to be left unanswered in the law, to be decided ultimately by the Secretary. In the light of the advisory committee's experience, some groups wondered whether Secretary Freeman would be able to make the *right* decisions under the shadow of the budget cutters, or whether he would be allowed to stay in office if he did make the right decisions.

6. *New Directions: Rural Renewal*

IN OCTOBER, while programs were being developed, Undersecretary Murphy received a cable from Secretary Freeman, who was visiting Ambassador John Galbraith in India, in which Freeman suggested the form that the 1962 legislation should take.

It would again be a comprehensive approach, introduced with fanfare. Yet it would not be called an omnibus bill, on the assumption that the sundry provisions of the bill could really be formed into a single entity. Again education would be required for stimulating popular support of the bill, particularly the new ideas involved.

New perspectives would be emphasized. Given an urban society, the administration would think not of farm commodities but of food. Instead of subtracting acres from farm production, they would be planning to meet the many new demands on land—for highways, recreation, scenic strips, and "green belts" to run around and through the metropolises.

Freeman said the new 1962 legislation should tackle all the many problems of rural America. Assistant Secretary John Baker's phrase "rural renewal" was to be the complement to the urban focus upon land and food.

The format of the 1962 Act would be largely Baker's, not Willard Cochrane's, though the controversy in Congress undoubtedly would still center on commodities. For decades rural congressmen had been far more interested in farm prices than in broader plans to improve rural America.

The phrase "rural renewal" was an outgrowth of old ideas which had guided Baker's work in earlier USDA jobs and recently as Washington Director for the Farmers Union. True to its tradition,

Farmers Union even in late 1961 was organizing a nationwide committee to conduct a three-year study of "pockets of poverty" about half of which were still located in the rural areas.

Early in 1961, Freeman had named Baker to coordinate efforts to implement the rural redevelopment program which Secretary Benson had begun on a pilot basis. The several large agricultural credit agencies had been put under Baker's wing, as well as the Soil Conservation Service which helped farmers to plan and carry out land improvement programs, including the construction of many farm ponds. Under additional authority in the proposed legislation for 1962, Baker would be given still more tools to rejuvenate rural society.

Land for Other Things

As the yields went up and the need for crop land went down, new land uses were taking priority over agriculture. (See Illustration 15.) Of course residential, commercial, and industrial uses traditionally took precedence over farming, although on the San Francisco peninsula where tract developers were gobbling this way and that into the rich, delightful, specialty farming areas, some local planners and their constituents were working against great odds to find ways to intersperse green belts within the growing miles of crackerbox houses.

Just because most people no longer farmed did not mean they no longer appreciated nature and the land. In addition to keeping their backyard gardens, suburbanites wanted to see the open spaces and to visit them. So many people sought escape from one another's elbows that they found themselves almost rubbing shoulders in the few state and national parks.

Recreation was a subordinate activity in quite a number of federal agencies. The Forest Service in the USDA took care of recreation in primitive and wilderness areas of our national forests; the Health Education and Welfare Department provided playgrounds in urban housing projects; the Department of Interior had three offices in the area: (1) the Bureau of Land Management, ad-

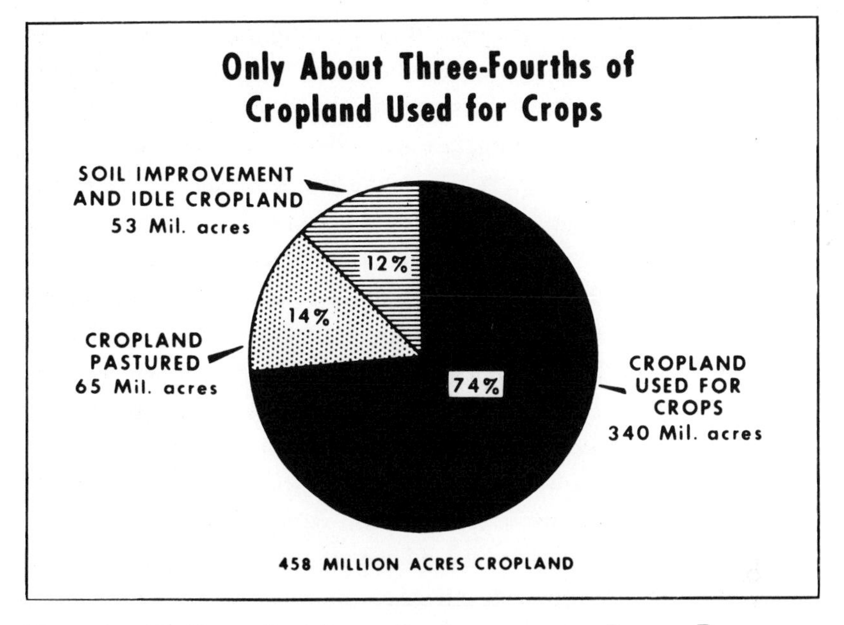

Illustration 15. COULD IDLE LAND BE CONVERTED TO PAYING RECREATION AREAS? As the above USDA chart shows, 12 percent of U.S. farmland, or 53,000,000 acres, was retired from production in 1963. The Food and Agriculture Act of 1962 asked authority to aid farmers in converting this land to other uses, such as picnic areas, wildlife preserves, and other forms of recreation.

ministering primitive and wilderness areas, (2) the National Park Service, operating the national parks, (3) the Bureau of Reclamation, providing camping spots and boat docks in the vicinity of government man-made lakes. The U.S. Army Corps of Engineers also provided services similar to those of the Bureau of Reclamation. The Fish and Wildlife Service had also yielded to popular demand and set up trash cans and benches at their installations.

CONSERVATION AND RECREATION

In 1958, some farsighted congressmen had got authorization for an Outdoor Recreation Resources Review Commission (ORRRC) to study recreation needs. After conducting opinion polls and land surveys, the commission prepared a six-volume report which was about ready to be submitted in late 1961. At the same time some of the ORRRC staff members were finding their way into the USDA, and ORRRC ideas went with them. Other ORRRC people became associated with an interacting group of liberal farm staff people who worked in congressional offices, in organizations such as the National Rural Electric Cooperative Association, the Farmer's Union, and in the AFL-CIO. The group kept a semi-formal relationship which was symbolized by a weekly luncheon.

Among this group were thinkers about rural and outdoor living, including some contemporaries of the depression-time rural homestead projects under which city people were moved out to raise country gardens. There were others who had belonged to the era of rural electrification. Most in this group were oriented by job or past experience toward the Department of Agriculture, which had reached a temporary truce in an old struggle with the Department of Interior over who should manage which portions of the public domain, and for what purpose.

Centered around the Department of Interior and the Committees on Interior and Insular Affairs in the Congress, however, were other enthusiasts for preserving and enjoying our natural heritage. These government employees were the progenitors of the ORRRC Report.

Outside government were thirty small "conservationist" groups which kept in touch with one another through a consultative Natural Resources Council. One such group was the Izaak Walton League, whose director served on the ORRRC Commission. This venerable 50,000-member organization had already been able to get federal help to use land idled in soil bank and conservation reserve programs as wild game habitats and feeding grounds.

Against the conservationists, however, was a strong American belief in the sanctity of private property (even if its owners let the top soil go down the river), as compared to a small value placed on outdoor recreation facilities (notwithstanding the American love for the out-of-doors).

And now the Department of Agriculture proposed to turn corn fields into parks! Congresswoman Catherine May (R., Wash.) disapproved, in behalf of her rural constituency:

> American agriculture is perhaps the greatest success story in the world today. . . . Are we now going to reward our farmers by having them give up a part of their most valuable asset— . . . their good farm land, for recreational purposes for our cities?
>
> In addition to putting farmers in a straightjacket of controls, are we going to penalize them by having them set aside a portion of their farms as fishponds or picnic areas to be used, or abused, by swarms of folks from far-off cities?
>
> Must we add to the already numerous problems of our farmers by having them assume the burden for supplying the Nation's recreational facilities? [1]

According to the ORRRC report, however, metropolitan residents needed outlets to nearby privately owned land, much of it producing burdensome surpluses. New uses could provide new income to owners. Recreational development had already brought youth and new vigor to some rural communities. As Congressman Frank Stubblefield (D. Ky.) put it, humorously and perhaps too optimistically:

> One of the phases of new land use, relating to recreation, is a very popular category of land use in my part of the country. A few years ago I recall a trip to Florida and talking to a man there. He had picked cotton in Mississippi until he found out that one tourist would equal two bales of cotton and was twice as easy to pick.[2]

Could a farmer learn to "pick" a tourist? If a man owned a big hill in Illinois, could he turn his farm into a profitable ski resort? To help him, an agency within the Department of the Interior would give him technical advice, and a USDA agency would lend him credit, while the Rural Electrification Administration piped in electricity to operate his lift. (An Illinois rural electric cooperative had already loaned federal money to finance the purchase of a

[1] *Congressional Record* (daily edition), Feb. 21, 1962, p. 2698.

[2] *Hearings on the Food and Agriculture Act of 1962*, House Committee on Agriculture, p. 198.

snow-making machine for skiing, which detractors dubbed "another REA snow-job.") Other USDA agencies would help groups of farmers and local communities coordinate development of recreational complexes.

Exciting new directions for the sprawling old Department of Agriculture! Its concern would shift from farm land to land in general, and maybe even include some rural zoning, through the use of various financial inducements. And if the USDA were to sponsor recreational and industrial development in rural communities it might eventually be concerned with virtually all aspects of nonmetropolitan communities. It would become a Department of Rural Affairs, perhaps to be complemented by a Department of Urban Affairs, although some wondered about the wisdom of dividing work along geographic lines within an interdependent society.

In still another area, it seemed that the USDA's old interest in producing and pricing farm commodities might ultimately take second place to an interest in providing ample good food for consumers. At one point during the fall of 1961, consideration was given to changing the name of the USDA to "The Department of Food and Agriculture." This idea was dropped, but the actual bill title was lengthened in departure from long precedent, to read: The Food and Agriculture Act of 1962.

The shape of things was certainly changing. In response to these changes, the new bill was to take small steps in the new directions and, above all, to be a vehicle to educate decisionmakers—all the way down to the farmers—as to what should be done to reverse the decline of rural communities, to lift their spirits in anticipation of a moderately bright future.

A "book project" (for purposes of educating the public) proceeded apace with the drafting of the comprehensive bill.

Revision from Friendly Farm Groups

An early draft of the book was leaked, perhaps as a test balloon, to *Wall Street Journal* reporter Joe Western. Response to his story[3] came from the friendly farm groups. In a public letter to Secretary Freeman, Farmers Union President Patton lambasted the anticipated program. He felt it placed too much emphasis on retraining farmers and preparing farm youth for urban employment, and too little emphasis on preserving the family farm. Patton said the farm income goals of the program were far too low. Neither his vigorous protest, however, nor later efforts, including an interview with President Kennedy by Master of the National Grange Herschel Newsom, swayed the administration in its determination to reduce federal farm expenditures substantially, while providing for only modest per capita increases in farm income.

December Curtain Call

By late December, the Budget Bureau, USDA, and CEA had come to terms on most matters. On an afternoon just before Christmas, representatives of these agencies gathered in Sorensen's White House office to review for him the major points of agreement, and to get his decision on the unresolved question as to what level of price supports should be set for feed grains.

The 13 men at this meeting had much in common, though their stations ranged from Cabinet member to budget technician. During twelve-hour workdays (and add an hour or more on the road) and six day weeks, they had lived as do so many professional people and public servants in our society—at a point near physical exhaustion.

Yet, they obviously thrived. They had angled painstakingly for their present jobs, were working hard to keep them, and perhaps to merit tougher ones. Now they reaped a reward in experiencing the drama of this meeting.

Together they had fashioned a bill of major importance, that would straighten out the farm mess of which others had despaired. It would turn the faces of decisionmakers and rural communities toward the future, and would help balance the national budget

[3] *Wall Street Journal*, December 18, 1961, p. 1.

and stabilize prices throughout the economy. Or so they hoped and believed.

They knew the bill was far from being a law. Though the President's full power was to be used—"all the stops would be pulled" to gain its passage—Congress would surely shear off many of its provisions and ruin its symmetry and coherence, if indeed Congress could be persuaded to pass it at all. And would two-thirds of the wheat and corn farmers favor production controls in subsequent referendums? There were many other hurdles to cross.

Still, this meeting marked the end of an act, when some would move to the sidelines and other crews would come on. The little circle in Sorensen's office faced a kind of curtain call after so many phone calls, scribbled notes, heated words. (And they had missed the Army-Navy football game.) It is appropriate to call the roll of those at this meeting. In addition to presidential assistants Sorensen and Feldman, those present were as follows:

Orville Freeman, Secretary of Agriculture
Charles Murphy, Undersecretary of Agriculture
Willard Cochrane, Director, Agricultural Economics, USDA
John Schnittker, Staff member, Staff Economics Group
David Bell, Director of the Bureau of the Budget
Philip S. Hughes, Assistant Director for Legislative Reference, Bureau of the Budget
Charles Kraus, Director, Agriculture and Farm Credit Administration, Bureau of the Budget
Eric Robinson, Examiner for Price Supports, Bureau of the Budget
Don Horton, Agricultural Economist, Bureau of the Budget
James Tobin, member of the Council of Economic Advisers
Vernon Ruttan, Staff Agricultural Economist, Council of Economic Advisers

Director of Agricultural Credit John Baker should be mentioned also, although he was not present—presumably because his format emphasizing new land uses was no longer at issue.

After Christmas, Secretary Freeman and Undersecretary Murphy journeyed to Miami where President Kennedy, Budget Director Bell, CEA Chairman Heller, and other presidential advisers were reviewing final plans with Cabinet members, one department at a time. Apparently no important staff decisions were reversed at the Miami session on agriculture.

State of the Union Message

In his State of the Union Message which followed on January 11th, the President said:

> American farmers took heart in 1961—from a billion dollar rise in farm income—and from a hopeful start on reducing farm surpluses. But we are still operating under a patchwork accumulation of old laws. . . .
>
> I will, therefore, submit to Congress a new, comprehensive program—tailored to fit the use of our land and supplies of each crop to the long-range needs of the Sixties—and designed to prevent chaos in the Sixties with a program of common sense.

In his Budget Message of January 18th, the President added that his new farm program would provide substantial budget savings.

The Congress showed little interest in the anticipated new legislation, because the 1961 voluntary legislation had brought increased farm income. Rural constituents were writing few letters, and those who did were satisfied with the status quo.

In the absence of pressure from home, legislators surely preferred to stay clear of farm program hornets' nests, especially in this election year. And after all, farm program costs were down a tiny bit. President Kennedy even found it difficult to persuade the Agriculture Committee Chairmen to introduce his bill. Ellender objected, particularly, to the new land-use provisions.

The Need for Understanding

During January, Secretary Freeman did all he could to stir grass roots interest in his forthcoming legislation, giving new emphasis to the themes that he, and other officials in the USDA, had repeated in many speeches to all types of audiences in the previous year.

The major, integrating theme was "the need for understanding." If farmers should fully understand their predicament, they would surely accept rational controls on production, and if urban people understood the blessings of a healthy agriculture, they would be willing to help support the costs of supply management. (See Illustration 16).

Freeman also publicized his new directions in agriculture, always in a context of urgency. He frequently said that time was running out for those who would save our existing efficient structure based on the family farm.

As a way to call attention to his new directions, the Secretary had organized a series of regional conferences to consider what should be done with America's new food abundance, and how new demands for land could be met. Freeman himself set the tone at each of these conferences, which culminated in a national Conference on Food and People, held January 10th, and a Conference on Land and People, January 15th.

On January 21st, Freeman told the Extension Services which spanned rural America that it was time to broaden their role beyond teaching farmers how to be more efficient.

On January 23rd, Freeman met with a National Conference on Milk and Nutrition, one purpose of which was to emphasize that milk contributed to good health, and to cast doubt on highly-publicized findings that some adult ailments might be caused by milk products.

He also tried again to persuade the dairy industry to be concerned about the overproduction of milk. But the dairy industry refused to support the forthcoming administration bill, just as they had refused to accept control programs in the past, in the expectation that the federal government would, as before, create outlets for the dairy surplus.

Cultivating Urban Voters

To cultivate urban voters was a major reason for including recreation and food provisions in the new farm bill, and for the new directions of the USDA. As he had often done before, Freeman invaded the New York City metropolitan area a few days before the bill went to Congress, to tell consumers how the USDA served them:

I suspect that one of the best kept secrets in Washington is that the Department of Agriculture carries out more activities which are of . . . service to the consumer than any other Department or agency in the Federal government. . . .

He mentioned some of the services: providing meat and other food inspection and grading, lower cost foods, development of refrigerated and dehydrated products, flameproofing and wash-and-wear fabrics, and providing ever wider varieties of food. Freeman concluded:

Over the next 100 years, I suspect that this Department will continue to become an even more familiar and integral part of the daily lives of every American.

Nor did he fail to get in a plug for the family farm.

Despite Freeman's public-relations efforts throughout 1962, however, his image of the efficient "underpaid family farmer" took a back seat, in the mass media, to a wheeling-dealing farmer-swindler named Billie Sol Estes. In the *New York Times* and other major dailies, Estes was the lead story, time and again, from May through November. Freeman and his new bill made the *New York Times* front page only half-a-dozen times in 1962.

When the Estes investigation was over, Freeman could tell the congressional investigating committee that Billie Sol had not cost the taxpayers anything (except the days spent by high officials investigating the scandal) and that, to the contrary, the Estes affair had inspired healthy reorganizations and changes of personnel within the USDA. The fact remained that farmer Billie Sol had become part of the vocabulary in millions of households where Orville Freeman's name and story had not been heard.

Between speeches Freeman visited many congressmen, beginning as soon as they returned from Christmas vacations, bearing the same message at this higher policy level that he continued to preach to the general public.

Illustration 16. THE PROBLEMS, ACCORDING TO "THE BOOK." In an effort to package the new concept in farm programs so that it would gain wide public understanding and support, the USDA proposed the "ABCD" approach: abundance, balance, conservation, and development. These two pages show selected paragraphs from Secretary Freeman's opening statement in *Food and Agriculture–A Program for the 1960's,* the government brochure prepared for the public.

In the congressional debate about the legislative package, particularly in the shock of defeat encountered in the wheat referendum of 1963, the significance of the Kennedy program was lost. Nevertheless, the administration did get a large percentage of its requests through Congress. The years to come will show whether the administration was successful in its major purpose–to shift farm-problem solutions away from the commodity-by-commodity method and toward an approach aimed at the economic development of rural America.

STATEMENT

By Orville L. Freeman

Secretary of Agriculture

A fresh start has been made in 1961—toward better lives for rural people and toward better farm programs. We approach the challenge of further improvement with optimism and gratitude. Having not only enough food and fiber—but too much at a given time or place—is less a problem than an opportunity. It is in that spirit that we present . . .

Food and Agriculture: A Program for the 1960's.

Let us consider four major problem areas—all interrelated:

(1) The problem of underconsumption. Incomes—and diets—are generally good in America. Yet even here we have some inadequate diets in the midst of plenty. And in many parts of the world, tomorrow's hunger is as certain as tomorrow's sunrise.

(2) The problem of overproduction. We have the capacity to produce far more than can be utilized at home and abroad. This excess capacity to produce is greater in some commodities than in others, but the problem is common to all of agriculture.

(3) The problem of conservation and resource use. On the one hand, more land is being used to produce food and fiber than

is needed. On the other hand, there is a growing demand for recreation, wildlife, and simply open space in and around the cities of our increasingly urban Nation. This may well be *the critical decade* in determining how wisely our land will be used for generations to come.

(4) The problem of opportunities for farm and rural people. Problems of people on land that does not employ them fully and does not enable them to earn a decent living are closely related to the problems of land use. Opportunities for these people—both in farming and in other work in their communities—can be improved.

It is in the above conceptual setting that we propose a broad new program—a program that moves on four fronts—each equally important and all highly interrelated.

Abundance—one side of the quadrangle—emphasizes food and its uses, both in the affluent society that is America, and in a world which is a long way from satisfying the food needs of its people. It is aimed at expanding domestic and international uses for food and fiber. It is intended to utilize food as an instrument of development and good will—to strengthen friendly economies and to develop export markets.

Another side of the quadrangle is *balance* in the management of abundance—to maintain farm income through the establishment of a reasonable balance between supplies and needs. The overall goal—a food and agriculture program which will strengthen both America and the family farm system—can be reached by common sense and cooperation in managing the abundance which our family farms produce.

A third part is directed at *conservation* and the efficient use of land resources. Its goal is to provide adequate food for all, to conserve soil and water, to expand opportunities for recreation, and to insure that land resources are used and improved—not simply set aside and forgotten.

Finally, the Food and Agriculture Program for the 1960's is aimed at *development*—the creation of new opportunities and new incentives for those who gain a living from the land and who depend upon it indirectly, and the improvements in education and training which will enable them to use such opportunities. Enlarged opportunities for our rural people are, in fact, closely allied to the development and utilization of our land resources.

Illustration 17. THE PRESIDENT'S MESSAGE TO CONGRESS. When President Kennedy sent his message on farm legislation to Congress in January, 1962, the package was complete. A comparison of the message and the selections from Secretary Freeman's statement (see Illustration 16) shows how the two complement each other. Selected paragraphs of the president's message are shown here, as published January 31, 1962, in the *Congressional Record*. Note that the new program still had to include a good bit of the old way—specific commodity recommendations for wheat, for feed grains, and (not shown here) for cotton and other crops and commodities.

To the Congress of the United States:

Management of our agricultural resources to meet the triple goals of increased farm income, lower cost to the taxpayer, and reduced farm surpluses continues to be one of the most difficult problems confronting the Nation. A good start was made last year. Net farm income rose $1 billion, and income per farm increased almost $350. Government stocks of farm products were reduced for the first time in 9 years. Budgetary costs were below those that would have been incurred under the programs that were replaced. All this was accomplished at the same time food prices were reduced below their level a year earlier.

But the emergency programs enacted last year are expiring. There is a critical need for permanent legislation to consolidate the gains of 1961 and to provide a realistic and comprehensive program for agriculture in the years ahead—a program with which we can continue to move forward toward full utilization of our abundance. The drift toward a chaotic, inefficient, surplus-ridden farm economy, though halted last year, will resume unless prompt action is taken. In addition, new problems have developed in commodities not covered by the 1961 legislation. Unanticipated changes in consumer demand have produced still further surpluses. A reversion to the former programs for wheat and feed grains will inevitably bring both enormous surpluses and depressed farm income, seriously injuring a large segment of our economy.

Four independent studies, by Cornell University, Iowa State University, the Joint Economic Committee of Congress, and the Senate Committee on Agriculture and Forestry, show how sharp would be the drop in farm prices and farm income if farm programs were abandoned. These studies agree that wheat prices would be sliced almost in half, oats prices 25 percent, barley 28 percent, soybeans 38 percent, grain sorghums 22 percent, and dairy 17 percent. Non-price-supported commodities would also suffer. Livestock commodities would drop 24 percent, egg prices 20 percent, cattle prices 25 percent, hogs 30 percent, and broilers and turkeys even lower than this year.

Nor can the Federal Government be expected to undertake an indefinite program of large and unpredictable budget expenditures to acquire stocks of commodities that we do not need and cannot use. By the beginning of 1961—when the emergency legislation was introduced to reduce inventories—the Commodity Credit Corporation had over $9 billion in loans and inventories. Carrying costs exceeded $1 billion a year.

OBJECTIVES

The new program should use the successful emergency legislation passed last year to establish guidelines and should also rely upon those proven techniques and methods that have been employed in the past. It should be designed:

1. To make maximum use of our productive abundance. Our agricultural resources can advance the cause of peace and freedom throughout the world; they assure Americans of a high standard of living; they can be an important weapon against poverty and disease.

2. To seek a balance between production and demand that will avoid the waste of private effort and public resources. Rice, peanuts, and tobacco already enjoy well balanced programs whose principles can be extended to other crops. Properly balanced, agriculture can make a major contribution toward economic stability. The farmer, the consumer, and the taxpayer can all share in the benefits; without such balance, all may suffer.

3. To provide for conservation of our land and water resources. Land and water not needed to produce food and fiber should be directed to alternative uses of benefit to the Nation.

4. To initiate and expand programs for the development of human resources and renewal of rural communities. Each year 1 million people move from the farm to the city. Many others seek part-time employment to supplement

meager returns from farm labor. The hardship and suffering this often entails should be alleviated, and these workers assisted in their efforts to acquire needed skills, obtain jobs, and further their education.

Abundance, balance, conservation, development—these are our commonsense goals—as commonsense as A, B, C, D.

The feed grain program I recommend is designed to reduce feed grain output to a level that will maintain prices and incomes in the feed grain and livestock sectors of the farm economy without continuous ever-higher surplus accumulation. This can be accomplished by establishing a mandatory acreage allotment on all feed grains large enough to meet annual domestic and export requirements, for all purposes under all programs, less that amount which is to be deducted from the carryover stocks to reduce them gradually to a level no higher than that required for stability and security. Producers would share in the national allotment on the basis of past production, adjusted for unusual circumstances. Payments for diverted acreage would, of course, continue to be made to support farm income while surplus stocks are being reduced.

Initiation of this program is proposed for the 1963 crop year, subject to approval by a producer referendum.

WHEAT

The problems of wheat production are much the same as for feed grains. Large inventories and high program costs were inherited from the 1950's. The temporary 1962 wheat program is expected to halt the accumulation of wheat surpluses, but the old programs—which have already failed—will become effective again for the 1963 crop unless legislation is promptly enacted.

I recommend a wheat program which will reduce wheat stocks to manageable levels, improve the competitive position of American wheat in world markets, and maintain the incomes of wheat producers. To achieve these objectives, national wheat acreage allotments will be established by estimating the actual requirements each year for milling, seed, and for export, and deducting a number of bushels that will permit us to draw upon our surplus stocks on hand to gradually reduce the carryover to the level required for stability and security. Marketing certificates would be used to assure growers a price-support level between 75 and 90 percent of parity on the domestic allotment and up to 90 percent on the export allotment. The national allotment would be apportioned among all growers, including small growers, on the basis of past wheat acreage. The Secretary of Agriculture will have authority to make payments, which will help to maintain producers' incomes, for mandatory diversion of acreage from wheat to soil-conserving uses, and to offer such payments as an incentive for further voluntary acreage diversion.

Initiation of this program is necessary for the 1963 crop year. As in the case of feed grains, it would be subject to approval by a producer referendum.

RURAL RENEWAL AND EDUCATION

In some rural areas the general level of economic activity and family income is so low, and the lack of community facilities so acute, that a complete new development operation is the only sensible solution—a program of rural renewal.

For these areas, in addition to the nationwide rural area development program, I recommend a new legislative program under the Area Redevelopment Administration, to provide loans and technical assistance to local public rural renewal corporations. These corporations would aid in developing new uses for land and water, create forest industry parks, assist small farmers in farm consolidation and enlargement, and develop needed public facilities, including outdoor recreation. The bill would permit loans to approved public agencies to acquire, develop and dispose of land for these purposes, and provide for other loans to individual farmers to establish recreational facilities and other income-producing enterprises. Consideration might also be given to making loans available to rural citizens, both young and old, for vocational and other educational training not otherwise available but essential to their preparation for nonfarm jobs.

We will enjoy the fruits of the technological revolution in American agriculture only if we recognize its implications. We must learn to live with an agricultural economy of abundance rather than scarcity. That is the purposes of the approach I have outlined—a comprehensive, long-range program to replace the present patchwork of short-run emergency measures.

JOHN F. KENNEDY.

THE WHITE HOUSE, *January 31, 1962.*

Final Touches

For USDA staffers, January was a time for working out technicalities, polishing the bill and the book, and drafting the President's message. (See Illustration 17.)

A controversy was developing over the way in which the proposed two-price or wheat-certificate program would be operated, in which the wheat producers were at odds with the traders and speculators who operated the grain markets, and the flour millers and others who processed the grain. In all the years of advocating a two-price wheat program, few administrators or growers had bothered to consider how two prices could be maintained in a grain market which recognized only one price, or how the price of wheat could be drastically changed in a day without creating confusion which might lead to windfall profits or considerable losses to individuals, or actual shortages of grain for processing.

After initial study it appeared that all the complex problems of transition and pricing were surmountable, but the USDA was in no hurry to announce a specific plan which might make one or another of the interested groups unhappy. Instead, experts were set to work on the problems, in consultation with a committee representing interested groups, which would try to find solutions satisfactory to all. (Some of the basic decisions were never announced, even though, by the time of the wheat referendum in May of 1963, the major technical problems had been solved).

After Cochrane, Schnittker, and other economists had roughed out the substance of the "book," they asked Freeman's assistant George Barnes—who had written speeches for such notables as Elmer Davis, Ralph Bunche, and Eric Johnston—to help shape its final, polished prose. Meanwhile USDA lawyers were reading, rereading, and continually perfecting the bill. Words and phrases were being carefully weighed in constructing the President's agriculture message, which had to be revised in the final hours when White House aides rejected a few passages in the message because they were nearly identical to some passages in the book.

On January 30th, on schedule, the 14-page message went to "the Hill" along with the 100-page book and the 107-page bill.

7. *The Farm Bill and the Hearings*

BILLS MAY be introduced in the Congress without much fanfare. Chairman Cooley threw the administration's Food and Agriculture Act of 1962 into the hopper at the Speaker's desk on January 31st, and Senator Ellender, who had been ill, introduced the bill in the Senate on Februray 2nd. Both men submitted a digest of the bill to be inserted in the voluminous daily *Congressional Record,* along with a few remarks. Senator Ellender said the bill was a working document, not a final blueprint. The President was willing to compromise. But farm groups must be willing to cooperate, he warned, if any legislation was to be obtained. Cooley's remarks were in the same vein.

The 61-word descriptive title of the Food and Agriculture Act of 1962 clearly indicated to the parliamentarians in each house that the bill was to go to the Agriculture committee in that house. The provisions which signaled new directions for both the USDA and the Agriculture committees prompted no challenges from other committees.

The bill was numbered and ordered to be printed by the parliamentarian in each house, and referred to committee the day following introduction. Meanwhile Chairmen Cooley and Ellender were scheduling public hearings.

Though President Kennedy's farm message and legislation prompted the normal number of news stories, cartoons, editorials, and flavored comments by farm organization officials, congressmen, and other farm spokesmen, there still existed an obvious wall of apathy and indifference in the countryside and in Congress. To strike at least a tiny spark of interest in the new farm program, Senator Humphrey criticized New York's Governor Nelson Rockefeller for his remarks about the new program.

The farm organizations were at work during early February informing local groups, and planning strategy. President Charles Shuman of the Farm Bureau warned, "This bill makes the Secretary a czar. We learned how to fight last year, and we will certainly fight this bill tooth and nail." Farmers Union thought the bill was too mild.

Freeman paused from his nationwide speaking tour to make a two-hour presentation before the House Committee on Agriculture on February 4th.

Freeman and the House Agriculture Committee

The House committee sat in a double-tiered, elevated semicircle at the far end of a large, but warm, chamber adjoining the committee staff offices in the Longworth House Office Building. In happier days the chambers had felt the reverbrations of Farm Bureau President Ed O'Neal, who had often seemed to be Master of Ceremonies, and who helped to orchestrate the varied regional, commodity, and party interests. When O'Neal retired, former Republican Chairman Clifford Hope had carried on reasonably well as mediator until the early fifties. Then the many divisive influences had overwhelmed him. Hope retired from Congress rather than live as circumstances forced remaining members to do. Because the Committee seemed short on good fellowship and the ability to get farm legislation passed, other able men avoided it or sought to get off it.

But the early session with Freeman was a quiet one, in which Freeman laid out his program and no questions were allowed. The gloves were taken off when he reappeared on February 19th. Questioning then, mostly by Republicans, came to ninety pages of verbatim text, consuming both the morning and afternoon.

Most committee hearings are dull and poorly attended, even though in some of these listless sessions important work may be proceeding. But when a Cabinet member appears, so do the photographers, newsmen, and a large audience. Ordinarily Cabinet members bring with them enough assistants and experts to fill an elevator—all of them with carefully pressed suits, felt hats, and bulging brief cases, all hovering closely behind the Secretary like chicks to the mother hen, and all in the proper pecking order.

This time the Secretary brought only his chief counsel, John Bagwell. Freeman was knowledgeable enough after a year in office that he seldom felt a need to turn to experts for data. To allow the Committee maximum exposure to the farm program, some top USDA assistants would be questioned individually in subsequent sessions, except for Assistant Secretary James Ralph, who had just traded his high position (see chart page 38) at Freeman's suggestion for a job as an agriculture attaché to the Philippines, and who would be dismissed altogether when the Billie Sol Estes story came to light.

Also in attendance at full committee hearings were the principal committee staff members. Chairman Cooley had used his prerogative to select the staff, which included veteran draftsman John Heimburger. Heimburger helped to carve and recarve legislative language to reflect such harmony and compromise as had been suggested in the hearings, and in subsequent private sessions. Committee consultant Frank LeMay, a one-time newsman, wrote Chairman Cooley's speeches, press releases, and some letters. Mrs. Christine Gallagher, the chief clerk, was responsible for notifying members and witnesses about committee meetings, and for supervising the record-keeping staff.

The only staff member not working for the chairman was the minority (Republican) counsel Hyde Murray, son of a distinguished former member. Murray, who came to the staff in 1958 after graduation from Georgetown University law school, and a brief internship in the Department of Agriculture, had within three years become a leading, overworked, legislative technician on the Republican side of agriculture.

Republican Strategy

Republican strategy in the House committee was determined by the ranking (senior) committee Republican, Charles Hoeven, who was finishing his twentieth year in Congress as representative from a rich feed-grains district in northwestern Iowa. The proposal which Hoeven chose to support, as the Republican alternative to Freeman's proposed mandatory-controls program, was to continue the temporary feed-grains program. Questioning Freeman at the House hearings, Hoeven sought to show through Freeman's testimony that the administration's existing legislation was working well:

MR. HOEVEN: Mr. Secretary, before we get into the details of the bill, I would like to have some information from you as to the success or lack of success of the 1961 feed grain program.

In Omaha, on February 6, 1962, you addressed a meeting in which you said, among other things, "that the 1961 feed grain program was a smashing success—it more than met every target that I told the Congress I expected it to reach." I assume you made such a statement?

FREEMAN: Yes, Sir.

HOEVEN: Will you please, for the record, tell us in what respect the program was a success? . . .

Freeman proceeded to do so, guided and assisted by Congressman Hoeven. Hoeven then asked—

Well, if the program was so successful—and I'm not denying the fact that there have been some benefits—why do you want to discontinue it?

FREEMAN: Because there has been a substantial increase in production by noncompliers which has created additional costs. And over the long run I do not think that this program would work out satisfactorily.

HOEVEN: If the program is cutting down on production and saving the taxpayers so much money and is raising the farmer's income, I cannot quite understand why you do not want to continue such a successful program. . . . Would you be opposed to having the committee extend the present feed grain program with some modifications, rather than to impose your compulsory program on the farmer?

FREEMAN: I have recommended to this committee, and do recommend now very strongly, that the program as presented be enacted into law, rather than the present feed grain program for a third year.

HOEVEN: That is not the question. I am asking you whether you would be opposed to extending the Feed Grain Act of 1961–62 into the calendar year 1963 and the subsequent years.

FREEMAN: If I may say so—if I were in favor of it I would have testified in favor of it, instead of bringing a new program before this committee.

HOEVEN: I understand, but it seems to me that your arguments against extending the program are rather weak.[1]

Hoeven had not voted for these 1961 voluntary programs, nor did he have reason to believe that a majority of Republican legislators had been won over to the programs within the past year. However, these temporary programs had proved relatively popular among producers, and could be used to emphasize the many unattractive features of the new mandatory programs.

In pursuing this strategy of criticism, Hoeven faced an age-old tactical problem of the minority which, because it exists, obliges them to make a considerable contribution to our system of government. The problem is that adept majority leaders take account of minority criticisms, and thus improve the bill. For example, the new farm bill provided stiff fines and even prison sentences for dairy farmers who falsified their production records. In the morning question period with Freeman, Hoeven and Congressman Page Belcher (R., Okla.) had protested repeatedly that farmers might have to go to jail for being poor bookkeepers, though USDA Counsel Bagwell said that the government would first have to prove intent to perpetrate a fraud.

In the afternoon session a second-term Republican from Ohio, Delbert Latta (remembered for having dared as a freshman to criticize the committee chairman for abusing a witness—Secretary Benson) turned attention again to the criminal penalty, insisting that criminal intent need not be proven in order to send farmers to jail. He insisted so hard that Secretary Freeman was finally moved

[1] *Hearings on the Food and Agriculture Act of 1962*, House Committee Agriculture, pp. 123–24.

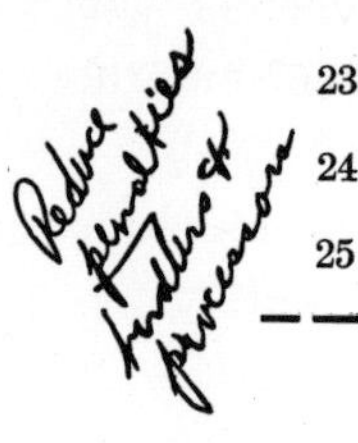

23 "PENALTIES

24 "SEC. 379i. (a) Any person who violates or attempts
25 to violate or who participates or aids in the violation of any

79

1 of the provisions of subsection (b) of section 379d of this
2 Act shall forfeit to the United States a sum equal to two
3 times the face value of the marketing certificates involved in
4 such violation. Such forfeiture shall be recoverable in a
5 civil action brought in the name of the United States.
6 "(b) Any person who violates or attempts to violate
7 or who participates or aids in the violation of any provision
8 of this subtitle, or of any regulation, governing the acquisi-
9 tion, disposition, or handling of marketing certificates shall
10 be deemed guilty of a misdemeanor and upon conviction
11 thereof shall be subject to a fine of not more than $5,000
12 for each violation.
13 "(c) Any person failing to make any report or keep
14 any record as required by section 379h shall be deemed
15 guilty of a misdemeanor and upon conviction thereof shall
16 be subject to a fine of not more than $5,000 for each
17 violation.

Illustration 18. MARKING UP THE BILL. *First Stage.* The House Agriculture Committee produced fifteen prints, or revisions, of portions of the administration's farm bill, H.R. 10010, before arriving at a *final* version which was introduced as a "clean bill" (H.R. 11222). Revisions of the wheat section (Title IV, Subtitle B) were contained in Committee prints 2, 3, and 10. Line by line, the bill was changed as it progressed from one print to the next. The three parts of this illustration display such changes in portions of the bill concerning penalties. Above is from the first printing (H.R. 10010). A USDA staff member noted on his copy a change to be urged: "Reduce penalties handlers and processors."

12 civil action brought in the name of the United States.
13 ~~"(b) Any person who violates or attempts to violate~~
14 ~~or who participates or aids in the violation of any provision~~
15 ~~of this subtitle, or of any regulation, governing the acquisi-~~
16 ~~tion, disposition, or handling of marketing certificates shall~~
17 ~~be deemed guilty of a misdemeanor and upon conviction~~
18 ~~thereof shall be subject to a fine of not more than $5,000~~
19 ~~for each violation.~~
20 ~~"(c) Any person failing to make any report or keep~~
21 ~~any record as required by section 379h shall be deemed~~
22 ~~guilty of a misdemeanor and upon conviction thereof shall~~
23 ~~be subject to a fine of not more than $5,000 for each~~
24 ~~violation.~~
25 *"(b) Any person, except a producer who is subject to*

Illustration 18. A Later Stage. A portion of the bill in a later printing, with subsections (b) and (c) lined out in accordance with intended revisions. The revisions are in italics, beginning with line 25.

to respond "You are correct, and I think that that section is a very stringent one, and I am sure that this committee will be able to write a better section." They did, but by achieving a change in the bill the Republicans had impaired a political issue which even President Eisenhower had helped to build. Eisenhower had earlier publicized his willingness to go to jail rather than live with the Democratic farm program. (See Illustration 18.)

Alternative legislative strategies were open to Hoeven, which some congressional Republicans would have preferred over the one he chose. Some younger committee Republicans were inclined to try to form a bipartisan coalition united in support of modified long-range voluntary programs. If such a group could oblige a re-

78

1 such violation. Such forfeiture shall be recoverable in a
2 civil action brought in the name of the United States.
3 "(b) Any person, except a producer who is subject to
4 subsection (c) of this section, who violates or attempts to vio-
5 late or who participates or aids in the violation of any pro-
6 vision of this subtitle, or of any regulation, governing the
7 acquisition, disposition, or handling of marketing certificates
8 or who fails to make any report or keep any record as re-
9 quired by section 379h shall be deemed guilty of a misde-
10 meanor and upon conviction thereof shall be subject to a fine
11 of not more than $5,000 for each violation.
12 "(c) Any person who, in his capacity as a producer,
13 knowingly violates or attempts to violate or who participates
14 or aids in the violation of any provision of this subtitle, or of
15 any regulation, governing the acquisition, disposition, or
16 handling of marketing certificates or fails to make any report
17 or keep any record as required by section 379h shall, (i) for-
18 feit any right to receive marketing certificates, in whole or in
19 part as the Secretary may determine, with respect to the farm
20 or farms and for the marketing year with respect to which
21 any such act or default is committed, or (ii), if such market-
22 ing certificates have already been issued, pay to the Secretary,
23 upon demand, the amount of the face value of such certifi-
24 cates, or such part thereof as the Secretary may determine.

Illustration 18. Final Committee Stage. The penalty provisions of the clean bill, reported out of Committee as H.R. 11222.

luctant administration to accept the voluntary route, Republican participants would have taken a step to shake off the obstructionist image which congressional Republicans had gained while in the minority during most of the past thirty years.

Prominent among the young farm Republicans was Congressman Albert Quie of Minnesota, respected both for his political acumen and his expertise in farm legislation. He, and to a lesser extent Representatives Catherine May (R., Wash.) and Don Short (R., N.D.) worked during 1962 to improve the administration bill.

Representative Robert Dole (R., Kans.) might also have taken a constructive approach had administration Democrats not barred him from any active role. Dole's unique problem was that his Kansas district was being merged with that of administration stalwart Floyd Breeding, chairman of the wheat subcommittee. As Dole put it, "The administration did not want to give me credit for knowing the time of day," since he was to be Breeding's campaign opponent.

It was difficult for these young Republican congressmen to move—let alone to achieve their political goals——against the wishes of Republican leaders. And there were other roadblocks to this strategy of bipartisan action. The Farm Bureau insisted on a no-compromise position, as did the Farmers Union and in addition the administration seemed prepared at the time to push through the mandatory programs without any considerable Republican congressional support.

Two other strategies remained to the Republicans:

One would be to register a strong protest, and then let the mandatory programs go through—"give the Democrats enough rope to hang themselves." Aside from the gamble involved in awaiting such distant rewards, and the fact that any Democratic legislative success put the Republican leadership in a bad light and also might prove contagious in other areas, there was the plain fact that Republicans were convinced the Democratic farm program was bad for farmers and for the nation.

In the other strategy, Hoeven could have embraced an alternative long-range program such as the ones recommended by the Farm Bureau and other groups which fit the principles of conservative Republicanism but which seemed to have even less political appeal than the administration's program. Such programs would get nowhere in the Congress, and the President would not have been embarrassed to veto them.

Republicans were, after all, not expected to pass legislation. They were the minority whose privilege was to criticize and to oppose. The farm issue was a good one for the "outs." The Democrats had stalled while surpluses accumulated under Benson, so why should Republicans now worry about solutions, especially since surpluses were being reduced under Kennedy's own temporary programs? So despite the range of choices, Hoeven, House minority leader Charles Halleck, and other Republican leaders seemed never to have been tempted to organize forces in support of any alternative program.

It would have mattered little what the Republicans did if the administration had the means to control the large Democratic majority. But Democratic party ties were so tenuous in the decentralized Congress, particularly across the Mason-Dixon line, that the natural majority on most issues belonged to a conservative coalition of most Southern Democrats and most Republicans. The Truman Administration had once run a farm bill (the Brannan Plan) against that coalition, with disastrous results.

The Kennedy-Cochrane bill, in contrast, was framed to come to terms with most Southerners, and with the urban Democrats, and still to win about twenty maverick Republican votes. If Hoeven and his party-minded Republican committee members could keep all Republicans in opposition, and if the Farm Bureau could wean away enough Southern Democrats the bill would fail. As one Republican committee member said of their strategy, "About the only thing to do was to make it [the bill] as bad as possible and then defeat it."

So it was a party issue from the beginning.

Alienating Southerners

Opponents of the bill had an opportunity which they used to strike the weakest spot in the Democratic coalition. That was the question as to whether racial segregation might be permitted in recreation areas developed under the bill. If Freeman were to insist on integration of the recreational facilities, the Southerners who held the eight senior seats on the House committee would not vote for the bill, nor would such a bill ever leave the Senate committee. (Possibly Senator Ellender's early objections to the recreation feature were borne of a desire to stay clear of the explosive race issue.)

The Department of Agriculture likewise tried to skirt the subject, but Illinois Republican Paul Findley would not let them. He first raised the issue with Administrator Gladwin Young, whose Soil Conservation Service would help develop community recreational projects—

FINDLEY: Is the question of segregation apt to be involved in any of these recreational areas?

YOUNG: I think that that could be entirely a local situation. However, the . . . regulations with respect to the use of Federal funds would have to be taken into account.

FINDLEY: As you know, there is a great deal of controversy on that. I wondered if the Administration had thought out what its attitude would be in regard to segregation in these recreational facilities?

YOUNG: I think that we have not thought it out specifically in that respect.

At which point Mississippi Congressman Thomas Abernethy, also an opponent of the bill, commented—

I do not think it will take you more than 5 minutes to make a decision on that. (*laughter*)[2]

[2] *Hearings on the Food and Agriculture Act of 1962*, House Committee on Agriculture, pp. 293–94.

When Findley put the question to Secretary Freeman a month later (March 15th), Freeman answered "This is a question that, very frankly, I have not had the opportunity to consider before. I would want to reserve judgment in connection with it until I had time to review the conditions and circumstances of the present law to determine what would be the soundest practicable judgment to make."

FINDLEY: Will you place an answer to this question in the record?

FREEMAN: Surely.

And the answer, though in the most obscure lawyer language, was that segregation would in fact be allowed:

> It has been deemed in line with the intent of Congress to provide in the agreements with local organizations only those requirements necessary to achieving the benefits on which the projects are justified with a minimum burden on local initiative and control. It is contemplated . . . that there will be no change in the general administration of the program.[3]

So Representative Findley seemed justified later in suggesting an amendment to prevent the Secretary from spending funds for recreation "unless he finds that any recreation facilities established under the Act will be available for the use and enjoyment of all persons, regardless of race, creed or color. . . ." [4] This amendment, well known as the Powell amendment, brought a vigorous rebuke from Vice-Chairman Poage:

> This amendment has not a thing in the world to do with anything except the pure politics of the matter. The hope of course is that somehow he will sow the seeds of dissension over here on our side. He heard the fire alarm, so he comes running with a can of gasoline in each hand. . . .[5]

[3] *Hearings on Cropland Retirement and Extension of Expiring Conservation Reserve Contracts*, House Committee on Agriculture, pp. 176–77.

[4] *Congressional Record* (daily edition), June 20, 1962, p. 10403.

[5] *Congressional Record* (daily edition), June 20, 1962, p. 10404.

Congressman H. R. Gross (R., Iowa) countered that Findley's amendment had as much to do with the farm bill as "golf courses, swimming pools, ski rides, and what have you." Congressman John Lindsay (R., N.Y.) thought Poage should apologize for questioning Findley's motives, and then Lindsay himself questioned the motives of Vice-Chairman Poage, an outspoken segregationist:

> . . . The gentleman from Texas is very willing to make taxpayers' money available . . . to one limited group only. . . . He would exclude one-half the public. This is the oldest story in the world. It's the story of bigotry. And every time the question of doing something about it, of giving U.S. taxpayers equal opportunity in the enjoyment and use of federal land or federally supported institutions, the gentleman and his friends get up and say, "You are trying to rock the boat." What boat? How can you rock a boat that is already sunk in a muddy sea of bigotry and petty bureaucracy? [6]

Nevertheless, Findley's amendment did not pass, and his particular tactic may have backfired slightly, in that this challenge from the other party seemed to tighten somewhat the ranks of urban and Southern Democrats.

Functions of the Public Committee Hearing

Public hearings are supposedly to educate committee members as to the substance of legislation and how groups feel about it, but they have many other, perhaps more important, functions. Junior members of the committee can learn a lot from them and are urged to be constant in their attendance. However, the men on the committee's top tier who ask most of the questions, and who usually make the decisions, hear little from witnesses that is new.

More often than not senior members were seeking, like laywers in a court-room cross-examination, to bring out facts and opinions favorable to their point of view. While Republicans continued to draw attention to the blackjack alternative of low prices which

[6] *Congressional Record* (daily edition), June 20, 1962, p. 10404.

would be offered farmers in the referendum as an alternative to the administration programs, leading Democrats sought testimony that the choice offered wheat and feed grains producers was in fact a fair one. The Democrats confronted witness after witness, in both House and Senate Hearings, with the question that Democrat Paul Jones (Mo.) put to President Patton of the National Farmers Union:

JONES: I take it that you believe that in return for support that the producer has an obligation to cooperate in bringing his production in line with the demand?

PATTON: I certainly do.[7]

Assistance could even be gained from unfriendly witnesses. Although Farmers Union Patton came to put in a plug for the bill, Congressman Hoeven recalled that Patton had criticized the USDA staff report which was the basis for the administration's program. Patton had said the administration's income goals were "totally unacceptable," even "preposterous." So Hoeven asked:

Then you do not feel that the bill is going to afford the kind of farm income you desire?

PATTON: Well, I think it needs a constructive amendment that will put the income higher than it is, higher than what seems to be contemplated as now written.

HOEVEN: We have tried very hard to have the Secretary of Agriculture tell us just how this bill will increase the farmers' income, and I for one don't think we received a satisfactory answer. . . . The most I can gather . . . is that he thinks farm income will remain status quo. Would you be satisfied with that?

PATTON: No sir; no, sir, and I said so. I said any number of times . . .

HOEVEN: Mr. Patton, I am delighted to have your frank appraisal.[8]

[7] *Hearings on the Food and Agriculture Act of 1962*, House Agriculture Committee, p. 513.

[8] *Hearings on the Food and Agriculture Act of 1962*, House Committee on Agriculture, p. 518.

Vice-Chairman Poage countered with a different perspective:

Now you talk about getting more than we have—now, first, Mr. Patton, would you agree that it is important that we hold onto what we have?

PATTON: I agree with you.

POAGE: And that we make sure that we hang on to what we have before we try to get more than that—

PATTON: I agree with that, too, but—

POAGE: Since you are talking about raising the parity and raising the income. I think you will agree that about the most important thing right now is to try to maintain as far as the price structure—to keep what we have rather than have it taken away—

PATTON: Yes.[9]

Urging Revisions in the Legislation

Many of the questions and much of the testimony, as in the case of Mr. Patton's, sought really to get the proposed law changed. Congresswoman Catherine May worked in the public hearings, as she later did in executive (private, closed) sessions of her subcommittee, to achieve the major revisions in the bill that the National Association of Wheat Growers, the Grange, and the Farmers Union had proposed and failed to get before the bill was introduced. As a Republican whose vote the administration still hoped to get, she was in unique position to give Wheat Grower President Bayne chances to qualify his support for the administration bill when he testified before the House Committee:

MAY: . . . If the proposal for a wheat certificate program were voted down in favor of the only alternative in this bill—no program—what would it mean to the wheatgrowers' economy in the Nation?

BAYNE: Well, certainly, I do not believe that the wheatgrowers' economy is in any position to stand a complete removal of controls without complete chaos in the industry.

MAY: Should the Committee in its wisdom look at this section of the

[9] *Ibid.*, pp. 518–519.

bill and revise it with another alternative? Would you be in favor of some floor protection? . . .

BAYNE: It certainly should offer better protection for the wheat industry, as you point out. However, this complete choice between a reasonable control and no support and no control, is the choice that many growers have indicated they want to make . . . I think that, perhaps, it is a dangerous choice . . . We certainly would not be opposed to a change.[10]

Partly through the efforts of Mrs. May—who did not finally vote for the bill—wheat growers were guaranteed some price support in the event of a "no" vote which, as it happened, they dearly needed. They also were authorized, at the Secretary of Agriculture's discretion, to interchange wheat and feed-grains acres, and a single wheat certificate (two price) was provided for in place of the more complicated two-certificate (three price) plan, though the value of the certificate would not be allowed to fluctuate freely as the Wheat Growers Association had hoped. (See Illustration 19.)

Nor did the administration give in to their demands for higher subsidies for diverted acres. The sum of the public hearings in the House and Senate actually convinced national officials of the Wheat Growers, the Grange, and the Farmers Union that they should—indeed must—fight for and be prepared to live with the administration bill.

MULTIPLE ACTION POINTS

Both Mrs. May and Representative Dole were faced with divided opinion at home which was keener than legislators normally have to deal with. They resorted, as politicians must, to a zig-zag course along what one scholar called "multiple action points." [11] As sponsor of the original Wheat Growers bill and helpmate to the

[10] *Ibid.*, p. 614.

[11] Charles O. Jones, "Representation in Congress: The Case of the House Agriculture Committee, *The American Political Science Review* (June 1961), 367.

37

1 "SUBSTITUTION OF WHEAT FOR FEED GRAINS

2 "SEC. 360i. Notwithstanding any other provision of law,

3 the Secretary ~~may~~ shall permit producers of wheat to have acre-

4 age devoted to the production of wheat considered as de-

5 voted to the production of feed grains to such extent and

6 subject to such terms and conditions as the Secretary de-

7 termines will not impair the effective operation of this sub-

8 title A.B.

O K Mrs May

Illustration 19. A SCORE FOR MRS. MAY. As the USDA staff member marks up his copy of the bill during the Committee action, he acknowledges the source of one of the changes. His margin comment reads: "O K Mrs. May."

Wheat Growers in securing committee changes in the administration bill, Mrs. May could count on the Wheat Growers Association to forgive her for her vote against the bill on the floor, which would in turn please constituents who had no sympathy at all for the wheat bill.

Likewise, Dole indicated in his home visits, newsletters, and in his separate statement in the Committee's Report [12] that he did not oppose the certificate plan as such. But in evidence presented at the hearings, Dole found ample grounds on which to oppose the administration's wheat-certificate bill, particularly in the answers he helped solicit which indicated wheat farmers' income would not go up much, if at all, as a result of the new controls program. This political zigging and zagging required great skill, and perhaps considerable sincerity as well, if he was to emerge before his constituents as a statesman rather than a doubledealer. The returns

[12] *Report on H.R. 11222 (87th Congress)*, House Committee on Agriculture, p. 151.

from his fall contest with senior Democrat Floyd Breeding showed he had done a convincing job. Breeding's enthusiastic supporters knew that their candidate, as the influential chairman of the House wheat subcommittee and a member of the conference committee that finally wrote the bill, had wrangled many changes which made the bill more compatible to Western Kansans, but in the fall elections Breeding's supporters were far from being a majority of the voters.

Making a History

Legislation which authorizes an administrative effort within our kaleidoscopic, very complex environment, as this farm bill did, must leave many things for the administrators to decide. Often a philosophic statement of purpose or intent included in legislation must seem as helpful to the administrators as the specific guidelines which are in the law. But while legislators cannot cover all contingencies in the law, they can and do further embroider their intent in lengthy committee reports, in public hearings, and in the congressional debate.

Administrators are supposed to observe this legislative history along with the words in the law itself. So senior committee members of both parties were occasionally occupied in writing a history at these public hearings. As an example, Republican Clifford McIntire from Maine, a softspoken, careful veteran, was concerned that under a new authority in the bill to distribute our food surpluses through some future multilateral or international authority, the participant nations might decide, over the protests of the U.S. government, to give U.S. surpluses to Communist China, Russia, or Cuba. He raised the matter with Raymond Ioanes, the Administrator of the Foreign Agricultural Service:

McIntire: Are you in position to advise us at this time as to whether these agreements [setting up an international food agency], which are at the discussion stage, place these commodities completely and solely for administration or distribution in the hands of an international agency?

IOANES: We would assume that in the case of each agreement in which the United States would participate that the United States would have the right to either approve the particular program or disapprove of the program.

In other words, once the United States agreed a particular program could go forward, then the particular program would be in the hands of the international agency. . . .

MCINTIRE: But our participation in there is simply as one of the group of signatories and we are not in a controlling position at all? . . . And there would be nothing to prevent our contribution here up to the statutory limit of being used by the international agency over our objection . . .

IOANES: It would be possible . . . I doubt that it would happen, sir.

MCINTIRE: Ray, this is happening every day in the U.N., isn't it? . . . There would be nothing to prevent . . . our funding up to whatever the statute permits for a program of feeding into the Communist countries. . . .

IOANES: Well, there is no provision in this law that indicates to which destination commodities could go. . . . But I think I can assure you without question today that there would be no intention of permitting any of the food under a program of this kind to go to Red China . . . I am certain that in the international agreement that is finally written that the United States would reserve the right to restrict shipments to certain destinations of the world.[13]

Having gained this declaration, McIntire found his position seconded by Representative D. R. (Billy) Matthews of Florida, another member of the subcommittee which handled such matters, who expressed confidence that U.S. negotiators were as concerned about this as the Committee apparently was. McIntire replied that "this is not in any sense a criticism, but a record is what we are making here and I just wanted to develop these questions as a part of the record." [14]

[13] *Hearings on the Food and Agriculture Act of 1962*, House Committee on Agriculture, pp. 383–384.

[14] *Hearings on the Food and Agriculture Act of 1962*, House Committee on Agriculture, p. 384.

But in the experience of Congressman Paul Jones, bureaucrats were slippery. He felt in this case that the Committee should state the intent in the law itself. Ultimately the Committee decided to delete the authority for multilateral food distribution, and the bureaucrats lived up to Mr. Jones' expectations by going ahead with negotiations anyway on the basis of scraps of authority found in other legislation.

Congressmen are accustomed to bureaucrats who seek their ends by mild subterfuge in the apparent belief that the congressmen would not appreciate their problem if it were clearly put to them. Congressmen often catch them at the game. Howard Bertsch, administrator of the Farmers Home Administration which made loans for rural water systems under the rural redevelopment programs, pleaded before the Committee for authority also to finance sewerage systems, on the ground that

> . . . when we loan funds for a community water system and the trenches are dug connecting all the homes in the area, pipelines for a community sewerage system could be laid at the same time, resulting in economies in equipment use, making essential surveys, etc. Yet there is no source of credit available to these people for sewerage system construction.[15]

Something about this statement was so distasteful that the chairman checked on it over the lunch hour and returned to it in the afternoon questioning:

> CHAIRMAN COOLEY: Did you make some statement indicating that when the trench was open for the water pipes, that they could also put in the sewer pipes to save money?
>
> BERTSCH: No. I indicated that when the members of an association saw that open trench there in which they were laying the water pipes, they realized the advantage which would accrue to them if they could also simultaneously combine their engineering costs and installing sewage disposal systems at the same time.
>
> CHAIRMAN: Well, that was the observation of other people. But since this morning, I have learned that you have a sanitary law that

[15] *Ibid.*, p. 343.

prevents putting sewage pipe in the same ditch with water pipes. . . .

McINTIRE: . . . Then it is recognized that undoubtedly there would be many local ordinances . . . that would not permit the use of any trench for a water system and a sewage system?

BERTSCH: That is correct. . . . [But] economies in the utilization of engineering facilities, construction facilites, etcetera, could be achieved if the job was done simultaneously . . .

POAGE: Your purpose is not engineering—your purpose is financing, is it not?

BERTSCH: Right.

POAGE: So that if we assume these things can be adequately financed without your agency then, obviously, they will never come to you.

BERTSCH: That is correct.

The Farmers Home Administration did not finally get authority to finance rural sewerage systems, although such authority was included in the bill as reported by the House committee.

REA's Problems

The problems and aspirations of another rural lending agency, the Rural Electrification Administration (REA), consumed more than 150 of the 1,000-plus pages of the House committee testimony on the Farm bill. The 971 rural electric coops organized and financed by REA had modernized rural America and had set records in providing a yardstick of low-cost electric power which the embarrassed, once-indifferent, private electric monopolies were obliged to equal. Now that the job was done, and with farmers moving to town (though their electric fences and electrically powered machinery continued to increase loads on many rural lines), these coops were fighting with municipalities and private companies in an effort to serve the portions of cities and suburbs which stretched into what was once REA's geographical domain. REA's urban and industrial users were sometimes angry hostages who had been offered cheaper power from the city utility or private company, despite the fact that the financing of REA's lines and generating facilities was still somewhat subsidized by federal taxpayers.

REA was also enthusiastic about rural renewal, hoping to serve the industrial complexes and cities which might grow up in rural America, and the new recreational developments as well. But their political base was fast disappearing. Many within the thinning ranks of rural congressmen thought it distressingly immoral that an institution which had given lights to rural students, ended mother's trips to the well and outhouse, and taken the drudgery out of vigils in the dairy barn, should now be eagerly outfitting and lighting lake resorts and roadhouses. As a youthful Illinois Republican, Robert Michel, protested on the floor of the House—

> . . . (if) REA funds could be used to finance at least part of the cost of a night club in the country it is not at all unlikely that part of this cost financed by the REA would cover the spotlights and other lighting devices used to illuminate the talents of exotic dancers. If the REA funds could be used to finance such appliances at lower interest rates than regularly available, the REA inadvertently could become a party to development of a center of sin and debauchery.
>
> Mr. Chairman, is this what was intended for the REA? [16]

Most objectionable to representatives of private power companies, who took their turns before the House and Senate committees, was the cloak of secrecy under which REA decisions were made on granting loans to electric coops for purchase of additional generating facilities. Although REA's well-heeled National Rural Electric Cooperative Association brought in numerous coop officials to rebut the private power representatives, the House committee finally decided to delete all of REA's requests for new authority. In its report, the House committee not only rebuked REA for what Chairman Cooley called its "star-chamber proceedings" [17] but in effect told REA that its aggressive campaign for suburban and industrial users violated the intent of the law.[18] The Senate committee report, though milder, contained much the same

[16] *Congressional Record* (daily edition), June 19, 1962, p. 10181.

[17] *Congressional Record* (daily edition), June 20, 1962, p. 10399.

[18] *Report on H.R. 11222 (87th Congress),* House Committee on Agriculture, pp. 71–72.

message.[19] It was a bitter pill for this venerable bureaucracy, and for those who had viewed REA as one instrumentality through which the electric power industry might ultimately be made a government enterprise.

The hearings on the farm bill had many other purposes, sometimes unrelated to the legislation at hand. Congressman Charles Teague of California took the opportunity to alert Secretary Freeman publicly about legislative proposals by the Health, Education, and Welfare Department to require better housing for migratory laborers, which Teague feared would be too costly for some California farmers. Congressman Ralph Beermann of Nebraska criticized the Secretary for remarks he had made in an Omaha press conference, and Representative Ralph Harding rewarded the Secretary, at the end of his last three-hour stint as witness, with a bag of quality Idaho potatoes.

Kinds of Witnesses

Secretary Freeman and other administration witnesses together consumed about one-third of the time during the 13-day House committee sessions. Another third of the time was used by the familiar farm organization lobbyists whose basic message did not vary much from previous years. Chairman Cooley chose to allow a ten-minute hearing to all other comers, including a number of farmers who paid their own way into Washington to plead for some small concession, or perhaps to present their personal solution to the farm problem. Mr. and Mrs. Emmett Simmermon from Ohio had even put their farm program to verse, which the recording clerk transcribed to read, in part:

> Set a price for my fiber and food
> That is just and fair to the Nation's good.
> And if I overproduce which sometimes I might
> I could pay the surplus cost to set things right.

[19] *Report on S. 3225 (87th Congress)*, Senate Committee on Agriculture, pp. 22–24.

Free-lance "economist" Carl Wilkens, perennial favorite because of his "one to seven" theory that every federal dollar spent in agriculture multiplies itself seven times, was bested this year by an Ohio farmer, Charles Oler, who asserted that the relationship was in fact one to ten.[20] Two congressmen brought constituents who had problems or theories for the Committee to consider, and another congressman testified in his own behalf.

Since these public hearings were a threshold for getting attention in the national media, many phrases were turned in the hope of activating a reporter's pen. Questioners and publicity-seeking witnesses had learned that the press likes preposterous language—which might in turn cause a ruckus in Committee, which is what the press likes most. Perhaps with this in mind, Earl Hughes, a former Benson official appearing for the Illinois Chamber of Commerce, decried the "boondoggle" in the USDA, the "vast horde" of county ASCS employees, politically determined prices, and labor-union monopoly power, but committee Democrats let his lures go by.

However, when Walter Garver appeared for the U.S. Chamber of Commerce, Democratic Representatives Poage, and Lester Johnson of Wisconsin, made their own capital in an extended bitter exchange, the flavor of which was as follows:

POAGE: You decided that it was not in the public interest to give to agriculture the same kind of treatment that you give to others. You find it is in the public interest to protect business, to protect the oil industry, to protect almost every activity except where it is in agriculture.

GARVER: I would like the record to show that I do not accept all of these sweeping words as an interpretation of what we believe in.[21]

[20] *Hearings on the Food and Agriculture Act of 1962*, House Committee on Agriculture, p. 727.

[21] *Hearings on the Food and Agriculture Act of 1962*, House Committee on Agriculture, p. 947.

The most effective witness for the opposition was President Charles Shuman of the American Farm Bureau Federation, who spent a four-hour afternoon session with the House committee, and testified at length again in a unique four-day separate hearing devoted to the Farm Bureau's program, which followed consideration of the administration's bill.

Farm Bureau Hearings

As in 1961, the Farm Bureau was uncompromising toward the Freeman program, though its own program contained some similar mechanisms. Shuman offered several reasons, in response to criticism of the Farm Bureau's unbending opposition, why the Farm Bureau could not seek a compromise. First, he said, the Farm Bureau and Freeman were going in different directions: Freeman's bill sought permanent controls, while the Farm Bureau's program was to be transitional toward a free market in agriculture—to protect farm income while government controls and market-depressing surpluses were being removed and while individual farmers were making the adjustment.

Secondly, Shuman said, the Farm Bureau's top leaders could not change the policy set by members at conventions. "Wherever you see a farm leader who says 'We will change and we will compromise,' " Shuman said, ". . . then you find an organization where the direction of policies is from the top down." As a third reason Shuman pointed out, on another occasion, that consistency is an element of organizational strength. Members would become confused if the organization's position changed from time to time. Finally, the Farm Bureau viewed its function as making the best possible case for its program, and letting the Congress, like a jury, reach the decision. The trouble with using this adversary approach of the court room in farm politics was that the committees themselves were drawn into it. When constituent organizations and party leaders told congressmen "You are with me or against me," there might be no one left to compromise.

The Farm Bureau bill was not a serious effort to legislate in 1962 nor, regardless of its economic merits, did it seem possible that the Congress would find the Farm Bureau program acceptable in future years. Almost all Democrats opposed it, as did many rural Republicans. Though urban Republicans had not yet been asked to commit themselves, some had loudly denounced a similar principle represented in the 1956 soil-bank program, which had been phased out during the last Benson years as it lost political support. Perhaps a determined Republican President might ram through the Farm Bureau program, as Kennedy was trying to ram through mandatory controls, but that was a matter for the future.

Like the administration's farm bill, the Farm Bureau's would reduce production by diverting acres. But except during a two-year interlude when the Farm Bureau's Illinois state President William Kuhfuss insisted that farmers should be required to divert some acres in order to get price supports, the Farm Bureau's basic mechanism was to have government rent surplus cropland outright. The Secretary of Agriculture would decide how much land should be idled to keep production in line with demand, and he would offer a rental price high enough to induce farmers to rent that much land to him. This rented land would remain completely idle. The Secretary would try to rent whole farms, and thus to rent the good as well as the poor land, and to give many farm operators an opportunity to move to other employment. Land would be rented for three-year periods or longer. The acres not rented to the government could be planted to any crop except rice, cotton, peanuts, tobacco, and other crops whose acreage was still regulated under mandatory programs.

Meanwhile, price supports on wheat and feed grains would be allowed to slide downward to a point where, in a few years, supports would have no effect upon the market price. By that time production might have adjusted so that the land rental programs could also come to an end.

Hearings on the Farm Bureau bill—which was introduced by 16 congressmen and co-sponsored by 17 senators—produced many criticisms of the bill. The big criticism was cost to the government. President Shuman admitted it would be expensive even though temporary. He felt it was impossible to predict the costs. If it was so difficult for Mr. Shuman to peer into the future, wondered Committee Democrats, how then could he so confidently predict all the marvelous effects of the program, to occur five years hence.

Secretary Freeman was quite willing to project costs:

> The costs would be unjustifiably high because of the nature of the program itself. It uses the shotgun approach to taking acreages out of production.[22]

That is, according to the USDA, it would retire the poor acres often devoted to sweet potatoes, hay, and many other crops not in surplus. To rent enough productive cropland to really reduce overproduction would cost $1,880 million per year, according to the USDA, as compared with $760 million that would be spent under the administration's 1962 mandatory programs. While the government spent $900 million more, the farmers would be getting nearly a billion dollars less per year than under the administration's program, Freeman said, "based on a careful analysis by the professional career people within the Department of Agriculture," using "the soundest statistical techniques that we know." [23]

The Farm Bureau had said Secretary Freeman's mandatory feed-grains program could not be administered. Freeman returned the compliment, noting past difficulties in taking bids for farm-land rentals as Farm Bureau proposed to do.

What made the Bureau's bill objectionable to most rural congressmen, especially those from the poor-land areas, was that rentals of whole farms would speed the migration of rural people to cities, although the bill did authorize a limitation on the amount of acreage to be retired in any one county.

[22] *Hearings on the Cropland Retirement and Extension of Expiring Conservation Reserve Contracts,* House Committee on Agriculture, p. 139.

[23] *Hearings on the Cropland Retirement and Extension of Expiring Conservation Reserve Contracts,* House Committee on Agriculture pp. 140, 141, 167.

In the Senate Committee

The Senate Agriculture Committee received Secretary Freeman on the morning after his long day of questioning in the House committee. The line-up of groups to appear before the Senate was virtually the same as that of the House, and the Senate group was reconciled to getting a rerun of testimony previously presented to the House committee. Still it was worth a quip by the ranking minority member Senator George Aiken of Vermont, to Freeman:

Aiken (*grinning*): This statement is completely different from the one you gave the House, is it not?

Freeman (*also grinning*): It is somewhat different, Senator.

Chairman Ellender (*feigning sternness*): Why is it different—why should it be? It is the same bill.

Senator Allen Ellender of Louisiana had set the tone of his committee and guided its deliberations and decisions even more than Senate chairmen usually do. A product of Huey Long's rough-and-tumble regime, Senator Ellender ran a tight ship, tolerating no proliferation of subcommittees which would magnify the Committee's budget, but which might weaken his control over it. His staff consisted of an expert lawyer-counsel, Harker Stanton; a respected politician-economist, Henry Casso; and an amiable chief clerk, Cotys Mouser. The Republicans had their competent clerk, Jim Kendall. Most business was done with the full committee facing one another along the intimate, felt-covered table with a place for a witness at the end, which was centered in the chandeliered, carpeted room in the old Senate Office Building.

As indicated earlier (pp. 54–55), Ellender's Agriculture committee included some men of considerable prestige and some moderates and mavericks. Committee members were said to like the chairman's way of doing business, which he described as follows:

It is my job to give everybody a chance to say what they have to say. It has always been my way. I have never sat on a bill. My motto is a square deal, a good chance, be honest. Always lay out where you are going, no back door deals. And I always take the view that compromise is better than nothing.[24]

Chairman Ellender insisted on the logrolling, commodity-by-commodity approach to legislation, even while he looked ahead to a product defensible on the Senate floor. He proved in 1962 what could be done with a spirited vocabulary, a small staff, a good committee, and a willingness to compromise. His principal contribution was to help get Senate approval, on three different occasions, of a bill to which a majority of his committee were opposed. If this had not been one of the few times in his career that he had overridden his committee he might well have failed to do so. Of course, Ellender did not labor alone in the Senate; of particular importance was farm leader and Democratic whip Hubert Humphrey, a man of great prestige who often paved the way behind the scenes—on occasion persuading Ellender himself to take the next step.

[24] Interview by Hadwiger with the Senator in his office, June 1963.

8. *Reporting the Bill*

After the Senate committee finished public hearings it went into executive session behind closed doors, during which members ironed out changes in the bill as it was read slowly, paragraph by paragraph. This time-consuming, arduous, painstaking work is the heart of the legislative process, demanding different, more valuable knowledge of the subject, the language, the psychology of other members, and the whole political context than is required in the parliamentary stages of the process.

Besides looking for any remaining imperfections in the language, friends of the bill were weeding out the red flags—provisions which were not absolutely needed but might give an opponent a handle to criticize the bill, such as the criminal penalties which might have applied against farmers, and the authority the Secretary had sought but now said he already possessed to set up multilateral food assistance programs, and another provision to let the Secretary take farms by eminent domain to be used for community recreation programs (it seemed better to let the communities themselves buy this land). The Committee at one time deleted the whole section on recreation, feeling it was a red flag to segregationists, but then put it back in.

The Time Problem

Continually in mind was the matter of how to get the bill out of committee—or how to stop it there, and the key here was how a few undecided Southern Democrats and rural Republicans would react in the showdown vote with respect to the wheat and feed-grains provisions of the bill. These provisions faced an uncertain future in both the Senate and House committees, but the best strategy for supporters seemed to be to vote on them before Easter. Both sides assumed that delay permitted the building of opposition pressures.

Senators serve on as many as three committees, and often find that they can give full attention to only one of them. So each Senate committee has just a few individuals such as Chairman Ellender and ranking minority member Aiken who will be present and really functional in executive sessions. The party, constituency, and committee interests of these senior men combined to put them at odds and to give both a considerable stake in the decision on the controversial commodity programs.

Senator Herman Talmadge of Georgia was a knowledgeable member who had proposed his own program that would give a preference to the small farmer, but he was certain to vote for the administration bill, and he might even assist in lining up other Southern Democrats.

Another busy Ellender ally in the executive sessions was Senator Eugene McCarthy, Freeman's political colleague from Minnesota. McCarthy relied heavily on his agricultural assistant, former philosophy teacher Emerson Hines, who in turn found guidance in Aristotelian and Thomistic precepts even for decisions such as whether to pass a mandatory feed-grains program, and how to do it. Hines' expertise and good judgment were as well respected by the other liberals on the Agriculture committee as were his speeches on the morality of politics, delivered to church and university groups across the country.

McCarthy and the four other liberal senators had a different style than their committee cohorts. As liberals they desired much new legislation. Yet sitting as they did at the bottom end of the Committee, almost as outsiders, their direct influence within the Senate was fairly small, although some other liberal senators did look to McCarthy for guidance on farm bills.

Perhaps as an alternative role, but also because they took a more comprehensive view of the political scene than did some Senate-centered colleagues, these liberals laid more emphasis on the educational-propaganda function of their office. They had good staffs and used them to help in committee work and also to help educate a larger public about measures the Congress would be considering. To do this they introduced many bills for publicity only, made many speeches and "insertions" in the *Congressional Record*, and wrote articles for magazines and newspapers. But these legislators were uncomfortable on the Agriculture committee which dealt with established governmental functions increasingly for the benefit of well-fixed farmers. All but McCarthy moved off the Committee the following year.

Senator Proxmire

Besides McCarthy, the liberal Democrats were Senators Philip Hart of Michigan, Stephen Young of Ohio, Maurine B. Neuberger of Oregon, and also Senator William Proxmire of Wisconsin, who was expected normally to support the administration on farm bills. Proxmire, however, was unpredictable, and his constituents apparently liked him that way. One scholar of the Senate described him as the archetype of the Senate "outsider who does not abide by the many unspoken Senate rules for behavior, and therefore gets little fellowship or support from his colleagues." [1] In compensation he is free to shift positions quickly, to attack anything at any time, and in so doing often to destroy the best-laid plans of other senators. On this occasion he upset the administration's plans, and in the process made administration officials so furious that some could not speak of him in a level voice. The fact that he was subsequently proven "right" did not help matters. One official in the USDA said, "I can respect a man who speaks out when he differs with us, but I simply cannot stand one who thinks he has a mandate from God that makes him always right."

Briefly, Proxmire decided to oppose the administration's feed-grains provision because, based on a study of the economics of the program as well as of polls and statements by political observers,

[1] Ralph Huitt, "The Outsider in the Senate," *American Political Science Review* (September 1961), pp. 566–575.

he felt that farmers would reject the program overwhelmingly in a producer referendum. If farm income dropped drastically in the absence of effective price supports, farmers would blame the Democrats.[2]

Half of the potential referendum voters, Proxmire noted, were outside the corn-belt—cotton, tobacco, rice, wheat, beef, and dairy producers who wanted to be free to plant as much in feed grains as they wished on the acreage not used for their primary product. To prevent farmers from voting for controls on their primary cash crop, and against controls on feed grains if Congress insisted on enacting them, Proxmire suggested farmers be obliged to express themselves with respect to all controls, by a single vote in simultaneous referendums.

Proxmire predicted that the small feed-grains producers, given an option to stay out of the program, would sign for the program in order to vote against it. All these would be joined by Midwesterners who fed their feed grain to their own stock (85% of the feed grains were fed on the farm that produced them), who would not benefit directly from supported grain prices but would still have to cut back production.

In making his decision to oppose the feed-grains program, in mustering his evidence, and later in making a scholarly case that modified voluntary programs could be used over the long run, Proxmire got much guidance from Walter Wilcox, analyst in the Legislative Reference Service. For some time Wilcox had been telling all listeners that mandatory programs could not be passed, and Proxmire's turn-about was a victory for him.

Proxmire was not the first person to suggest that the referendum would probably fail. Stiff opposition had been voiced within the administration, earlier, on the same ground. But would the hard choice be any easier next year, or the year after? Some Southerners were inclined to say, "So what if it fails?" Farmers would be quickly educated by low prices, as were tobacco farmers when they voted "no" to mandatory controls in 1938, and voted back

[2] *Congressional Record* (daily edition) May 17, 1962, p. 8726.

controls the next year. Secretary Freeman did not publicly accept the latter reasoning, but clung instead to the hope that farmers would respond favorably to an intelligent educational campaign conducted before the referendum.

Proxmire told Freeman he was unrealistic:

I am sure your staff could and would conduct a vigorous educational program prior to the referendum. But farmers would be confused by woefully misguided farm organization officers and staff who disregard or deny the analyses of leading economists. These people, in spite of numerous studies showing the opposite, greatly minimize the current benefits to livestock producers of feed grain price supports. The local press and much of the farm press also would confuse and obstruct your educational programs by raising fears of excessive bureaucratic controls, the inequities of historical bases, and similar issues.[3]

Proximire's fear was shared by an important senator on the Republican side of the Committee, Senator Milton Young, another maverick though popular in the Senate as well as in North Dakota. With a substantial farm population, North Dakota could not afford to chance a wheat depression which might follow the rejection of the wheat-certificate or feed-grains programs.

Conservative Senators Bourke Hickenlooper of Iowa and Karl E. Mundt of South Dakota resisted the administration bill. Senator John Sherman Cooper of Kentucky, one of a small liberal Republican group that voted for administration domestic legislation more often than not, opposed this farm bill even while he worked to improve it. The other Committee members were Republican Caleb Boggs of Delaware and Democratic Senators James Eastland of Mississippi and Spessard Holland of Florida, all opposed; and B. Everett Jordan from North Carolina, whose preference for mandatory programs extended, unlike Cooper's, to other programs as well as tobacco.

The lineup was seven "sure" votes for the administration and eight against, with two on the fence or—as it turned out—on

[3] *Congressional Record* (bound volumes) May 17, 1962, p. 8726. See also *Congressional Record* (daily edition), April 17, 1962, 6238.

opposite sides of a teeter-totter. The sure votes in favor were Ellender, Talmadge, Jordan, Young, Hart, McCarthy, and Neuberger. The sure "no" votes were Republicans Aiken, Hickenlooper, Mundt, Boggs, and Democrats Holland, Eastland, and Proxmire. On the fence were Milton Young of North Dakota and Olin D. Johnston of South Carolina, normally a supporter of administration farm policy. Though an old-timer, second to Ellender on the committee ladder, Johnston was experiencing a moment of vulnerability in consequence of a primary challenge from a popular governor.

Deficit-Areas Provision

Johnston objected to the feed-grains bill as did several other Southerners on the grounds that feed-grains controls might halt the trend of expanding feed and meat production in the South. Just as the South maintained cotton controls to keep that product from moving West, some Southerners did not want to see controls that kept corn from coming South. As a way out for Johnston and other Southern Democrats who favored controls that would not hinder Southern growth, the administration suggested a "deficit areas" provision under which the Secretary could exempt counties, states, or whole regions from feed-grains controls if he found that these areas did not produce enough feed grain for their needs, and were suffering hardship. With such vague guidelines for its use, Southern politicians could offer voters the prospect that their whole region would be left free of controls but by the same token Republicans could alert the commercial feed-grains areas that they faced tremendous cuts in the event that deficit areas should be exempted.

The question as to whether government should allow migration of commodity production in response to economic pressures could be used to arouse regional jealousies, and also fears that the Secretary would use this discretionary power in an arbitrary manner. Both Benson and Freeman had already been accused of using existing discretion to increase their leverage in the Congress.

Black Friday

The Senate committee made its crucial decisions on Friday, April 13th. Throughout the bill-writing stage in Congress the USDA's political economists Jaenke and Schnittker had camped outside the committee rooms ready to explain the bill, to negotiate minor concessions, and to do whatever outsiders could to hurry the committee but still prevent them from watering down the feed grains and wheat provisions. On the day of decision these administration provisions were intact, and a bare majority of the Senate committee seemed favorably disposed to them.

Others in the USDA had been involved in seeking votes in committee—the Secretary of Agriculture most of all, but also other administration officials who could boast ancestral, regional, political, economic, or friendship ties with committee members or with intermediaries who could influence the congressmen. Party leaders in Congress were involved as were farm-group lobbyists, and even a group of state ASCS committeemen who had been brought to Washington on business. As long as the ASCS men were there, President Kennedy told them, they ought to visit their congressmen in behalf of the farm bill. Everybody who had influence was pressed into service.

Immediate responsibility for lining up favorable votes, however, rested on three people in a special section of the USDA called the Legislative Liaison Section, in the shadow of the Secretary's office.

Most USDA liaison work was drab: hunting down statistics for junior congressmen, and arranging for meetings between USDA officials and interested constituents. However, liaison people were also involved in the strategy and tactics of influencing the Congress, which included the distribution of favors to those who cooperated with the Department.

Chief of the liaison group was Ken Birkhead, a former congressional staff member, who dovetailed with Schnittker and Jaenke by lapping over a little into legislative policy, while they dipped heavily into his area of congressional politics. As the officer corps for tactical operations, these three men were permitted to be in on most of the big decisions and were expected to lay the ground work for them both as to substance and strategy as the two became ever more entwined.

Also in the liaison section were a knowledgeable journalist, Duke Norberg, who had renovated a defeat-oriented Iowa Democratic organization, and Mabel Snyder, who had been Senator Hubert Humphrey's agricultural assistant.

On the morning of the Senate vote, Miss Snyder and Birkhead visited Senator Proxmire, who told them he would indeed introduce an amendment to eliminate the administration's feed-grains program, and insert the existing voluntary program in its place. However, they misjudged the seriousness of Proxmire's effort, which was successful in the morning's tentative decision session, thanks to a supporting vote from Senator Johnston. Proxmire left forthwith on other business, quietly giving his proxy (the right to cast his vote) to his neighbor at the table, Mississippi's Eastland.

The morning vote on Proxmire's amendment was not the critical one, nor was his proxy in Eastland's hand necessarily to be the balance wheel on subsequent committee votes, though last-minute efforts were made in the afternoon to reach Humphrey and other influential leaders in the hope that they might persuade Proxmire to vote for the bill with a feed-grains provision in it. The critical vote came after Senator Johnston had been allowed to add the deficit-areas amendment to the feed-grains section. Johnston would now vote for the feed-grains program, unaffected by Proxmire's tentative morning amendment, and administration supporters jubilantly brought it to a final vote. But the amendment that made Senator Johnston change his vote also changed Senator Young's vote in the other direction, for reasons discussed earlier.

Young's change of vote had not been expected. The vote was tied, and hung 8-8 while Chairman Ellender waited anxiously for the remaining member, Senator Cooper, to be summoned from a Senate Banking and Currency Committee hearing.

Cooper respected Ellender, and would not lightly vote against the chairman on a matter so important to the latter. But after shuffling into the committee room, and gently explaining his position, Cooper did vote the provision down. Lacking a majority, Ellender might have been expected to halt proceedings at this point, but was somehow unable to do so, with the result that an amendment by Senator Mundt passed which offered wheat farmers a chance to choose the existing, more attractive voluntary program as an alternative to the proposed certificate program. In effect this left the wheat program, along with feed-grains provision, dead in committee. The Committee voted to report out the amended bill.

The Senate action coincided with a failure to get approval of the bill in the House committee, on this same Black Friday.

Committee Action in the House

After public hearings in the House had been completed March 15th, the various sections were pushed along in the five subcommittees, all but one of which had reported to the full Committee by the end of March. Lester Johnson of Wisconsin was having trouble getting a program out of his dairy subcommittee, mainly because the dairy cooperatives and other enterpriser groups, collectively called the "dairy industry," were unable to agree on a surplus control measure but also, again, because one Western and two Southern Democrats feared that controls would slow dairy expansion in their districts. Chairman Johnson noted caustically that his district had far more cows than all of theirs put together, but they had the votes.

Senator Ellender had already tried and failed to arrive at an acceptable dairy program, during a long private evening session with dairy-industry and USDA spokesmen. Even Johnson's "milk-toast" voluntary program still seemed unsatisfactory to the industry, but Johnson wanted it in the comprehensive bill, and got it there by threatening to vote against the administration program in committee unless its supporters pushed the dairy section through his subcommittee and then incorporated it in the committee bill. (This provision was expected to be deleted on the House floor, and indeed was.) After the dairy section was reported on April 2nd, there began a long count-down of seven full Committee meetings. The minority refused to permit early and late sessions, and insisted on reading each section of the bill. Feelings exploded time and again at these meetings.

Votes on individual sections were lopsided. Proceeding differently than the Senate minority, Hoeven had decided to let mandatory programs go by easily, perhaps making the Democrats overconfident, and to gamble that he could then muster enough strength on the final vote on the bill to stop the whole package in committee. (See Illustration 20.)

Chairman Cooley scheduled the April 13th showdown after he was certain of 17 supporting votes (all from Democrats). He needed an additional vote, which he hoped to obtain from one of the four recalcitrant Democrats. Of these, Mississippi Congressman Abernethy would likely follow his recent pattern of anti-Kennedy votes, and the young Louisianian Harold McSween's voting record indicated he would likely oppose the bill.

The First Effort to Report the Bill

So attention was first centered on Watkins Abbitt (D., Va.) and George Grant (D., Ala.). Abbitt was a protégé and rumored heir apparent of the aristocratic Byrd machine of Virginia, whose leader, Senator Harry Byrd, was philosophically at odds with President Kennedy. The administration no doubt made every effort to secure Byrd's sympathy for the bill, without initial success. Congressman Abbitt himself got a call from President Kennedy which Abbitt would no doubt have preferred to receive at another time and on another subject. He was "hotboxed" by administration lobbyists—and doubtless by the opponents as well—on the Thursday eve of the anticipated vote.

The friendly, elderly Grant of Alabama also had a chat with the President, and long Thursday evening sessions with administration people who tried to persuade him to support the bill.

Grant was personally inclined to vote for the bill after certain modifications acceptable to the administration had been made.

This 25-year veteran of a one-party district would probably have voted for the bill, if it had not been for an extraordinary political tangle in Alabama.

Alabama had lost a congressional seat because of relative population decline. Since the state legislature was obliged to redraw the district lines to eliminate one of the existing districts, all Alabama congressmen were sensitive to pressures exerted through the legislature. In 1961, the Farm Bureau had successfully threatened to use its influence within several Southern legislatures to redistrict congressmen who did not vote with it. In that year the Alabama legislature—locked in conflict over which district should be abolished—had not acted at all on this matter, so that the nine Alabama congressmen had to run at large for the eight available seats in 1962. Primaries were to be held in each old district on May 1st, and the winners (presumably the incumbents) would be candidates in a state-wide election which would eliminate one of the nine.

So pressure from all over Alabama could be put on Grant, who was certainly not regarded as one of the front runners in this race. (As it turned out, he ran fourth.) The Alabama Commissioner of Agriculture and other influential Kennedy supporters were urging Grant to vote "yes" to report the bill, while cattlemen's spokesmen, activated and joined by Farm Bureau groups in Alabama, warned him flatly they would work for his defeat in the approaching primary if he voted for the bill.

The Committee session on that Friday morning was a brief one. On Thursday night, Grant had apparently indicated a willingness to vote "yes" if one of the other three uncommitted Democrats would vote with him. But if the bill could not be carried without

Illustration 20. PAINFULLY, LINE BY LINE. As the House Agriculture Committee stormed through the rewrite of H.R. 10010, a USDA staff member made marginal notes on his copy of the bill, not only recording the changes the Committee was discussing but also keeping in mind the change of plans the USDA would have to make in putting the measures into action once the bill was law. These notes, with occasional comment and clarification, appear on the following pages.

4 "NATIONAL MARKETING QUOTA

5 "SEC. 360b. (a) Whenever prior to June 20 in any
6 calendar year the Secretary determines that the total supply
7 of feed grains in the marketing year beginning in the next
8 succeeding calendar year will, in the absence of a marketing
9 quota program, likely be excessive, the Secretary shall pro-
10 claim that a national marketing quota for feed grains shall
11 be in effect for such marketing year and for either the
12 following marketing year or the following two marketing
13 years, if the Secretary determines and declares in such
14 proclamation that a two- or three-year marketing quota
15 program is necessary to effectuate the policy of the Act.

Illustration 20. Concerning feed-grains marketing: "Winter wheat and barley–mktg year Sept. 1."

8 thereof; less (i) an amount of feed grains equal to the esti-
9 mated imports of feed grains into the United States during
10 such marketing year and, (ii) if the stocks of feed grains
11 owned by the Commodity Credit Corporation are determined
12 by the Secretary to be excessive, an amount of feed grains
13 determined by the Secretary to be a desirable reduction in
14 such marketing year in such stocks to achieve the policy of
15 the Act: *Provided*, That if the Secretary determines that
16 the total stocks of feed grains in the Nation are insufficient
17 to assure an adequate carryover for the next succeeding
18 marketing year, the national marketing quota otherwise de-
19 termined shall be increased by the amount the Secretary
20 determines to be necessary to assure an adequate carryover.

Illustration 20. Anent the Secretary's determining excessive stocks of feed grains: "Poage *no*." Numerous notes indicate the Committee's changing the text of the bill to take discretionary powers from the Secretary and hold him to specifics by naming crops, specifying numbers of acres, stipulating geographic units, and otherwise.

4 "APPORTIONMENT OF NATIONAL ACREAGE ALLOTMENT

5 "SEC. 360d. (a) The national acreage allotment for
6 any crop of feed grains, less a reserve acreage of not to
7 exceed 1 per centum thereof for use as provided in sub-
8 section (b) (2) of this section, shall be apportioned by the
9 Secretary among the several States on the basis of the base
10 acreage of feed grains for each State. The State base acreage
11 of feed grains shall be the average acreage of feed grains
12 in the State during the base period, adjusted pursuant to
13 subsection (d) of this section.

commercial areas. Jennings objects to any. No objection to 25,000 acres

Illustration 20. "Commercial areas–Jennings objects to any. – No objection to 25,000 acres.

11 "COMMERCIAL AREA

12 "SEC. 360e. Notwithstanding any other provision of this
13 part, if the Secretary determines that the establishment of a
14 commercial feed grain area will facilitate the administration
15 of a marketing quota program for feed grains and will not
16 substantially impair the effective operation thereof, he may
17 establish a commercial area for feed grains taking into con-
18 sideration with respect to the commercial area and the non-
19 commercial area one or more of the following factors: the
20 total production of feed grains, the number of farms normally
21 producing feed grains, the average production of feed grains
22 per farm, the value of the total marketings of feed grains, and
23 the extent to which marketings enter into commercial chan-
24 nels outside such area. In establishing a commercial area
25 the Secretary shall, insofar as practicable, observe ~~county~~ State

Poage

Illustration 20. "State–Poage." An objection to county-line boundaries for commercial areas.

31

1 boundary lines. The commercial area shall be proclaimed
2 at the time the national marketing quota is proclaimed pur-
3 suant to section 360b, and such national marketing quota
4 shall not be in effect with respect to feed grains produced out-
5 side the commercial area. The national acreage allotment
6 for any crop of feed grains shall be apportioned by the
7 Secretary among the States, counties, and farms in the
8 commercial area on the basis of the provisions of section
9 360d.

Illustration 20. "State only 25,000 acres."

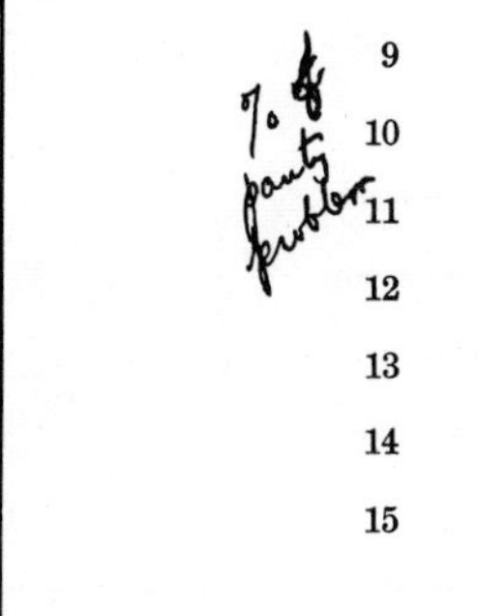

9 "(2) price support for each crop of barley, grain
10 sorghums, oats, and rye, respectively, shall be at such
11 level as the Secretary determines is fair and reasonable
12 in relation to the level at which price support is made
13 available for corn, taking into consideration the feeding
14 value of such feed grain in relation to corn and the
15 other factors specified in section 401 (b) of this Act.

Illustration 20. "% of parity problem." "Poage–strike out other factors."

3 "REFERENDUM

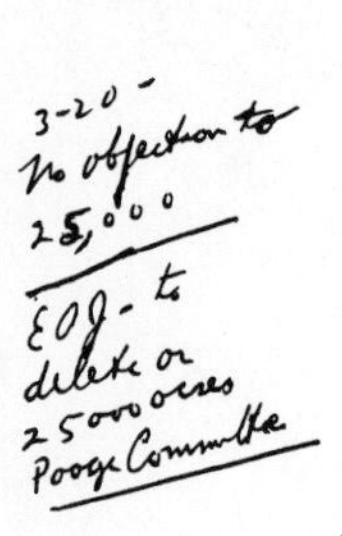

4 "SEC. 360g. If a national marketing quota for feed grains
5 for one, two, or three marketing years is proclaimed, the
6 Secretary shall, not later than sixty days after such proclama-
7 tion is published in the Federal Register, conduct a referen-
8 dum, by secret ballot, of farmers to determine whether they
9 favor or oppose marketing quotas for the marketing year or
10 years for which proclaimed. Any producer who has a feed
11 grain base shall be eligible to vote in any referendum held
12 pursuant to this section, except a producer who has a farm
13 feed grain base of twenty-five acres or less and who does not
14 elect, pursuant to section 360f, to be subject to the farm acre-
15 age allotment. The Secretary shall proclaim the results of
16 any referendum held hereunder within thirty days after the
17 date of such referendum, and if the Secretary determines that
18 more than one-third of the farmers voting in the referendum
19 voted against marketing quotas, the Secretary shall pro-
20 claim that marketing quotas will not be in effect with respect
21 to the crop of feed grains produced for harvest in the calendar
22 year following the calendar year in which the referendum is
23 held. If the Secretary determines that two-thirds or more

Illustration 20. "3–20– No objection to 25,000––EAJ–to delete or 25000 acres Poage Committee."

16 "(3) In determining the farm marketing quota and
17 farm marketing excess, (i) any acreage of a feed grain
18 remaining after the date prescribed by the Secretary for the
19 disposal of excess acres of such feed grain shall be included
20 as an acreage of feed grains on the farm, and the production
21 thereof shall be appraised in such manner as the Secretary
22 determines will provide a reasonably accurate estimate of
23 such production, (ii) any acreage of any feed grain classified
24 as wheat acreage pursuant to section 337 shall not be con-
25 sidered feed grain acreage, and (iii) any acreage of feed

substitution p 59

Illustration 20. Portion of page 34: "Substitution p 59" concerns substitution of feed grains for wheat; see the next note.

6 SEC. 417. Section 337 of the Agricultural Adjustment
7 Act of 1938, as amended, is hereby amended by deleting
8 the provisions thereof and substituting the following:
9 "SUBSTITUTION OF FEED GRAINS FOR WHEAT
10 "SEC. 337. Notwithstanding any other provision of law,
11 the Secretary ~~may~~ shall permit producers of feed grains to have
12 acreage devoted to the production of feed grains considered
13 as devoted to the production of wheat ~~to such extent and~~
14 ~~subject to such terms and conditions as the Secretary deter-~~
15 ~~mines will not impair the effective operation of this sub-~~
16 ~~title~~."

p34

Breeding

Illustration 20. Portion of page 59, with note referring to "p 34," change in line 11 substituting "shall" for "may," and a suggested deletion, by "Breeding," of three lines. This change cut the Secretary's discretionary authority concerning substitution of feed grains for wheat.

39

1 of the penalty under this section shall be liable also for in-
2 terest thereon at the rate of 6 per centum per annum from
3 the date the penalty becomes due until the date of payment
4 of such penalty.

5 "(2) The Secretary may require that the acreage on
6 any farm diverted from the production of feed grains be land
7 which was diverted from the production of feed grains in the
8 previous year, to the extent he determines that such require-
9 ment is necessary to effectuate the purposes of this subtitle.

10 "(3) The Secretary may permit the diverted acreage to
11 be grazed in accordance with regulations prescribed by the
12 Secretary.

13 "(b) The Secretary is authorized to formulate and
14 carry out a program with respect to the 1963, 1964, and 1965
15 crops of feed grains under which, subject to such terms and
16 conditions as he determines are desirable to effectuate the
17 purposes of this section, payments may be made in amounts
18 determined by the Secretary to be fair and reasonable to
19 producers with respect to acreage diverted pursuant to sub-
20 section (a) of this section. The Secretary may permit the
21 producers on the farm to divert from the production of feed
22 grains an acreage, in addition to the acreage diverted pur-
23 suant to subsection (a), equal to 20 per centum of the
24 farm acreage allotment for feed grains: *Provided*, That the
25 producers on any farm may, at their election, divert such

Illustration 20. "Give authority to graze adjoining fields." "Poage 3–20 formula for reducing payment–not to exceed ½ (?) or ¾ if nothing planted or grazed." "rates?"

40

1 acreage, in addition to the acreage diverted pursuant to sub-
2 section (a), as will bring the total acreage diverted on the
3 farm to twenty acres. Such program shall require (1) that
4 the diverted acreage shall be devoted to conservation uses
5 approved by the Secretary; (2) that the total acreage of
6 cropland on the farm devoted to soil-conserving uses, includ-
7 ing summer fallow and idle land but excluding the acreage
8 diverted as provided above and acreage diverted under the
9 land-use provisions for wheat pursuant to section 339, shall
10 not be less than the total average acreage of cropland devoted
11 to soil-conserving uses including summer fallow and idle land
12 on the farm during the base period used in determining the
13 farm acreage allotment adjusted to the extent the Secretary
14 determines appropriate for (i) abnormal weather conditions
15 or other factors affecting production, (ii) established crop-
16 rotation practices on the farm, (iii) participation in other
17 Federal farm programs, (iv) unusually high percentage of
18 land on the farm devoted to conserving uses, and (v) for
19 other factors which the Secretary determines should be con-
20 sidered for the purpose of establishing a fair and equitable
21 soil-conserving acreage for the farm; and (3) that the pro-
22 ducers shall not knowingly exceed (i) any farm acreage
23 allotment in effect for any commodity produced on the farm,
24 and (ii) except as the Secretary may by regulation prescribe,
25 the farm acreage allotments on any other farm for any crop

25.

Poage wants direction to adjust.

cross compliance (Poage wants 2-3 paragraphs added possibly)

Illustration 20. "25" acres instead of twenty. "Poage wants direction to adjust"—another reduction of discretionary authority. "cross compliance." ("Poage wants 2–3 paragraphs added possibly.")

6 payment of the penalty. The producer on any farm for which
7 a farm acreage allotment is established pursuant to section
8 360d (c) (2) (C) shall not be eligible for payments here-
9 under. The Secretary shall provide for the sharing of pay-
10 ment among producers on the farm on a fair and equitable
11 basis. Payments may be made in cash or in feed grains.
12 "(c) The Secretary may provide for adjusting any
13 payment ~~on account of failure~~ to comply with the terms
14 and conditions of the program formulated under subsection
15 (b) of this section.
16 "(d) Not to exceed 50 per centum of any payment to
17 producers under subsection (b) of this section may be
18 made in advance of determination of performance.

Illustration 20. "new farm." "Present procedure?" wilful violation?" "adv. payments." "to the extent that a producer has failed" instead of "on account of failure."

17 or advice to the extent the Secretary deems it desirable in
18 order to provide fair and equitable treatment.".
19 Sec. 402. Section 2 of the Agricultural Adjustment Act
20 of 1938, as amended, is hereby amended by striking out
21 "and" immediately following the last semicolon, by changing
22 the period at the end thereof to a semicolon, and by adding
23 immediately following such new semicolon the following:
24 "and to reduce the annual carryover of feed grains, to stabi-
25 lize the supply of feed grains at a level consistent with any

Illustration 20. "Broadens declaration of policy. P(22)." Page 22 of the draft bill is on p. 83 of this book, a part of Illustration 14.

44

1 "(6) (A) 'Market', in the case of cotton, rice, to-
2 bacco, wheat, and feed grains, means to dispose of, in
3 raw or processed form, by voluntary or involuntary sale,
4 barter, or exchange, or by gift inter vivos, and, in the
5 case of wheat and feed grains, by feeding (in any form)
6 to poultry or livestock which, or the products of which,
7 are sold, bartered, or exchanged, or to be so disposed of."
8 (3) Subsection (b) (7) is amended to read as
9 follows:
10 "(7) 'Marketing year' means, in the case of the
11 following commodities, the period beginning on the first
12 and ending with the second date specified below:
13 "Barley, July 1–June 30;
14 "Corn, October 1–September 30;
15 "Cotton, August 1–July 31;
16 "Oats, July 1–June 30;
17 "Grain sorghums, July 1–June 30;
18 "Peanuts, August 1–July 31;
19 "Rice, August 1–July 31;
20 "Rye, July 1–June 30;
21 "Tobacco (flue-cured), July 1–June 30;
22 "Tobacco (other than flue-cured), October 1–
23 September 30;
24 "Wheat, July 1–June 30.
25 " 'Marketing year' means, in the case of 'feed grains',

Poage Use July to July - Corn

Illustration 20. "added" before "feed grains." "Poage Use July to July–Corn."

45

1 the marketing years for the agricultural commodities
2 comprising the feed grains."
3 SEC. 404. Sections 361, 362, and 363 of the Agricul-
4 tural Adjustment Act of 1938, as amended, are hereby
5 amended as follows:
6 (1) Section 361 is amended by adding "feed
7 grains," after "wheat,", and by changing the period at
8 the end of the section to a comma and adding the follow-
9 ing: "and to the review of land-use penalties assessed
10 pursuant to sections 339 and 360j."
11 (2) Section 362 is amended by adding at the end
12 thereof the following: "Notice of the land-use penalty
13 assessed pursuant to section 339 or 360j shall be mailed
14 to the farmer."
15 (3) Section 363 is amended by adding "or land-
16 use penalty" after the word "quota" wherever it appears
17 in such section.
18 SEC. 405. Section 372 of the Agricultural Adjustment
19 Act of 1938, as amended, is hereby amended by adding
20 "feed grains," after "wheat," in subsection (a) thereof.
21 SEC. 406. Sections 373, 374, and 375 of the Agricul-
22 tural Adjustment Act of 1938, as amended, are hereby
23 amended by deleting "corn" wherever it appears and by
24 substituting in lieu thereof "feed grains"; and subsection (b)
25 of section 375 of the Agricultural Adjustment Act of 1938,

Mktg quota remains Committee on diverted acres as now or mktg quota penalties.

Illustration 20. The note may read: "Mktg quota remains Committee on diverted acres as now or mktg quota penalties."

3 (4) By adding at the end of section 407 the
4 following: "Notwithstanding any other provision here-
5 of, (i) if a marketing quota for feed grains for any mar-
6 keting year is disapproved by producers, the Commodity
7 Credit Corporation ~~is authorized to~~ may sell for unrestricted
8 use from its stocks at market prices during such mar-
9 keting year ~~up~~ not to exceed ten million tons, or the equivalent in
10 bushels, of feed grains, (ii) if a marketing quota for
11 wheat for any marketing year is disapproved by pro-
12 ducers, the Commodity Credit Corporation is authorized
13 to sell for unrestricted use from its stocks at market
14 prices during the marketing year up to two hundred
15 million bushels of wheat."

16 SUBTITLE B—WHEAT

17 SEC. 410. Section 331 of the Agricultural Adjustment
18 Act of 1938, as amended, is hereby amended by striking out
19 the last paragraph thereof and inserting in lieu thereof the
20 following paragraphs:

21 "Wheat which is planted and not disposed of prior to the
22 date prescribed by the Secretary for the disposal of excess
23 acres of wheat is an addition to the total supply of wheat
24 and has a direct effect on the price of wheat in interstate and

Leg. findings

H.R. 10010——4

Illustration 20. The interlineations are verbal refinements. Margin: "Leg. findings"; see Illustration 14.

3 Sec. 412. Section 333 of the Agricultural Adjustment
4 Act of 1938, as amended, is hereby amended to read as fol-
5 lows:
6 "NATIONAL ACREAGE ALLOTMENT
7 "Sec. 333. Whenever the amount of the national
8 marketing quota for wheat is proclaimed for any marketing
9 year, the Secretary at the same time shall proclaim a na-
10 tional acreage allotment for the crop of wheat planted for
11 harvest in the calendar year in which such marketing year
12 begins. The amount of the national acreage allotment for
13 any crop of wheat shall be the number of acres which the
14 Secretary determines on the basis of expected yields and
15 expected underplantings of farm acreage allotments will,
16 together with ~~(1) the expected production of wheat in~~
17 ~~the noncommercial area, if any, and (2)~~ the expected pro-
18 duction on increased acreages resulting from the small-farm
19 exemption pursuant to section 335, make available a supply
20 of wheat equal to the national marketing quota for wheat
21 for such marketing year."

Illustration 20. This portion of page 54 of the bill, and pages 55–57 which follow, concern acreage allotments. The deleted language above reads "(1) the expected production of wheat in the noncommercial area, if any, and (2)."

55

1 subsections (a) and (b) thereof and by inserting in
2 lieu thereof "five".
3 (2) By amending subsection (e) thereof by in-
4 serting the following sentence immediately following
5 the eighth sentence thereof: "The land-use provisions
6 of section 339 shall not be applicable to any farm re-
7 ceiving an increased allotment under this subsection, and
8 the producers on such farm shall not be required to
9 comply with such provisions as a condition of eligibility
10 for price support."
11 (3) By repealing subsection (g) thereof and by
12 redesignating subsections (h) and (i) thereof as (g)
13 and (h) respectively.
14 (4) By amending subsection (i) thereof, redesig-
15 nated by this section as subsection (h), by inserting the
16 following sentence immediately following the seventh
17 sentence thereof: "The land-use provisions of section 339
18 shall not be applicable to any farm receiving an addi-
19 tional allotment under this subsection."
20 (5) By striking out of the last sentence of sub-
21 section (i) thereof (added by Public Law 87–357, 87th
22 Congress, 1st session), redesignated by this section as
23 subsection (h), "or 1963".
24 SEC. 414. Part III of subtitle B of title III of the Agri-

Illustration 20. "Durum" at lines 3 and 16 refers to durum wheat. Lines 20–23 constitute a "technical amendment."

56

1 cultural Adjustment Act of 1938, as amended, is hereby
2 amended by adding immediately after section 334 thereof
3 the following:

4 "COMMERCIAL AREA

5 "SEC. 334a. If the acreage allotment for any State for
6 any crop of wheat is twenty-five thousand acres or less, the
7 Secretary, in order to promote efficient administration of this
8 Act and the Agricultural Act of 1949, may designate such
9 State as outside the commercial wheat-producing area for
10 the marketing year for such crop. If such State is so desig-
11 nated, acreage allotments for such crop and marketing quotas
12 for the marketing year therefor shall not be applicable to any
13 farm in such State. Acreage allotments in any State shall
14 not be increased by reason of such designation. ~~The national~~
15 ~~acreage allotment for any crop of wheat shall be apportioned~~
16 ~~by the Secretary among the States, counties, and farms in~~
17 ~~the commercial wheat-producing area on the basis of the~~
18 ~~provisions of section 334."~~

Hawaii + alaska

delete

19 SEC. 415. Section 335 of the Agricultural Adjustment
20 Act of 1938, as amended, is hereby amended to read as
21 follows:

22 "SMALL FARM EXEMPTION

23 "SEC. 335. Notwithstanding any other provision of this
24 part, no farm marketing quota for any crop of wheat shall
25 be applicable to any farm with a base of fifteen acres or less

Illustration 20. "Hawaii & Alaska" are or may be affected. The deletion in lines 14–18 takes from the Secretary his authority to apportion acreage allotments.

57

1 (hereinafter called 'small-farm base acreage') if the acreage
2 of such crop of wheat does not exceed the small-farm base
3 acreage determined for the farm, unless the owner or op-
4 erator elects in writing on a form and within the time pre-
5 scribed by the Secretary to be subject to the farm acreage
6 allotment. For the purposes of this section, the small-farm
7 base acreage for a farm shall be the average acreage of the
8 crops of wheat planted for harvest in the calendar years 1960
9 and 1961, or such later two-year period determined by the
10 Secretary to be representative, with adjustments for abnor-
11 mal weather conditions, established crop-rotation practices
12 on the farm, and such other factors as the Secretary deter-
13 mines should be considered for the purpose of establishing a
14 fair and equitable small-farm base acreage. If the owner or
15 operator of any such farm fails to make such election with
16 respect to any crop of wheat, (i) for the purposes of Public
17 Law 74, Seventy-seventh Congress (7 U.S.C. 1340), as
18 amended, the farm acreage allotment for such crop of wheat
19 shall be deemed to be the small-farm base acreage determined
20 for the farm, if the acreage of such crop exceeds such base
21 acreage, (ii) the land-use provisions of section 339 shall be
22 inapplicable to the farm, (iii) such crop of wheat shall not
23 be eligible for price support, (iv) wheat marketing certifi-
24 cates applicable to such crop shall not be issued with respect
25 to the farm, and (v) the producers on the farm shall not be

Illustration 20. Additions in lines 2–3 exempt from marketing quotas farms below the "smaller of (i) the small-farm base acreage determined for the farm, or (ii) 15 acres." "Senate?" "Breeding 5 years?"—a five-year rather than a two-year average for determining base acreage.

60

1 be subject to a penalty on such crop, in addition to any
2 marketing quota penalty applicable to such crops, as pro-
3 vided in this subsection unless (i) the crop is designated by
4 the Secretary as one which is not in surplus supply and will
5 not be in surplus supply if it is permitted to be grown on the
6 diverted acreage, or as one the production of which will not
7 substantially impair the purpose of the requirements of this
8 section, or (2) no wheat is produced on the farm, and the
9 producers have not filed an agreement or a statement of
10 intention to participate in the payment program formulated
11 pursuant to subsection (b) of this section. The acreage
12 required to be diverted from the production of wheat on the
13 farm shall be an acreage of cropland equal to the number
14 of acres determined by multiplying the farm acreage allot-
15 ment by the diversion factor determined by dividing the
16 number of acres by which the national acreage allotment is
17 reduced below fifty-five million acres by the number of acres
18 in the national acreage allotment. The actual production of
19 any crop subject to penalty under this subsection shall be
20 regarded as available for marketing and the penalty on such
21 crop shall be computed on the actual acreage of such crop
22 at the rate of 65 per centum of the parity price per bushel
23 of wheat as of May 1 of the calendar year in which such
24 crop is harvested, multiplied by the normal yield of wheat
25 per acre established for the farm. Until the producers on

Illustration 20. "Hagen–acre crops"–the thought is unspecified.

61

1 any farm pay the penalty on such crop, the entire crop of
2 wheat produced on the farm and any subsequent crop of
3 wheat subject to marketing quotas in which the producer
4 has an interest shall be subject to a lien in favor of the United
5 States for the amount of the penalty. Each producer having
6 an interest in the crop or crops on acreage diverted or
7 required to be diverted from the production of wheat shall
8 be jointly and severally liable for the entire amount of the
9 penalty. The persons liable for the payment or collection of
10 the penalty under this section shall be liable also for interest
11 thereon at the rate of 6 per centum per annum from the date
12 the penalty becomes due until the date of payment of such
13 penalty.
14 "(2) The Secretary may require that the acreage on
15 any farm diverted from the production of wheat be land
16 which was diverted from the production of wheat in the
17 previous year, to the extent he determines that such require-
18 ment is necessary to effectuate the purposes of this subtitle.
19 "(3) The Secretary may permit the diverted acreage
20 to be grazed in accordance with regulations prescribed by
21 the Secretary.
22 "(b) The Secretary is authorized to formulate and carry
23 out a program with respect to the 1963, 1964, and 1965
24 crops of wheat under which, subject to such terms and con-
25 ditions as he determines are desirable to effectuate the pur-

Illustration 20. "3-31-61—3-22-62." At line 21: "the Secretary, and may make payments on such acreage at a level not in excess of half the rate otherwise applicable taking into account the value of the use to be made of the land."

State rate.

62

1 poses of this section, payments may be made in amounts
2 determined by the Secretary to be fair and reasonable with
3 respect to acreage diverted pursuant to subsection (a) of this
4 section. The Secretary may permit producers on any farm
5 to divert from the production of wheat an acreage, in addi-
6 tion to the acreage diverted pursuant to subsection (a),
7 equal to 20 per centum of the farm acreage allotment for
8 wheat: *Provided,* That the producers on any farm may, at
9 their election, divert such acreage in addition to the acreage
10 diverted pursuant to subsection (a), as will bring the total
11 acreage diverted on the farm to fifteen acres. Such program
12 shall require (1) that the diverted acreage shall be devoted to
13 conservation uses approved by the Secretary; (2) that the
14 total acreage of cropland on the farm devoted to soil-
15 conserving uses, including summer fallow and idle land but
16 excluding the acreage diverted as provided above, and acre-
17 age diverted under the land-use provisions for feed grains
18 pursuant to section 360j, shall be not less than the total
19 average acreage of cropland devoted to soil-conserving uses
20 including summer fallow and idle land on the farm during
21 a representative period, as determined by the Secretary,
22 adjusted to the extent the Secretary determines appropriate
23 for (i) abnormal weather conditions or other factors affecting
24 production, (ii) established crop-rotation practices on the
25 farm, (iii) participation in other Federal farm programs,

Illustration 20. "State rate" refers to the section indicated by the marginal arrow-brace.

71

1 cation program shall be in effect as provided in this subtitle.
2 Whenever a wheat marketing allocation program is in effect
3 for any marketing year the Secretary shall determine (1)
4 the domestic component of the wheat marketing allocation
5 which shall be the amount of wheat which will be used dur-
6 ing the marketing year for human consumption in the United
7 States, less such portion not to exceed 50 per centum as the
8 Secretary determines of the amount established pursuant to
9 section 332 of this Act to be the desirable reduction during
10 such marketing year in stocks of wheat owned by Commod-
11 ity Credit Corporation, and (2) the export component of
12 the wheat marketing allocation which shall be the portion of
13 exports during the marketing year on which marketing cer-
14 tificates shall be issued to producers in order to achieve, inso-
15 far as practicable, the price and income objectives of this sub-
16 title, and (3) the national allocation percentage which shall
17 be the percentage which the national marketing allocation
18 (the sum of the domestic component and the export com-
19 ponent) is of the estimated production of wheat during the
20 calendar year in which such marketing year begins. Each
21 farm shall receive a wheat marketing allocation for such
22 marketing year equal to the number of bushels obtained by
23 multiplying the number of acres in the farm acreage allot-
24 ment for wheat by the estimated yield of wheat for the farm
25 as determined by the Secretary, and multiplying the result-

Illustration 20. "Belcher–adjust farm yields. – Perhaps should freeze certificate issue." "? Apportionment."

87TH CONGRESS
2D SESSION

H. R. 10010

A BILL

To improve and protect farm income, to reduce costs of farm programs to the Federal Government, to reduce the Federal Government's excessive stocks of agricultural commodities, to maintain reasonable and stable prices of agricultural commodities and products to consumers, to provide adequate supplies of agricultural commodities for domestic and foreign needs, to conserve natural resources, and for other purposes.

By Mr. COOLEY

JANUARY 31, 1962

Referred to the Committee on Agriculture

Illustration 20. On the back of his copy the staff member put a series of notes to himself: "3–20 To committee / White corn–contracts / P 38–Grazing payments–grain / 41–Guidelines on tenant and l. l. [landlord?] –same as rental share 41–1. 12–Guidelines on reducing payments / 44–Change dates of marketing years.–report / 47–a position on striking out "other factors" / 48–Storage provision for feed grains in high-risk areas / 49–make overseeded producer eligible for certificates but no p.'s for wheat / 49–not to exceed 10–200 / Rate of payment

Wheat / New commercial states–Present non commercial area / P 57–5 years on small farm exemption / P 57–30 acre feed grain wheat–feed grain base / Position on noncommercial areas / P 59–cut out all discretion."

his vote he preferred to postpone this decision so critical to his career. He finally gave the chairman his proxy in favor of postponement, with the intention of absenting himself the following day. But then he turned up at the Committee session, which led the chairman first to propose and pass the "deficit" area provision in hopes of winning Grant's vote and perhaps another of the holdouts. When Cooley ascertained that it won him no votes, he moved to postpone the final vote until after Easter and this motion carried 19–16.

Congressman Hoeven called this postponement a victory for the opposition, and predicted the administration would now abandon the mandatory programs. House Democratic whip Carl Albert quickly replied that the Easter recess would give time for the administration to muster enough committee votes to get the bill out. When the Senate committee deleted the feed-grains and wheat provisions that same afternoon, administration spokesmen did momentarily feel that this part of the bill would have to be sacrificed. Later on, some administration strategists wished they had jettisoned the feed-grains provision at this point, although it subsequently served as a battering ram behind which the wheat program and other features could pass.

Congressman McSween and the Deadlock

Within the following week, which ended on Good Friday, Senator Ellender decided to try to amend his committee's bill on the floor, restoring the administration's mandatory provisions. During the Easter recess, attention in the House turned to Congressman Harold McSween of Louisiana, after he flew with President Kennedy in a presidential plane to New Orleans. McSween was facing likely defeat in a primary contest against Gillis Long, member of the thriving family dynasty founded by the legendary populist Huey Long. In fact, McSween had served the present term under a cloud, having been defeated by Governor Earl Long in the 1960 primary. The Democratic State Committee had decided to give McSween another term after Governor Long died before the election.

Objections to the administration farm program within Louisiana arose less from the Long group (with which Senator Ellender was aligned) than from local Farm Bureau leaders, joined by segregationist leader Leander Perez and other extreme conservatives.

After extensive talks with McSween, American Farm Bureau leaders felt it necessary to warn him (as well as Grant) that they would use every resource to have him defeated if he voted to report the bill out of committee.

While in Louisiana for Easter, McSween apparently decided that his chances for reelection were so poor that what the Farm Bureau and their friends did would make little difference. On April 22nd, he told a group of his constituents that he would probably vote to report the bill. Secretary Freeman visited him after he returned to Washington, and emerged beaming that McSween "had cut the umbilical cord."

As a condition for voting "yes," McSween was permitted two minor amendments (the deficit areas amendment having already been added) and he reserved the right to oppose the bill on the floor, which implied he might ask further amendments there.

The dam had broken, or so it seemed. Chairman Cooley called a second showdown committee meeting for Wednesday, May 2nd, but had to adjourn this meeting too, because Congressman McMillan of South Carolina—an unenthusiastic "yes" voter—was home campaigning. A third try was made on Monday, May 7th, and this time "yes" voters Gathings of Arkansas and Hagan of Georgia failed to appear or give the chairman their proxies. On both occasions all the Republicans sat eagerly in their chairs, waiting to cast their "no" votes in person. "This is getting embarrassing," Chairman Cooley told reporters.

In the end it was just one episode in an embarrassing—even humiliating—year for the chairman and his House committee. Cooley himself had set a poor example in attendance, being absent during much of this critical period in order to argue an estate case in North Carolina. The series of three abortive meetings had frazzled administration representatives who were trying to keep their "sure" votes in line. McSween, Grant, and other wavering Democrats had been subjected to a crescendo of pressures from home, while having to confront—prior to each committee meeting —representatives of interested parties in Washington.

At the fourth meeting, "the ducks were finally all in a row," and the committee defeated efforts by Congressman Abernethy to remove the dairy provision (which would have lost Wisconsin Congressman Johnson's vote), and to remove the mandatory feed-grains program. The Committee went on to pass the bill with the deficit-areas provision and McSween's two amendments.

But by this time the haggling and delay in committee, and charges that the administration had improperly influenced McSween, had given the bill a questionable legacy. "This close vote simply means the bill is in for real trouble when it gets to the House floor," Secretary Freeman reported. Still, he thought this vote was a turning point.

Opponents of the bill still had one delaying tactic to employ in the House committee. The bill could not leave without the minority report, ultimately only fourteen pages in length, which took a week to be prepared and signed by all dissenting members. The 72-page majority report—prepared in the USDA—had been ready almost immediately after the final Committee vote. (See Illustration 21, at the end of this chapter.)

When the bill was finally reported on May 16th, with the hurdle of the House Rules Committee before it, debate was about to begin in the Senate. The powerful Rules committee, policeman of legislative traffic in the busy House, had been "packed" by adding two liberal members in early 1962, at President Kennedy's insistence. Presumably it would not be able now to pigeonhole any bill that the conservative Republicans and Southern Democratic members did not like, so the bill's chances of clearing this second committee were excellent. But Rules chairman J. Howard Smith suggested—and Cooley agreed—that they should wait to see what happened on the Senate floor before giving the House bill a rule. There was a chance that Senator Byrd (D., Va.) could be persuaded to vote for the bill, in which case his Virginia group which included Representatives Smith, Abbitt, and five other congressmen, might also favor it in the House.

The Senate's bill, which had been formally reported following the Easter vacation (on April 27th), had lain on the Senate calendar uncalled for three weeks. The delay was partly because the Senate had other business, but also the Senate Democratic leadership had wanted to be sure that the House committee first reported the bill. Then a Senate fight on it would be worthwhile. Debate in the Senate lasted a full week, ending with the final vote on Friday, May 25th.

Illustration 21. From the Other Side of the Aisle: *Minority Report.* Fourteen members of the House Agriculture Committee submitted a minority report opposing the passage of the Committee bill (H.R. 11222). An abridged version is shown on the following pages. Tables are omitted, together with text referring to them, and several pages describing the bill are also omitted.

MINORITY REPORT

Background

The administration has finally forced its bill, H.R. 11222, out of the Committee on Agriculture only by the repeated application of intense political pressure, the like of which we have never witnessed in the past.

In spite of this pressure, the bill just barely cleared the committee (which is controlled by a margin of 21 to 14 by the majority) by a vote of 18 to 17 with 1 proponent publicly stating he would oppose the bill on the floor of the House. And this action came only after three desperate attempts to report the bill on April 13, May 2, and May 7, 1962.

Administration tactics have included a Presidential suggestion to visiting State ASC committeemen to "not let your Congressman get lonesome," reams of printed propaganda by the Department of Agriculture and wholesale lobbying by a swarm of administration representatives.

This sharp division of opinion within the committee reflects a growing concern over the wisdom of the administration's basic policy goal of completely dominating and controlling all of American agriculture. While this legislation specifically earmarks wheat and feed grain farmers for new and stringent controls, livestock producers and other farmers now free of Government controls should recognize that they are next in line.

The bill sets forth the first steps for controlling dairy production by authorizing a lucrative payment plan under which the basic data and administrative machinery would be established for next year's sure-to-come dairy control plan. Dairy farmers need only look to the feed grain farmer as an example of this fact. For the last 2 years there has been a "voluntary" feed grain program often described by the Secretary of Agriculture as a "smashing success," but now described by the administration as "too costly and expensive" to continue. H.R. 11222 would replace the present feed grain program with an extremely inequitable and ineffective compulsory program.

To illustrate fully the undesirable trend toward Federal mastery of agriculture we need only refer to the recommendation for agriculture made by the administration last year. This fantastic proposal called for a shotgun attack on all of agriculture, including Federal production controls on each and every one of the 256 agricultural commodities produced in America.

These control plans would of course have been written, imposed, and enforced by the Secretary of Agriculture. Each new plan would automatically go into effect 60 days after being sent to the House and Senate. Congress could veto but not amend. Last year's wheat proposal didn't even include perfunctory consideration by Congress. Fortunately for America, Congress emphatically rejected this bizarre scheme.

After last year's defeat the administration changed its tactics, but not its purpose. A bill (H.R. 10010) was submitted to Congress calling for stricter wheat controls, tight new controls on feed grains, and a virtual licensing of dairy farming. By concentrating its efforts on a few commodities the administration apparently hoped to avoid its mistake of last year when it bit off a bit more than it could chew.

The dairy proposal ran into immediate trouble and was quickly discarded as unworkable, unacceptable, and unsound. The dairy industry virtually unanimously rejected the administration's dairy program.

For example, the National Milk Producers Federation described it as follows:

> Surely it would be the height of folly to require American producers to submit to rigid production controls to reduce total supply and then permit imports to come in and replace our own production. Without effective import controls domestic production could be rolled back without in any way reducing the surplus problem.

The Metropolitan Cooperative Milk Producers Bargaining Agency, of Syracuse, N.Y., said:

> We feel that this section as written allows the Secretary of Agriculture to virtually dictate what producers must do and that a referendum vote granted them would be as meaningless as a Russian election.

The administration dairy program (sec. 440 of H.R. 10010) also called for the imprisonment in a Federal penitentiary for up to 1 year, or a $2,000 fine, or both, for any dairy farmer who failed to keep proper books and records as determined by the Secretary of Agriculture.

Other major provisions in the original bill which were rejected included a request by the Secretary for authority to purchase and condemn farmland including whole farms, a request to turn over to the United Nations U.S. funds and surplus farm commodities, a request to impose strict production controls on producers of turkeys and turkey hatching eggs, prison terms for wheat farmers, and a request to establish a revolving fund subject to congressional review for the Rural Electrification Administration.

As the hearings on the bill progressed, it became readily apparent that there was no clamor or desire on the part of farmers for this legislation.

On the contrary, all members received and are continuing to receive heavy mail in opposition to the bill.

While we recognize that all opinion polls have limited application, we feel that the recent poll taken by one of the Nation's largest and leading farm magazines is highly indicative of farmer opinion on this bill. In a final tally of 64,560 ballots received from actual farmers these results were obtained:

	Percent
Total for compulsory quotas	4
Total for land retirement	43
Total for Government clear-out	53
Total	100

83991—62——9

During the consideration of the bill in the committee, the minority attempted time after time either to perfect or to strike from the bill provisions which we felt were undesirable, while also offering constructive alternatives to these objectionable features.

As is generally the case in omnibus legislation, H.R. 11222 contains some worthwhile provisions which, if left to stand on their own merits, would undoubtedly receive the approval of the House. It is unfortunate that such provisions must be attached to such an undesirable bill.

At the appropriate time in floor debate we will continue our attempts to improve and amend this bill.

General Statement

While specific objections to H.R. 11222 are legion, one basic objection is dominant: the objection to compulsion and control by the Federal Government to restrict and destroy the rights of farmers to use and enjoy their farms. While it is also apparent that this legislation is ineffective, discriminatory, unfair, wasteful, and unsound, the basic issue revolves around whether there should be a continuation of a system which recognizes the individual farmer and his right to enjoy the success or suffer the failure of free enterprise decisions, or whether our national policy should embrace the concept of a tightly regimented agriculture established as a federally sponsored monopoly.

Secretary Freeman was quoted by the Associated Press on Friday, May 11, 1962, when this bill was ordered reported to the House as saying he regarded this bill as a turning point in the farm program.

The Secretary's statement is indeed a true one. If the Congress adopts H.R. 11222 in its present form, the turning point will be passed and all of agriculture will be committed to the "supply management" or planned scarcity concept. Experience on the five crops now under Government control shows that once imposed these controls are not removed.

We also feel that it is appropriate to consider H.R. 11222 in the light of recent and continuously disturbing reports on the activities within the Agricultural Stabilization and Conservation Service of the Department of Agriculture: The controversy engendered by that agency's operation policies; its "section 22" shipping actions; the "Free Enterprise Wrecked This Train" exhibit at the South Dakota State Fair last fall. The current allegations of favoritism and maladministration have seriously impaired public confidence in this important agency of Government. We do not, therefore, feel that it is at all appropriate to grant new and sweeping power and authority over wheat, feed grain, and dairy farmers to this agency until the dark clouds of doubt and distrust have been publicly and openly removed.

[At this point, the minority report contains several pages describing the bill's provisions; these are not printed here.]

Analysis of Bill

TITLE I—LAND-USE ADJUSTMENT

While the Secretary's authority to purchase and condemn farmland has been deleted from the bill, broad authority still remains for the development of new land-use programs. The Secretary and other Department officials have continually spoken of an intensified recreation effort. Specific recreation and land-use programs have already been planned and announced. These include grassland demonstration, family forest demonstration, watersheds, town and country recreation, farmer-sportsmen, and urban renewal. In his speech at the Mayflower Hotel before the National Federation of Grain Cooperatives on April 3, 1962, Secretary Freeman stated as follows:

> Four metropolitan areas would be selected where a unit of government—such as a suburb—would be willing to cooperate with an association of farmers—such as a soil and water conservation district—in an outdoor recreation program. The citizens from the urban area would help develop recreational facilities, such as camping and picnicking facilities, riding and hiking trails, and other projects to improve and protect the scenic attractions of rural areas.

While the full impact of this new Government-sponsored recreation activity upon the privately owned and operated recreation industry is still unknown, the civil rights of the persons using these new facilities should certainly be clarified in order to insure that Federal funds not be expended for the establishment of racially segregated facilities.

TITLE II—PUBLIC LAW 480

The most glaring inconsistency in H.R. 11222 exists in the proposal to allow the Secretary of Agriculture to purchase those farm commodities he deems to be in surplus directly from private stocks and then donate these commodities to needy people overseas. While producers of wheat and feed grains are forced to take sharp cuts and strict controls on production, the producers of noncontrolled crops could find their surplus production purchased and donated overseas by the Government. Thus, the advocates of "supply management" are hereby endorsing the concept of unlimited production with a price-support removal operation.

TITLE III—MARKETING ORDERS

The amendment to exclude potatoes for dehydrating from the coverage of marketing orders is obviously processor oriented. We regret that this proposal was never brought up or discussed in the open hearings on the bill, and that potato farmers were never given an opportunity to present their views on it.

TITLE IV—COMMODITY PROGRAMS

Subtitle (A)—Feed grains

1. *Allotments and quotas previously repealed.*—In 1954 Congress repealed marketing quotas on corn. In 1958 Congress repealed acreage allotments on corn. H.R. 11222 would reimpose both acreage allotments and marketing quotas on corn, oats, rye, barley, and grain sorghum. Quotas and allotments were repealed by both Republican-controlled and Democratic-controlled Congresses for a good reason. They were simply unworkable. Marketing quotas can be made to appear to work on a crop like cotton or tobacco because virtually all of the production of these commodities goes into the market for sale to merchants and processors. This is not true of feed grains. Some 80 to 85 percent of all feed grains never leave the farm. They are fed to livestock. Thus the marketing quota is relatively meaningless. In spite of this long-recognized distinction H.R. 11222 would establish a farm marketing quota for every eligible feed grain farm in America. A violation of this quota would result in a civil penalty based on double the normal production of the farm (or the actual production) times 65 percent of the parity price.

2. *Impact on farm income.*—There can be no doubt that feed grain farmers' income would drop under this bill. It offers no increase in price support. Diversion payments would be reduced from 50 percent in 1963 to 40 percent in 1964 to 30 percent in 1965 to zero in 1966 and thereafter when farmers would be "donating" their valuable farmland to the Government.

Of course farm income would be devastated if farmers failed to vote "right" in the loaded referendum. In response to a specific question on the economic effect of the disapproval of marketing quotas, the Secretary at page 159, serial EE of the printed hearings said:

> With no price supports in effect, utilization of this level of current production plus the specified quantities from CCC stocks would mean prices well below those of recent years, probably in the general area of 70 to 75 cents per bushel for corn. Prices received for wheat would be in about a feed value relationship to corn, that is 5 to 10 cents per bushel higher.

3. *No real choice in referendum.*—Those feed grain farmers who were fortunate enough to be allowed to vote in referendum would truly be faced with a "Hobson's choice." Either they must accept the punitive and restrictive program asked by the administration or take nothing plus the threat of the Government dumping the equivalent of one-third billion bushels on the market. This "blackjack" provision makes a complete mockery of the referendum process. No other producers now under marketing quotas are subjected to such duress. If wheat, rice, peanut, or cotton farmers should vote down quotas,

price support at 50 percent of parity would be available to cooperators (those farmers voluntarily staying within their allotments) and the surplus could not be sold in the domestic market for less than 5 percent above this support price plus reasonable carrying charges. If tobacco quotas are disapproved there would be no price-support program, but there is a very small surplus of tobacco in Government hands; thus there is no threat of dumping tobacco.

4. *Many farmers ineligible to vote.*—While certain feed grain farmers (generally the larger growers in the Corn-Sorghum Belt) would be faced with the impossible choice offered by the referendum, many thousands of other feed grain farmers (generally the smaller growers and those farmers in the deficit areas) would not even vote.

Feed grain farmers in feed deficit areas are specifically denied the right to vote in the referendum by the last clause of the committee amendment which states:

> * * * and (iv) the producers on such farms shall not be eligible to vote in any referendum on marketing quotas for such crop.

The total number of these farmers is unknown to us because we do not know what criteria the Secretary might use in establishing feed-deficit areas. If he uses the normal definition of a State which consumes more feed grains than they produce, this would exclude all the feed grain farmers in some 35 to 40 States from voting.

The voting eligibility of small feed grain farmers is set forth in sections 360(g) and 360(f) of H.R. 11222 which provide in part as follows:

> Section 360(g) "* * * Any producer who has a feed grain base shall be eligible to vote in any referendum held pursuant to this section *except a producer who has a farm feed grain base of 25 acres or less and who does not elect, pursuant to section 360(f), to be subject to the farm acreage allotment.*" [Emphasis added.]
>
> Section 360(f) "* * * Notwithstanding any other provision of this part, no farm marketing quota for any crop of feed grains shall be applicable to any farm with a farm base acreage of 25 acres or less if the acreage of such crop of feed grains does not exceed the farm base acreage determined for the farm, *unless the owner or operator elects in writing on a form and within the time prescribed by the Secretary to be subject to the farm acreage allotment.*" [Emphasis added.]

Thus it can be seen that this complicated burden falls on the back of the small farmer. If he wants to vote he must sign in writing his promise to comply with the farm acreage allotment. If he fails to commit himself ahead of time, he cannot vote. Yet in either instance he is subject to severe marketing quota penalties for overplanting. Larger growers on the other hand need not go through this procedure. They are automatically eligible to vote. This discrimination against small growers is another intolerable gimmick in the effort to "rig" the outcome of the referendum and is incompatible with the referendums on all other commodity programs (except wheat) which give one producer one vote, regardless of the size of his farm or his allotment.

What this means in numbers of farmers is again problematical. At page 162 of the printed hearings, serial EE, the Secretary responded for the record in reply to a request for statistical material as follows:

> The Department of Agriculture does not have information on the number of feed grain farms by size of acreage planted.

Suffice it to say, there are many thousands of these small growers who will find very little democracy in the democratic choice offered by H.R. 11222.

5. *Unfair to corn-sorghum belt.*—While grain farmers in the "non-deficit" States (or areas) would be cutting back production, the Secretary under the last-minute politically motivated committee amendment could excuse feed grain farmers in deficit areas from cutting their production. Suppose there were two dairy farmers, one in Indiana and one in Kentucky. If the Secretary declared Kentucky a "feed deficit" area the dairy farmer in Indiana who may need all the corn he is raising for his dairy herd would have to cut back on feed grain production, while his Kentucky neighbor would not. This provision simply represents regional favoritism and political maneuvering at the expense of one part of the country. It is based on neither equity or economics.

6. *Unfair to feed deficit areas.*—Whatever initial joy that producers in feed deficit areas might experience by virtue of the special provision will soon evaporate when it is discovered that this exemption is really a two-edged sword. The exemption is conditioned on the Secretary's definition of "hardship," "unduly increase prices," "disrupt normal farming practices," and finally "feed deficit areas." Since there was no discussion of this provision in open hearings or with the departmental witnesses these terms are at best nebulous and are subject to just about whatever interpretation the Secretary cares to make. The arbitrary decision of the Secretary this year in regard to "section 22" rates for grain shipped to the Southeast clearly illustrates the lack of sufficient guidelines in this area.

Assuming the designation as a feed deficit area, farmers in such an area would not be able to expand their production beyond their historical production during the base period. This would, of course, freeze current production patterns and prevent the growth of an expanded livestock economy in many parts of the Nation. Except for a very small reserve, new growers would also be precluded from becoming feed grain farmers, and finally feed-deficit-area growers would be subject to marketing quota penalties while not being eligible to vote in the referendum or be eligible for price support or diversion payments.

Subtitle B—Wheat

1. *Impact on income.*—The wheat farmer can look for a reduction of income under H.R. 11222. Commonsense dictates that a wheat farmer under the present program receiving a diversion payment of from 45 to 60 percent plus a price support of $2 per bushel on all the wheat he can grow on his allotment will have more income than he would under the proposed program where his diversion payment would slide down from 50 percent in 1963, 40 percent in 1964, 30 percent in 1965 and zero in 1966 and thereafter, while at the same time receiving a price support from $1.95 to $2.05 per bushel on approximately 85 percent of the production on his allotment and a

price support of $1.40 per bushel on the remaining 15 percent of his production. In addition the bill repeals the long-standing provision in present law which allows wheat farmers in high-risk areas some measure of protection against the elements by allowing excess wheat stored under bond from a previous year to be applied to a subsequent year's crop. To other producers on the approximately 10,000 farms which are currently taking advantage of this provision, H.R. 11222 could easily spell economic disaster.

2. *Unsound legislation.*—We recognize that the wheat provisions of H.R. 11222 are not the programs for "domestic parity" or "wheat stabilization" long advocated by several farm and commodity organizations. During the course of hearings this fact became apparent to a number of individual members and local units of these organizations as witnessed by a growing number of withdrawals of endorsement. The program proposed in H.R. 11222 would unquestionably be one of the most complex ever instituted. Each step of wheat production processing and export would be tightly policed. Farmers, processors, taxpayers, and consumers would all be required to bear the burden of this program. Feed grain farmers would suffer because of the Government policy of artificially encouraging wheat for feed. Our exports would suffer because of international repercussions to an artificial multiple-price plan for our domestic market. Taxpayers would pick up the bill for heavier export subsidies while consumers would suffer from inefficient production patterns and advancing costs. Wheat farmers producing those classes of wheat not in serious surplus supply would suffer from further cuts in acreage.

3. *Unfair to small growers.*—This bill is probably the most harsh and vindictive measure ever aimed at the small wheat farmer. He is flagrantly discriminated against in voting and in marketing.

Voting eligibility for small growers is set forth in sections 335 and 336 which read in part as follows:

> SEC. 336. * * * Any producer who has a farm acreage allotment shall be eligible to vote in any referendum held pursuant to this section, *except a producer who has a small farm base acreage for such crop of wheat and who does not elect, pursuant to section 335, to be subject to the farm marketing quota.* [Emphasis added.]
>
> SEC. 335. Notwithstanding any other provision of this part, no farm marketing quota for any crop of wheat shall be applicable to any farm with a base of fifteen acres or less (hereinafter called small-farm base acreage) if the acreage of such crop of wheat on the farm does not exceed the small-farm base acreage determined for the farm, *unless the owner or operator of the farm elects in writing on a form and within the time prescribed by the Secretary to be subject to the farm acreage allotment and marketing quotas* * * *" [Emphasis added.]

As in the case of the small feed grain farmer, the small wheatgrower must bear the complicated burden of signing in writing his promise to comply with the farm acreage allotment. If he fails to commit himself he cannot vote. If he doesn't vote he is still subject to the marketing quota penalty based on production in excess of his farm allotment. Again, larger growers are not burdened by this discriminatory provision. They are automatically eligible to vote. This again prevents the majority of farmers who raise wheat from voting in the referendum.

Perhaps the most unfair provision of all is the denial of marketing certificates to these small farmers electing to use the small farm exemption provided for under the bill. This means that small growers could not even plant up to the farm wheat base without losing the right to receive certificates (and hence the right to sell wheat for food and for export).

[The minority report contains a number of tables in substantiation of statements. These tables and text referring to them are omitted here.]

The effect of H.R. 11222 on the income of these small growers would also be devastating . . . at least $107 million less than in 1962. Under present law wheat growers with allotments of 15 acres or less may grow the lower of 13½ acres, or the highest planted acreage in 1959, 1960, or 1961. These small producers sell their wheat in the open market and receive a price fairly close to the price support. For 1962 this is about $2 per bushel.

This affects over 600,000 wheat producers—about half the wheat growers in any year. Under H.R. 11222 the 13½ acre exemption would end. The small farm base acreage would be the 1957–61 average wheat acreage. However, any farmer who plants above his allotment would not be eligible for price support and would not receive a marketing certificate. This means that these small producers would receive fairly close to $1.40 per bushel or about 60 cents less than for 1962.

4. *Base period changed.*—H.R. 11222 changes the base period for calculating the National and State acreage allotments from a 10-year period to a 5-year period. As can be seen in table No. 3, most of the major wheat-producing States lose acreage by this change while minor wheat-producing States gain acreage. Thus, H.R. 11222 would result in a double cut to most commercial growers—a loss in State acreage and a 20 percent farm allotment cut.

Subtitle C—Dairy products

The dairy provisions of H.R. 11222 are the ineffective remnants of the original dairy control plan. While the bill now calls only for payments, the administrative machinery and the program data for the control program would be established for subsequent controls. Each dairy farmer would be interrogated to find his 1961 production which would become his base in future years. The same line of argument that the feed grain program in 1961 and 1962 would "save" millions of dollars is now being proposed to dairy farmers in this bill.

If the Government makes these "Brannan plan" compensatory payments to dairy farmers for not producing milk, the advocates of H.R. 11222 say, it will "save" millions of dollars because the Government won't be purchasing the dairy products which farmers were paid not to produce. The fallacy of such "savings" is obvious. At best it would be a theoretical expenditure of less money than under the present program.

The real foolishness of the proposed dairy plan lies in its complete and obvious ineffectiveness. While it has been described as a "feed grain program for dairy farmers," there are three very important distinctions between the programs.

1. The present feed grain program retires an agriculture resource (land) for a period of time. The proposed dairy payments would not insure the retirement of dairy cows which might be sold to other noncomplying farmers who would keep them in production.

2. The present feed grain program is funded substantially by payments-in-kind out of the surplus stocks of CCC. The dairy program in H.R. 11222 doesn't propose payments in dried milk, butter, and cheese. On the contrary, it proposes cash payments direct from the funds of CCC without prior appropriation by Congress.

3. Under the present feed grain program, price supports are available only to farmers who participate. Noncompliers aren't eligible for price support. Under the proposed dairy plan, price support would be available to all producers, compliers and noncompliers. This sets the stage for a sharp increase in production by noncomplying dairy farmers, the net result of which would be large sums of money expended by the Government with very little result.

It is also appropriate to point out that the current dairy surplus situation has been a child of this administration.

The record shows that 2 years ago, on March 31, 1960, the Commodity Credit Corporation had 72.3 million pounds of butter, 264.6 million pounds of nonfat dry milk, and no cheese in its inventory. As of March 31, 1962, CCC had 271 million pounds of butter, 425 million pounds of nonfat dry milk, and 67 million pounds of cheese.

TITLE V—FARMERS HOME ADMINISTRATION

The addition of recreation loans to the Farmers Home Administration program appears to be particularly unwise at this time. The many requests for FHA loan funds already create an overburdening demand. We also have some serious reservations about the nature of the recreation activities to be sponsored by FHA loans and again express our concern over the availability of these facilities to all citizens.

We also object to the inclusion of sewer loans to municipalities because such a program would be a complete duplication of the legislative authority contained in several other statutes.

Charles B. Hoeven.
Paul B. Dague.
Page Belcher.
Clifford G. McIntire.
Charles M. Teague.
Albert H. Quie.
Don L. Short.
Catherine May.
Delbert L. Latta.
Ralph Harvey.
Paul Findley.
Bob Dole.
Ralph F. Beermann.
Ben Reifel.

9. *The Debates and the Votes*

FARM BILL debates are usually poorly attended in both Houses. Urban legislators are not much interested in them, and legislators not on the Agriculture committees are reluctant to spend the time needed to understand these complex measures.

TIMING

In the first Senate debate on the Food and Agriculture Act of 1962, many of the speeches to a nearly empty chamber were presumably for the record—as explanations for individual votes, or as interpretations to guide administrators and judges who would subsequently apply the law.

Speeches on the Senate floor were also the basis for press releases and newsletters, as well as a way to delay the votes. Opponents of the administration hoped to spark a "grass-roots" reaction against Senator Ellender's amendments to restore the mandatory programs.

Mail did pour in from the rural areas. Senator Wayne Morse (D., Ore.) inserted into the *Congressional Record* sixteen letters favoring mandatory controls, and thirty-seven opposing. Several are given here. Except for the first, they were addressed specifically to Senator Morse.

May 21, 1962. To Members of the U.S. Senate: Passage of the Food and Agricultural Act of 1962 as reported by the Senate Agriculture Committee would be a step toward the development of a farm program that will lead to a sound agriculture economy.

Its enactment would strengthen farm income and curb the cost to the Federal Government.

However, to further these goals the following amendments are needed:

1. Reinstate more realistic choices in the wheat referendum.

2. Replace the temporary extension of the feed grain program with the permanent program.

3. Reinstate the provision that would allow wheat to be grown on feed grain acres or feed grain on wheat acres.

We respectfully request your support of the Food and Agriculture Act of 1962 with these amendments.—*National Grange, National Farmers Union, National Association of Wheat Growers, Missouri Farmers Association, National Farmers Organization.*

Pendleton, Oregon, May 17, 1962. The farmers of this area will appreciate your effort to amend S. 3225, to restore administration feed and grain and wheat program as they were introduced in the original Ellender Bill. *W. C. Rosewall, President, Morrow County Farmers Union.*

Ontario, Oregon, May 19, 1962. Malheur County Livestock Association views with alarm the section in farm bill allowing grazing of acres which have been idled because of provisions of this bill for which payment is being received. Strongly urge this section be deleted. *William G. Ross, President.*

McMinnville, Ore. I am writing you in regard to the Kennedy-Freeman farm bill. The version sent to the Senate floor by your Senate Agriculture Committee isn't so bad, but it undoubtedly will be changed back to try and conform to the one on the House floor (H.R. 11222) and that bill I feel we can't live with. It will completely stifle the initiative and ability of a farmer to get ahead, and will make just another government hired hand out of him. Inasmuch as you own a farm yourself, I felt you should be in a position to see the danger in this sort of approach to the farm problem. *Respectively, M. E. Toliver.*

Holdhill, Oregon, May 22, 1962. We do not favor Senate bill 3225 and amendment or substitute. *Ernest Radomske, Chairman, County Farm Bureau.*

Imbler, Oregon, May 12, 1962, Union County Farm Bureau opposes return of administration amendments to Senate farm bill S. 3225. *H. Clayton Fox.*

La Grande, Oreg., May 19, 1962. Opposed to agriculture bill S. 3225. Favor S. 2786 as revised. *Dale Carson.*

Vale, Oregon, May 19, 1962. Please oppose Senate bill 3225 or any amendments from Senate bill to S. 2786. *John G. Tucke, President, Malheur County Farm Bureau.*

National Rural Electric Cooperative Association, Washington, D.C. May 18, 1962. Two parts of the Food and Agriculture Act of 1962 which you have under consideration are of direct concern to rural electric systems throughout the country. . . . We would appreciate your support of our position on these issues. Kermit Overby, director, Legislation and Research Department.

The Ellender amendments were the real issues, so Republicans were obliged to beat the air until Senator Ellender introduced them on the afternoon of the second day of debate, apparently in hopes they would be voted on next day (a Wednesday).

Minority member Aiken protested that the Senate should delay the vote until Thursday in order to allow opportunity for Texas cattlemen and some other affected producers to express their opposition to the amendments.[1]

Majority whip Humphrey, replying for the Democratic leadership, said the majority did not want "to force precipitate action." Given the fact that Senate debate may not be regulated except by unanimous consent (or by a rarely used cloture procedure), Humphrey offered to enter a unanimous-consent agreement that "would give senators who are vitally interested in the question time for study, and the advance notice required for orderly debate." Aiken approved. Ellender too agreed, after protesting that he had always intended to give the senators every opportunity to discuss his amendments.

After a discussion in private, leaders from both parties produced a hastily drafted unanimous-consent agreement, in which it was agreed to vote on the wheat amendment following a two-hour debate which would begin at noon Thursday, and after the wheat-amendment vote, to debate for two hours on the mandatory feed-

[1] *Congressional Record* (daily edition), May 22, 1962, pp. 8276 ff.

grains amendment before voting on it. This unanimous-consent agreement was passed late Tuesday afternoon.[2]

The time problem was still not settled.

On Thursday, debate went as expected on the wheat amendment, but Senator Case of South Dakota and others who wanted to propose amendments to the crucial Ellender feed-grains amendment began to realize that the scheduled two-hour period would be insufficient for their purposes.

To gain more time they exploited an error in the wording of the unanimous-consent resolution. When the presiding officer announced, following the vote on the wheat amendment, that debate on the feed-grains amendment would close in two hours (at 4:15) Senator Case was on his feet:

> As I read the unanimous-consent agreement, it says: "Two hours, to be equally divided and controlled as above, shall be allotted for debate on the Ellender feed grain amendment or any amendment thereto." It does not say, "and all amendments thereto." It seems to me a clear reading of the unanimous-consent agreement provides 2 hours of debate for any amendment to the feed grains amendment.

Majority leader Mansfield argued in reply that the amendment should be interpreted as its writers' had intended, rather than on the basis of the literal wording:

> I think the Senator from South Dakota has put his own interpretation on this. . . . Certainly this was not the intent of the distinguished minority leader [Mr. Dirksen], of the Senator from South Dakota [Mr. Mundt], of the Senator from Vermont [Mr. Aiken], of the Senator from Louisiana [Mr. Ellender], or other Senators, when that proposal was made. If that were the consensus, it would have been useless, in my opinion, to offer the unanimous-consent agreement. . . .

The presiding officer endeavored to support Mansfield by a formal ruling:

[2] *Congressional Record* (daily edition), May 22, 1962, p. 8295.

PRESIDING OFFICER: The written agreement differs from the memory of the Chair of the verbal agreement. . . . The word "and" was in the original agreement which was agreed to.

CASE: The word "and" was used? Does the *Record* show that?

PRESIDING OFFICER: That is what the Chair rules actually happened.

SENATOR ALLOT OF COLORADO: . . . I should like to know on what basis the presiding officer can rule that the printed unanimous-consent agreement . . . does not mean what it says, but means what somebody else says? . . . We are making a very serious mistake to set a precedent. . . .

Senator Morton of Kentucky broke in to announce that the astronaut Scott Carpenter had landed. The senators went back into orbit. Majority leader Mansfield started to offer another unanimous-consent agreement clarifying the language, and stopped when Case indicated he would object. Humphrey provided more evidence of the true intent of the resolution, and minority leader Dirksen momentarily ended the revolt in his ranks by endorsing the original understanding.

But as time again pressed, Case appealed the ruling of the Chair, causing a babel of questions, comments, and protests. To erase the whole parliamentary tangle, the majority leader asked unanimous consent that debate stop at 5:00, instead of 4:20. When no one objected, he tried to revise it downward to 4:45, but Senator Williams of Delaware suggested instead that 10 minutes be allowed each side on each amendment to the Ellender amendment, without setting a final deadline for voting on the Ellender amendment itself. This was agreed to, and debate began again.

Among the proposed amendments to the administration's feed grains program were one by Senator Young of North Dakota to exempt all corn used for silage and one by Senator Eastland (D., Miss.) to exempt all feed grains which were fed on the farm where they were produced. Neither amendment was acceptable to the administration which feared that either might have opened a huge, perhaps fatal, loophole in the feed-grains control program.

Another amendment by Senator Jack Miller (R., Iowa) would have eliminated the major loophole already in the bill—the exemption for those who produced twenty-five acres of feed grains or less. This was defeated, and the Ellender feed-grains amendment—still intact and with mandatory controls—was passed by the comfortable majority of 46 to 37.

No other major amendments to the bill passed. McCarthy's mandatory dairy bill, Proxmire's voluntary dairy bill, Republican Senator Keating's amendment to prevent racial discrimination in recreation, and a late effort by a harried Oklahoma Democrat, Mike Monroney, to pass a revised Eastland amendment (see p. 186)—all these opposition amendments were defeated, though by only three votes in the case of the Keating and Monroney amendments, either of which would in turn have jeopardized passage of the bill.

As a safeguard against passage of the Monroney amendment, Senate majority leader Mansfield stood ready with a motion to table it; such a tabling motion had to be voted on prior to the vote on the amendment itself. Had Mansfield's tabling motion lost, he planned to adjourn the Senate until the following week, at which time the Democratic leadership would hopefully have regained their majority in support of the bill and against Monroney's amendment.

The final vote on the bill followed the tabling of the Monroney amendment, and it was almost as close—42–38.

Senate passage of the bill was thought by some to presage an easy victory in the House, though others felt it had been possible only because some senators were relying on the House to defeat the bill.

In any case it was a major victory for backers of the bill. How did they win it?

A Party Vote

The vote was along party lines. Only one Republican, Senator Young of North Dakota, voted for the bill, and only eight of the forty-nine Democratic votes were cast against it. The ties of party were manifold, but on this administration farm bill, the differing philosophies of the two parties were very prominent motivating forces. Republican leaders in both Senate and House said they had little difficulty arranging virtually unanimous opposition to the bill because this was a chance for Republican members to vote their convictions and not be hurt by the vote. Democrats too were voting on concepts which had been woven into their party platform over decades. Even Southern Democrats, intransigent in varying degrees, found in farm bills an avenue for a romantic return to party principles dealing with the role of government in economic affairs which had been initiated by the great agrarian, William Jennings Bryan, and which had been elaborated further under Woodrow Wilson, the New and Fair Deals, and the New Frontier. So to explain the vote we must briefly note the party principles which oriented it.

Although the ideological division along party lines has not been clearcut, we can point out several compatible attitudes within each party which have guided its presidential wing and the more conservative congressional wing as well.

One attitude which has guided the Democratic party in its approach to farm policy and other domestic issues is related to the party's conception of itself—as the representative of farmers, workers, and small businessmen.

Complementing the view of the Democratic party as the "little man's party," as President Truman had called it, was the commitment of this party to active, strong government. To serve the less privileged members of society (and the public interest), government should become the master rather than the servant or the victim of the irrational and often ruinous forces in the private economy. In line with this view was the effort in the Kennedy administration farm bill to control production and prices in order to protect the family farm and to discourage the trend to corporation farms, and monopolistic vertical control of agriculture.

A third factor guiding Democratic economic doctrine and farm policy was a deep dissatisfaction with the way wealth was shared under unrestricted capitalism. Democrats had advocated regularized and rather far-reaching governmental intervention designed to assure that all got a minimum share of the economic rewards of capitalism. Although many Democrats worried that price-control programs provided little help for millions of subsistence farmers, the Kennedy bill did adhere to the idea of parity of income—fair return for all commercial producers.

The fourth among the attitudes guiding Democratic farm policy was derived from the experiences of the great depression. These prompted a view in the Roosevelt administration, made emphatic in the "full" Employment Act under Truman, that it is the government's responsibility to maintain prosperity. Though perhaps only a few of the New Frontier Democrats believed the axiom that "national depressions are farm led and farm fed" there was recognition that prolonged hardship in any segment of the economy could ultimately weaken the whole interdependent structure.

A different set of attitudes—also mutually compatible—relating to the role of government in economic affairs, had been expressed in the Republican platforms and campaign speeches, and in the interpretations which historians gave to the record of twentieth century Republican administrations. The most obvious and inclusive Republican attitude about government's role was suggested in a question proposed in a 1958 speech by Secretary of Agriculture Ezra Benson which, he felt, raised the major issue in the 1958 elections:

"Shall we manage our own affairs or shall the government manage them for us?"

We should manage our own affairs, he answered, because the generally satisfactory conditions of life in this country are attributable to the existing arrangement which stresses individual freedom in economic affairs:

> There is no other nation on the face of the earth so richly blessed as ours. There is no other span of time so bountifully endowed as the years of our generation. We occupy a very special spot of the world's surface at a very special time in history.
>
> In large measure, these abundant blessings have come to us through an economic system which rests on three pillars:

Free enterprise: the right to venture—to choose
Private property: the right to own
A market economy: the right to exchange.[3]

Another side of this confidence in free enterprise, and a second attitude influencing Republican domestic policy was the belief that tragic consequences could result from attempts by government to make decisions for the economy. Republicans have felt that government entrance into business results in poor administration because of the need for checks and balances, and in poorer leadership than would come from the free atmosphere of competition. Worst of all was the damage which would be wrought by the growth of bureaucracy: permitted to expand, bureaucracy would not only be relatively inefficient, it would ultimately stifle freedom of speech and the spirit of independence. Based on this view Vice President Richard Nixon stated in the 1960 campaign that the Kennedy farm program would actually encourage Soviet agricultural supremacy.[4]

On the whole, Republican congressmen in 1962 also felt little need for government intervention. According to a compilation of votes in *Congressional Quarterly* they voted 63% of the time for a smaller federal role, while the average Democratic congressman voted 74% of the time for a larger federal role.[5]

When Republican leaders responded to demands for novel or more vigorous governmental intervention, their actions were often motivated less by the conviction that they were really necessary than by the desire to forestall radicalism. The objective in these cases was to satisfy the demands on government with a minimal governmental response—to lead and thereby to moderate.

Pressures on the Democrats

On the farm bill, the pressures on the Republicans in the House as well as in the Senate tended to reinforce their philosophical

[3] Speech to the United Republican Fund of Illinois, Chicago, Illinois, June 2, 1958.

[4] *Des Moines Register*, October 5, 1960.

[5] *Congressional Quarterly*, December 28, 1962, P. 2290.

leanings. On the other hand many urban and rural Democrats who liked the principles underlying the bill were nevertheless tempted to vote against this hard choice due to unfavorable constituency reaction to it. The dilemma was particularly severe for the majority leader who was obliged on this occasion to risk his senate seat in service to the party.

Mansfield, his whip Hubert Humphrey, and others who were informal lieutenants in the brokerage of votes, reassured urban liberals that a vote for the farm bill would be repaid when programs such as urban development were voted on. As a result all of the Northeastern and Western Democrats finally voted for this farm bill in which they were not much interested. Some had privately threatened to vote against it two months earlier when rural Democratic votes defeated Kennedy's proposed Department of Urban Affiairs.

Urban constituents resented farm subsidies, when aware of them, but not enough that opponents of incumbent legislators could make their farm votes a good election issue. To ward off urban reaction against farm votes, Senator Joseph Clark (D., Pa.) had frankly introduced voters to the way legislative business was done: if you expect to get industrial redevelopment funds and other programs Pennsylvania needs, he told them, you must let me swap votes with those who have other interests.

Such cooperation in the form of logrolling was understandable to local politicians in metropolitan areas, where victory at the polls was due more to political organization than to the candidate's personality or his campaign pitch.

Union-oriented urban Democratic legislators found some appeal in a program which helped a group discipline itself in order to improve its income (though the unions took no active part in this farm struggle). They were also influenced, without doubt, by the "Supplemental Views" of Agriculture committee liberals Hart, McCarthy, Young (Ohio), and Neuberger, which had been appended to the majority's report on the bill. Theirs was a short, simply worded, moderate plea for passage of the bill together with the Ellender amendments added.

Many big-city Democrats felt safer than usual in deciding to vote for the bill because President Kennedy—generally popular in their districts—had said the program would cut down government costs and would not raise the price of food.

The bill had been designed to appeal to Southerners, from whom more help than usual was needed since urban Republicans would be voting no. Many Southerners were accustomed to mandatory controls and thought dairy, corn and wheat farmers ought also to accept them.

Additional Southern votes no doubt came in response to a personal appeal by the embattled Senator Ellender, or in response to the leadership of the respected Georgia Senator Richard Russell, who may in turn have been influenced by his colleague Senator Herman Talmadge, or by Assistant Secretary of Agriculture John Duncan from Georgia.

Mansfield and Humphrey lost only five of the Southern Democratic senators. These included Agriculture committee members Eastland and Holland, and Senator Strom Thurmond (D., S.C.), former Dixiecrat candidate for President whose total voting record in 1962 was more anti-Kennedy than that of any other Democratic senator.[6] Senator John McClellan (D., Ark.) also followed his conservative leanings.

Senator Harry Byrd of Virginia apparently surprised vote counters on both sides by voting along with his equally conservative Viriginia colleague Senator Willis Robertson in favor of the Ellender amendments. Perhaps for the same unrevealed reasons rather than the official reason of sickness in the family, Byrd abstained on the final vote, while Robertson voted against the bill.

Even the abstainers may have played a part in this close vote. Six were Mountain-state Democrats under heavy pressure from cattlemen to vote against the bill even though its provisions had no direct bearing on the cattle industry. Although Humphrey officially announced that all these legislators would have voted for the bill had they been present, the administration was enough in

[6] *Congressional Quarterly Almanac*, 1962, p. 707.

doubt that it took pains to find a "live" pair for Senator Hickey of Wyoming so that he might stay in the wings while the vote proceeded.

Farm Bureau people later pointed out proudly that Hickey and another fence sitter—John Carroll of Colorado—were defeated in the fall, although possibly for reasons additional to the fact they did not please the cattlemen on this particular vote.

Action in the House Rules Committee

Victory in the Senate raised hope of victory in the House, by means of Southern votes such as those of the doubtful Virginia congressmen who might follow Senator Byrd's lead, and the doubtful Georgia congressmen who might follow Senator Russell. Opponents of the bill—recognizing that the House was the last chance saloon on this particular highway—went into high gear.

Everyone agreed time was on the side of the opposition as grassroots resentment continued to build. Yet the bill was not out of the Rules committee and once reported, a place had to be found for it on the busy House calendar—and in a Tuesday-Wednesday-Thursday sequence at that, in order to command the votes of many eastern-seaboard congressmen collectively dubbed the "Tuesday-Thursday club." These legislators invariably spent a very long weekend in their districts.

On June 5th and 6th, the Rules committee heard Chairman Cooley's plea for a rule. In compliance with Cooley's request, they granted the ordinary "open" rule which allows amendments from the floor so long as they are germane. Six hours of general debate were authorized, three to be distributed by Chairman Cooley, three by the ranking minority member Charles Hoeven. These two men could themselves consume as much of this time as they wished, with the next priority being given to fellow members of the House committee. The other 400-odd House members could make a bid for any remaining time.

Debate would take place as usual under a procedure called Committee of the Whole House, in which only one hundred persons needed to be present to constitute a quorum. Under this procedure, amendments would be proposed following the general debate, with the proponent and a principal opponent of an amendment each having five minutes to discuss it.

Debate would move with dispatch under the discipline of the powerful presiding officer's heavy gavel.

For speakers to command attention of the mulling House membership required artistry in histrionics, though some members relied on a loud voice amplified by a loudspeaker to the magnitude of thunder.

Since this body was so much larger than the Senate, more work and more machinery were needed to organize the voting. Numerous congressmen and staff members participated in sizing up the situation by prevote polling, and then committee members, lobbyists, even Secretary Freeman and his staff were involved in extensive follow-up activities directed at undecided members. In the vote on this farm bill, all the men and machinery were put to work. In this case the Republican party machinery operated at near perfection.

The Republican Effort

After the Rules committee had cleared the bill, Republican leaders discussed strategy at the next weekly meeting of the Republican Policy Committee, a 36-member group chosen on the basis of geography and seniority. At this meeting the minority leader and the whip made a few remarks before giving the floor to Congressman Hoeven, who described the administration's farm bill in unflattering terms. Hoeven was followed in the order of seniority by several other members of the House Agriculture Committee, all of whom recommended that the party oppose the administration's bill.

Instead of the frank disagreement often heard at these private meetings, comment from the floor was invariably against the bill, prompting leaders to call for a vote which, as they had hoped, was unanimous in opposition to the farm bill.

The results of this meeting strengthened party leaders' effectiveness. With unanimity among the House Agriculture Committee minority, and among the Republican Policy Committee as well, the Republican leadership could make votes on this bill a rare test of loyalty to party as applied to the twenty or so Republicans whose support the administration still hoped to get. If virtually all Republicans voted against an administration bill, it would likely be defeated, according to a rule of thumb based on 1961 experience.

No meeting was called of the Republican Conference (to which all Republican House members would be invited). Instead, contact with the rank and file was through their whip—elderly, conservative Leslie Arends of Illinois, who called "indefinite" members and reported to Halleck the names of those from whom he could not get a commitment.

Arend's principal task, however, was to see that all were present and voting. To emphasize the importance of this vote he sent all Republicans a specially worded formal signed notice used only three or four times a year. The notice read as follows:

> On Tuesday June 19th, the farm bill (HR 11222) will be brought to the floor.
>
> This is an extremely important measure. It is imperative that all members be present and voting during the consideration of the bill.

Whip's assistants for each region and for each state kept track of all Republicans. Representative Katherine St. George, for example, was in charge of Eastern United States, and under her, Representative William Bates of Massachusetts contacted New England's 22 House Republicans; Pennsylvania Representative Carroll Kearns contacted the 16 in his state, and Mrs. St. George herself took New York's 23 Republican members. Throughout the debate the whip and his assistants worked closely with the Farm Bureau's national office, whose task of keeping count of Democratic voters against the bill was hardest, because these were the voters most likely to be swung back by administration pressure.

Minority Leader Halleck

Charles Halleck of Indiana, familiar to the public as the dour member of the televised "Ev and Charlie" team, had unseated the veteran Republican House leader Joe Martin of Massachusetts in 1959. He had since lived up to his backers' hopes by welding Republicans into an effective opposition group, although some Republican members in and out of Congress feared Halleck was building a public image of a hidebound, too conservative group.

On the farm-bill vote Halleck had a chance to prove that a political party does not need control of the White House or the Congress to achieve nearly perfect harmony. Farm legislation was one of those subjects in which the troublesome liberal Republicans had little interest and were inclined in any case to stand with the conservatives. Most rural-based Republicans might actually profit at home by voting for the bill, and a few tended to feel as did Senator Young that their declining farm population might better take what they could get at this time than wait for a pot of gold at the end of the Republican rainbow. Against this, however, was the psychological pull that goes with a test of party loyalty, in this case invoked by a unanimous Policy committee and all Republicans on the House Agriculture Committee, by close Republican colleagues, by meetings of Republican state delegations, and by pressures and enticements of a tough, blunt, party leader.

Republicans Halleck and Hoeven meanwhile wrestled with the familiar minority dilemma: should they simply unite in opposition to the bill, or should they offer an alternative approach? Hoeven wanted to offer an amendment to the administration bill— and he later did—which would have continued the existing voluntary programs, as the Senate committee bill had done. But he knew that many Republicans would not support such a bill if it stood a chance of passing, partly because the party had voted against these temporary programs in the previous year.

This dilemma became a public question because of the publication of a letter uncovered in the Billie Sol Estes hearings, written by a former Benson assistant, Martin Sorkin, which described a secret meeting of the Republican National Committee and the chairmen of the House and Senate Republican Campaign committees where "it was agreed that it was not the responsibility of the Republicans to propose solutions but to criticize the Administration wherever feasible." [7]

On the first day of debate in the House, Vice-Chairman Poage read excerpts from the Sorkin letter on the floor, and then concluded:

> I mention this letter . . . and merely suggest that this will give you a key to much of the proceedings that are going to take place in the next 2 or 3 days. . . . You are going to listen in the next two or three days to more proposals that have no intention of helping the farmers but merely to embarrass the Administration. You are going to have the Powell amendment [prohibiting discrimination in projects financed by federal funds] dug up on the banks of the upper Mississippi. You are going to have every sort of amendment that has nothing in the world to do with agriculture thrown out here in the hope that it may embarrass the administration and may prevent the passage of this legislation.[8]

Much reference was made to the Sorkin letter, which may have tightened party lines a bit on both sides but apparently had little effect on the total vote.

Scheduling the House Debate

Although most observers agreed that the House would have passed the bill had it acted in May, Democratic leaders were obliged to seek a week's postponement when the bill came up for debate in early June, because according to their whip count they did not have enough votes to pass the bill.

The decisions to postpone debate, and a week later to bring the bill to the floor, were made in four meetings in the House Speaker's office. These meetings were attended by White House lobbyists, by Secretary Freeman and Ed Jaenke, by Cooley and Poage, by

[7] *Congressional Record* (daily edition), June 19th, 1962, p. 10162.
[8] *Ibid.*, p. 10163.

House Speaker John McCormack, and by House Democratic leader Carl Albert. Albert—a former Agriculture committee member—spoke for the House leadership since McCormack was uninterested in and frankly unenthusiastic about the administration legislation.

There was disagreement at these meetings as to the prospects for passing the mandatory programs in the House. Albert preferred to send the bill back to committee for major repair, in the light of a Democratic whip count which indicated defeat. Freeman felt the count was inaccurate with respect to several presumed "no" votes, and Cooley was optimistic that additional "yes" votes could be gained through minor concessions on the floor, though he was unable to name anticipated switch voters.

Freeman was anxious to schedule the debate for the week June 19th–21st. He warned that President Kennedy might veto a bill passed at a later date because there would be insufficient time to educate farmers before the summer wheat referendum. White House lobbyists promised full presidential support, and on this basis House leaders reluctantly agreed to gamble their own prestige.

Pressure on the Uncommitted

A week before the debate, the White House lobby team joined the USDA liaison group, full time, in an effort to get crucial votes from the relatively few uncommitted "battleground boys."

Heading the White House lobbyists was presidential assistant Larry O'Brien, a long-time Kennedy associate who had helped create the organizations which had run President Kennedy's primary and election campaigns. In the harried atmosphere of legislative debate and later in the subtle politics of the congressional conference committee, O'Brien became a vehicle for last-minute appeal to the President from earlier decisions of the administration. No doubt O'Brien's on-the-spot judgment carried weight with those in the White House. Major concessions had to be cleared with Kennedy's legislative assistant Myer Feldman. He in turn first sought an opinion from Budget Bureau experts who received proposed changes by teletype as fast as they came up on the floor.

Congress expected to be cajoled by the President, almost as a prelude to action, but the administration lobbying on this farm bill was fiercely criticized by the opposition as going beyond previously accepted bonds of propriety, and as being too massive in nature. Minority leader Halleck quoted from a newsletter of Democratic Congressman Otis Pike, of New York, who wrote that a Post Office official with nine applications for new post offices in Pike's district had been in to talk to him about the farm bill. "The arm aches this week," wrote Congressman Pike, who decided to vote against the bill, "but the voice is still loud and clear."

Some implied that a president who made such use of his vast discretion could become a dictator. Others said they decided to vote against the bill after observing the methods used by the administration to sell it, though it seemed all these individuals had previously found ample reason to oppose the bill.

While the executive inducements appeared necessary to gain congressional cooperation and were sanctioned by long useage, apparently the public still did not understand this, because these inducements were kept absolutely secret. Farm-bill critics could give only a few examples of such "coercion," and these were mostly in connection with some other legislation. Since everyone admitted that the executive branch did barter for votes on a fairly large scale, four of the gifts ordinarily available for distribution by an administration might be listed.

1. *Jobs.* Many top federal jobs—all the federal judgeships, some ambassadorships, and most appointive positions at high levels within the administration were available to be bartered for votes. A few crucial votes on this farm bill would clearly have been worth a number of fine appointive positions. One lame-duck Republican who voted consistently with the administration on the bill, was hired by the Department of Agriculture in 1963, though in a situation where his efforts and reputation were presumably quite helpful to the USDA. A retiring Iowa Democrat, Merwin Coad, later served briefly as a high-level foreign-aid adviser, resigning after Iowa Republicans charged this was a pay-off for his vote on the farm bill.

2. *Federal agencies and installations.* Many decisions were being made by the executive branch with respect to the construction, improvement, or removal of post offices, veterans' hospitals, military bases, bridges, highways and so on, any one of which could be of consequence to a congressman and his district.

3. *Logrolling.* As the most powerful lobbyist, a president could give life to congressional proposals if he wished, or veto them. He could amend administration legislation, just as the farm bill was permitted to be amended to better fit the needs of particular constituencies. For that matter much law was by executive decree, as in the definition of "family farm" which one congressman who was at first opposed to the farm bill wanted broadened in order that certain benefits could be given to his large producers. The congressman subsequently supported the bill.

4. *Use of USDA expert services.* With USDA help a farm legislator could appear far wiser then he might actually be, and more powerful too if USDA top brass were always ready to make themselves available to visitors from his constituency. Though the USDA's wealth of expertise could be tapped even by hostile legislators, it was ready in abundance for those who would support the administration's farm bill.

Administration representatives asked wavering congressmen, "Is there anything we can do for you?" What they were willing to do very likely did not go beyond what the executive branch has been willing to do for years, and what the Congress often seems to demand. It was but one manifestation of the logrolling inherent in the democratic process. Despite the growing capacity of the executive branch to do favors, executive patronage did not prove to be enough in this case.

Freeman as Lobbyist

Debate on the bill got underway before the rule to debate the bill had been approved. Democrat Richard Bolling of Kansas City, who brought in the rule, urged city legislators to vote for it. A fellow Rules committee member, Clarence Brown of Ohio, asked the House to turn it down for lack of merit, and also because it had a shady past, and promised to have a shady future as well. According to Brown, the Agriculture committee had "gagged on this bill three times before it was possible to obtain a sufficient number of votes to report the bill out of committee." The vote which finally cleared it, Brown recalled, was cast by a gentleman (McSween) who said he might not support the bill on the floor.

Congressman Brown felt he could predict that floor action on the bill would be similarly indecorous. He had heard this from the grapevine:

> Some of us . . . have learned to rely more or less on what we call the grapevine telegraph. . . . The grapevine telegraph has been sounding off rather loud and clear in the last 24 or 48 hours that when we reach the proper place in the consideration of this bill, under the 5-minute rule, some of the leaders of this House, or at least men of great substance and dominating influence, will rise in their places and offer certain amendments to strike out of this measure some of the controversial provisions now contained in it, in the belief and on the theory that after their amendments are accepted it will not be too difficult to get the leadership of the committee on Agriculture to accept some of these amendments under present conditions. I say this because the whispers have had it that this measure has been in trouble for some time here in the House.[9]

Congressman Brown also deplored the "hordes of lobbyists running around Capitol Hill in support of this legislation." Over the grapevine telegraph soon came word that Secretary Freeman himself was lobbying nearby the Speaker's office just off the House floor. *The Wall Street Journal*[10] said of his last-minute effort:

> Agriculture Secretary Freeman, employing the flair of a carnival pitchman, is championing the Administration's farm bill with a display of salesmanship that has left even seasoned politicians slightly popeyed.

Testimonials to his effectiveness were included:

[9] *Congressional Record*, (daily edition), June 19, 1962, pp. 10147–48.
[10] June 21, 1962.

Veteran Democrat: "This man is a snake charmer. I was all set to speak against the bill until Freeman started coming around to see me and he's almost got me convinced I should vote for it."

Wavering Southerner: "He's the most persuasive man I've ever listened to. He not only sells himself, but he sells his cause."

A Democratic leader: "If anybody is going to pull the bill out for us it's Orville."

No one slighted Secretary Freeman's effort, supported by a number of other administration lobbyists on the telephone or on the scene. With Farm Bureau and other opposition groups similarly occupied, the uncommitted congressmen and the potential backsliders had callers at their offices if they appeared to veer a bit, although personal contacts with those on the floor and those outside the chambers tended to be by congressmen who supported or opposed the bill rather than by lobbyists as such.

Debate on the Floor

In the Senate, debate had probably changed few if any votes, as was usually the case. But the House debate may have helped create an atmosphere unfavorable to the bill which ultimately hurt its chances. Chairman Cooley and Vice-Chairman Poage seemed so personally involved in behalf of the legislation that they made its merits seem unbelievable. They chose to question the motives of some of the bill's opponents—the Republicans with their Sorkin letter, the Farm Bureau leadership which had strayed from an earlier farmer-centered program, and the nit pickers who would reject a bill because it was not perfect.

The arguments were much the same in both Houses. Backers said the bill would cut down surpluses, save billions of dollars, and offer stability and prosperity to the farm economy. The alternative was to build up surpluses, and ultimately destroy farm programs, including Southern price-support programs.

They said the substitution clause allowing interchange of feedgrains and wheat acreage would benefit Great Plains farmers who could grow wheat but little else. Opponents, they charged, wanted only to destroy the program.

Opponents had a longer list of arguments. Every section of the country seemed to be discriminated against: the Southern feed-grains and beef economy would be stunted; Western cattlemen would be controlled next; the deficit-areas provision and other exemptions would make a martyr of the Midwest; Oregon and Washington white wheat, Midwestern soft red winter wheat, and the spring wheat of the Dakotas would all be controlled even though these varieties were not much in surplus. The Northeast would, of course, have to pay higher prices for its feed grains.

Much point was made of the evidence that farmers did not want the program. The biggest farm organization opposed it and the Wheat Growers, Grange, and Farmers Union were only lukewarm in their support. Polls in *Farm Journal* showed, as usual, that its subscribers did not like controls.

Critics gave several reasons why the program would not work—incompetence of the bureaucracy, corruption of the Billie Sol Estes type, failure of the cotton program and of all past government programs to control production and assure parity incomes. Much emphasis was laid on the presumed bad consequences of the program. Farm income would not rise, yet farmers would lose more precious economic freedom. The Secretary would become a czar of agriculture as more controls were subsequently added and more commodities made subject to them. Several speakers felt that American farmers might shortly be as regimented and as inefficient as Soviet farmers, in consequence of this program.

Rhode Island's Democratic Representative John Fogarty, a dependable foe of all farm programs, called the proposed wheat certificates a "bread tax," which at a penny a loaf would cost consumers $450,000 a day, "not counting the cake tax and the doughnut tax, the cookie tax, the spaghetti tax, the cracker tax, the Danish pastry tax, and the French pastry tax." [11]

The Logrolling Issue

The issue that may have swung the balance, however, referred to the manner in which the bill was debated and amended on the floor.

[11] *Congressional Record*, (daily edition), June 19, p. 10168.

Poage and Cooley gave their personal approval to one substantial floor amendment after another—twenty-one in all, feeling little need to make a case for them even when they had not been previously considered in committee. When opponents pressed Cooley to give reasons for an amendment by committee member Pat Jennings (D., Va.) which would exempt additional feed-grain producers from acreage controls, Cooley answered frankly that it was to attract additional votes for the bill:

REPUBLICAN CONGRESSMAN AVERY (R., Kansas): I have been trying to get the chairman of the Committee on Agriculture . . . to tell me why the 25 acre exemption was good 2 weeks ago and now it has to be 40 acres? The facts have not changed. . . .

COOLEY: The membership problem might be softened up by this amendment.

AVERY: What was that? Will the gentleman restate that?

CONGRESSMAN CHELF OF KENTUCKY [*walking down the aisle waving his arms in an excited manner*]: It is because he needs fellows like me to vote for the bill. That is why. I cannot vote for it unless you adopt this amendment.

AVERY: That clears that up.[12]

Were the Republicans again trying to take advantage of the lack of public understanding of the legislative process, to condemn the Democrats for seeking a compromise that a majority would approve? Logrolling was perhaps not the healthiest mode of compromise, but it was the way Congress did much of its business, and one reason why the administration had chosen to introduce a "comprehensive" bill.

Surely, the Republican objection was to how the logrolling was done, rather than to what was done. Ordinarily, vote-getting provisions were put together, or at least reviewed in committee, by legislator-experts who must be ready to tell their colleagues what the legislation would do, and to vouch for it. But the Agriculture committee could not vouch for these amendments added on the

[12] *Congressional Record* (daily edition), June 21, 1962, p. 10532.

floor. Although Chairman Cooley approved of them because they attracted votes, he could not always predict their consequences. For example, he could not give even an informed guess as to the number of farms the 40-acre provision might exempt, nor could he say how it would affect the cost of the program. Congressman Chelf exulted that 90% of his farmers could be exempted by the amendment, and others said Cooley's and Jennings' farmer constituents would be similarly relieved of controls, which neither man denied. Jennings maintained that only 20% of national feed-grains production would be affected, but Cooley corrected him, perhaps under prompting by a nearby USDA expert, to say that it would affect only 10% of total production.

Cooley drew the line between the 40-acre exemption, which he called a "misdemeanor" even while accepting it, and two other amendments (presumably felonies) which would exempt much larger groups. These were the Eastland amendment (see p. 186) to exempt all grain fed on the farm, which failed, and the amendment to exempt feed grains used for silage. Poage said the silage amendment "would tear down the wall" [13] and "open the door far too wide." [14]

Members of urban districts who knew nothing about the legislation surely wondered whether it was safe any longer to rely on Agriculture committee Democrats. To further confuse them, Republicans too introduced numerous amendments (23 amendments failed), including one requiring that the number of USDA employees at no time exceed the number of farmers. This one passed on a voice vote—thanks to "ayes" from anonymous Democrats. Democratic leaders reversed the decision by means of a "division" vote in which members walked down the aisle to be counted.

Always indifferent to farm bills, apparently many urban Democrats had by this time succumbed to a giddiness which was a blend of hilarity and disgust, as they waited impatiently to begin their Thursday evening trip to their constituencies.

[13] *Congressional Record* (daily edition), June 21, 1962, p. 10535.
[14] *Ibid.*, p. 10535

Democratic leaders now raced against the clock, to get to the final vote before crucial voters left. Congresswoman Iris Blitch of Georgia, seriously ill, had already gone.

Republican opponents were in no hurry, frequently interspersing time-using "preferential motions" to kill the bill, often insisting that lengthy amendments be read in full, and fully using all the minutes they could wrangle.

In desperation at 5:45 in the evening—with many amendments still pending—Chairman Cooley asked for unanimous consent that debate on the controversial feed-grains section and on amendments to it be ended at six o'clock. His request was objected to by Iowa Democrat Neal Smith, whose views on agriculture were respected and who wanted to discuss his own amendment which would postpone the mandatory feed-grains program for a year. Cooley was obliged to override Smith's objection by use of a motion to limit debate (quickly labeled a "gag rule"). Smith was unable to make his case and his amendment failed by a large vote. He subsequently voted against the bill. So did Congressman George Mahon (D., Texas), whom the USDA presumed to have satisfied with two earlier amendments to the bill. But Mahon still had two other amendments that he lacked time to discuss, and these lost.

In debate on the last section of the bill, Republicans engaged in a keep-away game to impede Congressman Cooley from securing a specific limitation on debate, while repeatedly calling attention to the unusual afternoon "vote-baiting" performance.

When the Committee of the Whole House finally rose and proceeded to formal session, Congressman Findley of Illinois insisted that there be a roll-call vote on the deficit areas provision which had been approved in the informal session. This vote consumed half an hour. It also became Findley's privilege, normally reserved to the Agriculture committee ranking member, to make the motion to recommit the administration's bill, on which the decisive vote would be held. Republican leaders thought this might help Findley in a tough November race (which he won) against Democratic Congressman Peter Mack with whose district Findley's had been merged.

At the start of the last day of debate, odds had been better than even that the bill would pass. Apparently those on both sides who had tried to keep a running score of votes continued to predict its passage. In the center of the vote-seeking group and experiencing its frustration in fullest measure were Speaker McCormack and his assistant John Holton, who manned a telephone in a small room near the floor from which Holton initiated such moves as were suggested by reports from the floor and from the House cloakroom where members went to rest and visit.

Democratic line officers were the following: the majority leader Carl Albert, House whip Hale Boggs of Louisiana and his amiable assistant D. B. Hardiman; Cooley and Poage, who were in charge of amendments and debate on the floor; administration liaison men Birkhead and O'Brien who headed a communications network counting votes, persuading voters, and seeking White House and USDA clearance for individual concessions designed to win a vote or two; John Schnittker and Edwin Jaenke at the USDA, clearing changes; Myer Feldman at the White House; and Philip Hughes at the Budget Bureau.

Win or lose, this had been an excellent day for the minority, especially for leader Halleck, the vigorous Republicans on the House Agriculture Committee, and Jack Lynn, Roger Fleming, and the other discreet but hard-driving Farm Bureau lobbyists who waited to see if they had finally stopped the bill. The vote would be close, and after the raucous afternoon session there would surely be some surprises.

The amendments aimed at attracting Southern votes had won Grant and McSween, the two Agriculture committee holdouts. These concessions, plus much negotiation, had made the Alabama, Georgia, Arkansas, and North Carolina delegations solid for the bill. Over half the Florida and Louisiana and South Carolina Democrats backed the bill, and one lame-duck Mississippian, Frank Smith, felt free to buck Senator Eastland, the Mississippi Farm Bureau, the National Cotton Council, and the mounting anti-Kennedy sentiment in his state.

But six Virginia votes went the other way, due apparently to

	Republicans		*Democrats*	
	Yes	*No*	*Yes*	*No*
Urban districts	119	1	31	138
Rural districts	48	0	17	66

Illustration 22. THE FINAL TALLY ON THE MOTION TO RECOMMIT H.R. 11222. Urban population is that which lives in places of 2,500 inhabitants, or more, or in suburban or rural areas with a density of 1,500 persons or more per square mile. Rural population is the remainder. Classification of districts is that of the *Congressional District Data Book* (Districts of the 88th Congress), Bureau of the Census.

a miscast in floor leadership on the bill. Secretary Freeman had persuaded Virginia's delegation leader Smith to vote for the bill, and Smith would have carried at least three other Virginia votes with him. Smith apparently changed his mind when the bill was so stoutly defended by Agriculture committee member Pat Jennings, a Virginian anathema to the Smith and Byrd group who was allowed to introduce the 40-acre exemption which, with the deficit-area, silage, and other amendments was designed to attract the Southeastern delegations.

Smith was resentful also because—though he was a most powerful senior figure—he had been unable to secure recognition on the floor to make a few remarks about the farm bill.

Neither were the Democrats able to hold the Southwestern cattle constituencies. Freeman had charged publicly that cattlemen were being misled in being told his program would lead to controls on cattlemen, and that segments of the cattle industry were using "concentrated pressures, big money, resources, and intimidation" to defeat the bill. All of these charges were denied by Cushman Radebaugh, President of the American National Cattlemen's Association, before the vote. Secretary Freeman assured cattlemen that the bill would not lead to controls on cattle, even though it would stabilize the cattle industry. Nevertheless, thirteen ordinarily loyal Democrats from Texas, Oklahoma, and New Mexico voted against the bill.

With these losses added to the five Virginia defectors and ten other Southern opposition votes, seven urban Northeastern Democrats in opposition, two Maryland Democrats, and one from West Virginia, two from the West, and three from the Midwest, compensated for by only one Republican vote, the Democrats did not have enough to win. Nor were they able to change six of these "no" votes in a frantic last-minute effort to reverse a 205–215 defeat.

10. *The Bill's Second Life*

IN FIRST reactions which reporters gathered from those flushed with victory or shaken by defeat, all felt the vote was of great importance. An election issue had been forged. A constitutional crisis had been revealed. The Kennedy farm program had been crippled or killed.

Spokesmen for both parties tried to capitalize on the outcome. Minutes after the final action the President's press secretary, Pierre Salinger, handed out a statement which asserted that defeat of the bill "will cost taxpayers of the United States an additional billion dollars next year," [1] and the Republicans were to be blamed. They had ignored the President's earlier plea for bipartisan support, voting 167–1 against the bill. "They now will have to bear the responsibility for the continuing chaos of our agricultural surplus situation," said President Kennedy.

Minority leader Halleck denied that this had been a party-line vote. Republicans voted against it simply because "it's a bad bill." But former President Eisenhower praised Republicans for defeating the Kennedy program at a Republican dinner held the following evening:

> In agriculture—we demand that the ground rule be not only economic health but also the return of freedom. . . . Thank heaven that viewpoint prevailed yesterday in the House of Representatives. I salute Charlie Halleck and Charlie Hoeven, our other House Republicans, and the band of courageous Democrats who joined with them in defeating the legislative monstrosity that was based upon a ruthless concept of ruling or ruining American agriculture.[2]

[1] *New York Times*, June 22, p. 1.
[2] *New York Times*, June 23, 1962, p. 8.

A Constitutional Question

The *New York Times* felt the psychological impact of a minority victory would hurt chances of other Kennedy programs such as the forthcoming reciprocal trade bill. This newspaper did not blame the Republicans who voted their principles. The fault lay with the Democratic Congressional leadership, which had "shown itself woefully ineffective all through the session." [3] For the first time in recent years the *Times* had backed a Democratic farm program, in order to keep farmers "from having their bread and eating it too."

New York Times columnist James Reston saw a constitutional question made poignant by the vote: even under the spurs of the President, the Congress had not been moved to deal with an already aggravated domestic problem. The Congress, conceived as a wholesome check on executive power, may well have stalemated our constitutional system.

Reston said President Kennedy tended toward that view in his news conference following the farm bill defeat. Even with the existing huge Democratic majority, said the President, Congress could not act:

> We should realize that some Democrats have voted with the Republicans for twenty-five years, really since 1938, and that makes it very difficult to secure enactment of any controversial legislation. You can water bills down and get them by, or you can have bills which have no particular controversy to them and get by. But important legislation, medical care for the aged, and these other bills, farm programs, they are controversial. They involve great interests, and they are much more difficult.

As remedies the President had urged that some Republican congressmen support his program and, almost in the same sentence, he had asked voters to return an even larger Democratic majority in the fall elections. That is, he felt (or so some Republicans would phrase it) that if Republicans would just help him make a good

[3] *Ibid.*, p. 22.

record, people would elect more Democrats in the fall, and the constitutional crisis would be past.

The Farm Bureau viewed the vote as a victory for constitutional government, rather than as a sign of a crisis. President Shuman said—

It was a much-needed victory for Constitutional government. The American people should know the extent to which the Executive Branch of the government sought to bully or buy votes with political pressure.

It's reassuring to know that a bipartisan majority of the House was able and willing to resist this shameful interference with the legislative process.[4]

The Future of the Bill

Would the administration try again to enact mandatory supply-management programs? President Kennedy's statement implied he would await a fall election mandate.

In the meantime—Chairman Cooley told reporters—the administration would likely allow the temporary wheat and feed grains program to expire.[5]

Chairman Ellender, soured by the vote, agreed it was better strategy to return to the "permanent" surplus-producing programs than to save producers again with a voluntary program. "Let them go ahead and fill up the bins," he told the press. "It will mean the whole farm program for crops will go down. People won't stand for these surpluses forever." [6]

The Farm Bureau also preferred to return to the permanent legislation which the organization had helped enact. The Farm Bureau's cropland-retirement program had no chance at all, though Farm Bureau leaders hoped it would nevertheless be reconsidered.

[4] *AFBF Newsletter*, June 25, 1962.
[5] *New York Times*, June 23, 1962, p. 1.
[6] *Ibid.*

Pressuring the President

Secretary Freeman was not ready to quit, however, despite his reputation as a man who knew when he was licked. "We plan to win," he told one reporter in the aftermath. He told another, "If you lose a battle, the war doesn't end." He immediately gathered his staff, exhausted from keyed-up campaigning and half paralyzed by defeat, to frame a compromise and rally congressional leaders and the President. Freeman, Murphy, Jaenke, Schnittker, Duncan, Birkhead, and Baker spent half an hour together immediately following the vote and then went to Chairman Cooley's office for an hour. Cooley favored going for a compromise, as did White House lobbyist Larry O'Brien who sat in. From 9:00 to 10:00 p.m. the group visited with Senator Ellender, who let off steam and then took a more conciliatory tone.

The exhausted Freeman then went home while the rest of the group worked until 2:00 a.m. rounding out a new legislative strategy, a compromise program, a presidential announcement, and arguments to be used the next morning when they went to lobby in the White House.

The group met with presidential assistant Sorensen between 9:00 and 10:00 the following morning and then spent a crucial hour with the President. As in his press release, the President gave the impression he was inclined to quit. The White House had done its best on the knotty farm problem. It had tried to make some sense of programs, and to get costs in line. It had already footed the bill for two years of costly temporary programs, during which everything possible had been done to get agreement in Congress on a practical, acceptable permanent program.

The President was exasperated by the evident tendency of farm constituencies to insist on more than they were capable of obtaining. He had won in 1960 without much support from the farming areas, and enactment of a mandatory program was unlikely in any case to make Midwestern farmers vote Democratic. The fact that farmers liked existing voluntary programs was one reason why

Congress had balked on the administration's permanent program. But the federal government could not afford the voluntary programs. Neither did the President want to try again for the mandatory programs only to fail again.

The USDA group had faced virtually the same arguments from Ellender the previous night. Freeman and Murphy, with help from presidential assistants Myer Feldman and Larry O'Brien, pointed out that the voluntary programs had saved money and that the alternative was to return to the old programs under which surpluses would quickly rebuild, farm income would go down, and government costs would spiral again. A responsible government could not permit that.

Besides, there was no need to assume that the mandatory programs were lost. O'Brien told the President that the actual margin of defeat was only two votes, since four "no" voters had stood ready to switch. The House could be relied upon to pass a bill containing an extension of the voluntary program and, since the Senate had already approved the administration bill, the House-Senate conference committee might then frame a compromise containing the mandatory wheat program which the House would probably approve. The mandatory feed-grains program—the principal target of opponents—could be sacrificed, if necessary, since the successful voluntary program had recently proved to be much less expensive than existing programs for cotton and wheat, if costs were figured as a percentage of the total value of production.

The President decided to try again. Freeman raced to a caucus of House Agriculture Committee Democrats, who liked the strategy of pushing a watered-down bill quickly through the House, and then seeking to shape a final version in the conference committee which would contain the vital provisions of the administration's program.

Subsequently, Committee Republicans sought to frustrate this strategy with a series of countermoves—first by delaying action until it was too late for the program to be implemented in 1963, then by seeking assurances from Chairman Cooley relative to anticipated conference action and then by threatening to defeat the conference bill if it was substantially different from that passed by the House.

The majority in turn found responses to these minority tactics. The interaction became somewhat intricate, though still visible to the outside observer. Several veteran participants later described the legislative battle of 1962—in particular the phase described below—as one of the most exhilarating and memorable episodes in their experience.

The House Committee Compromise Bill

Benefiting from the careful Republican survey which produced the earlier Senate commitee bill, House committee counsel John Heimburger and USDA commodity bill-drafter Claude Coffman quickly cut and pasted a rough draft of a bill designed to hurdle the House. This streamlined bill, lacking even the dramatic land-use section, was introduced on the evening of the day (Friday, June 22d) following the House defeat. On the next Monday, Committee executive sessions began.

Cooley had hoped that with immediate Commitee approval wheat farmers would be able to vote for a new program in late August. But Republicans were in no hurry. They insisted that the bill be read and discussed section by section. After a week of daily meetings the Committee voted to report a "clean" bill embodying the agreed-on text. This bill was introduced the week following. The July 4th holiday then intervened, after which the Committee majority was obliged to hold three more daily sessions before this new and now further-amended bill could finally be reported to the House on July 12th.

In the House committee sessions, supporters of the mandatory programs had revealed a new tactic: Congressman Ross Bass of Tennessee had proposed to extend the temporary feed-grains program for another year, but at the same time to abolish the existing (since 1958) "permanent" supports on feed grains. For 1964, then, the Secretary could threaten to end price supports if producers did not accept controls along with them. Given this alternative, Bass assumed, the mandatory controls would be accepted.

The Bass amendment passed, but amid such protests that it was replaced by a provision which would after 1963 let supports drop only to 50% of parity. Then the Farm Bureau's supporter, Congressman Findley, offered to substitute a Farm Bureau provision under which feed-grain prices would be allowed to fall 20% in 1964 the first year, and then edge further down in future years. In the view of leading Committee Democrats, this Farm Bureau provision would accomplish virtually the same thing as the Bass amendment. They viewed this as an opportunity to cash in on Farm Bureau opposition to permanent supports and so they supported this Findley amendment, as did most Republican members. The Committee had suddenly achieved an inverted harmony, which lasted through the House consideration of the bill.

However, Republicans extended their support only after they had seriously complicated the administration's plan to rewrite the bill in conference. The first concession House Republicans got was at the expense of the Senate, which was thereby obliged to pass the farm bill a second time. Senator Ellender had thoughtfully gotten his Senate-passed bill referred to the House the day following the House bill defeat, as a means of facilitating the Democratic shell game. Under normal procedure, the House committee would have substituted its own compromise voluntary bill under the Senate number (S.3225), and following its passage in the House, the final version of the bill would have been written in conference. Opponents of mandatory programs insisted that the Senate bill be tabled and allowed to die in the House committee as evidence that Cooley and Poage did not intend to introduce mandatory programs in conference. Committee Democrats perforce agreed to do this.

Ellender was furious at the action. "That's the end of it," he told the press, implying no farm bill would pass in 1962.

He resented being asked to compensate for failures of House leaders, who apparently expected him to carry the mandatory programs through the Senate again so that there could still be some conference committee chicanery. In effect they were asking him to pass the bill three times in the Senate, in the hope that they could finally get one favorable vote in the House.

Yet, there were good reasons for Ellender to get on with the job. He wanted the mandatory programs badly, and he felt next year might be too late. If Freeman's all-out effort failed in 1962, the administration would likely change its course thereafter. For another thing, Kennedy and Freeman pointed out to Ellender that if part of the mandatory program should become law under the circumstances, the credit for it would largely be Ellender's.

Ellender protested so violently that the administration at first tried to resurrect the Senate bill in the House by getting an extraordinary rule which would enable the House to reinstate the Senate number after it had passed the House bill. When such a rule was proposed at a hurriedly arranged meeting of the Rules committee—the day after the House bill had been reported—the gentle atmosphere which characterizes most Rules committee meetings vanished. Congressman Hoeven charged that the unusual rule was part of a plot engineered by Freeman and Ellender to foist the mandatory programs on the House, via the conference. "We will not be trapped," he said, and turned on Congressman Cooley, who admitted lamely that such a rule would violate the House committee's agreement relative to the Senate bill and the mandatory programs. Cooley did not know how the rule came to be proposed, nor did any nearby Democrat. Ultimately House parliamentarian Lewis Deschler took the blame, explaining that he had drafted two rules, and had sent the wrong one to the Rules committee. So the Rules committee forthwith acted on the right one, which in effect made it necessary for the Senate to take the House bill and act on it before a conference could be held.[7]

Freeman's Press Conference

The Rules committee action as well as the harmonious Agriculture committee vote seemed to show that Midwestern and Plains Republicans were in command of events in the House. The Commit-

[7] *New York Times*, July 14, 1962, p. 8.

Illustration 23. Two Farm-State Views of the CED. Conrad in the *Denver Post* ("He Doesn't Know the Territory") and Barrow in the *Omaha World-Herald* ("Know How to Get Off that Limb?")

tee's bill which was to be debated the following Thursday embodied virtually the same commodity programs which had been offered in an amendment by Republican Hoeven in the first House debate.

Perhaps to make it clear that the administration was not ready to

'KNOW HOW TO GET OFF THAT LIMB? JUST LET GO!'

let House Republicans take credit for passing the voluntary programs which they had opposed a year ago, Freeman attacked their motives at a press conference called the day before House debate was to begin. According to *Washington Post* writer Julius Duscha, Freeman angrily denounced the Republican members of Congress for "playing the narrowest, most partisan, most bitter kind of politics of agriculture."

His face turning white, his hands shaking, the Secretary told a crowded news conference that Republican opposition to his farm program constituted "the biggest piece of nonsense and contradictions that the mind of man ever conjured up. . . ." Freeman said he was "not trying to create a political or campaign issue situation," but that he was prepared to "go to city folks just as much as I would go to the farm people" with his farm program during the fall congressional elections.[8]

By declining to comment on the House bill, Freeman seemed to make it clear that only the mandatory programs would satisfy him.

Freeman had called the news conference specifically to state his views on another farm program just proposed by the Committee for Economic Development, a respected, business-oriented research group. The CED farm program had been written by a group of leading economists, headed by Professor Theodore Schultz. Building on Schultz's well-known "homesteads in reverse" plan to have the Federal government help surplus farmers move to the city, the report chose to emphasize that "agriculture's chief need is a reduction of the number of people in agriculture."[9]

As the Farm Bureau had done, the report recommended a five-year transition away from the existing protectionist programs, and would have used the cropland-retirement plan, but also compensatory payments, to take the place of price supports as a means to keep farm income up. During the five-year period it would encourage about one-third of all farmers to move to the cities, by means of farmer education and retraining programs, and by creating new urban jobs.

The report provided an easy target and supporters of mandatory programs made the most of it. (See Illustration 23.) It was brief, logical, and readable, as its writers no doubt hoped it would be, but in places it seemed almost calculated to make farmers and their spokesmen bristle. Besides, the group which took authorship of the report was dominated by bankers and big business. In footnote

[8] *Congressional Record* (bound volume), July 19, 1962, p. 14150.

[9] *An Adaptive Program for Agriculture*, Committee for Economic Development (New York, 1962), p. 29.

comments sprinkled through the text, some of this group frankly informed readers of their laissez faire, antigovernment participation, antiagrarian views.

In August Freeman happily referred to the CED report again and again as the "real alternative" to his mandatory programs. In the same spirit House committee Democrats called a special "CED" hearing to make the point that farmers must either work with their friends in programs to control production and thus to preserve the family farm, or let their traditional enemies force them to the cities, where these industrialists would use them to break the wage scale. The message reached members of the National Farmers Organization who burned piles of Sears catalogues in protest against that company's involvement in CED and got their Ford dealers to write the home office until both companies disclaimed any responsibility for the report.

Political Understanding

The CED report was cited often in the House debate by supporters of the administration's program. To force a choice between the Freeman and the CED plans, liberal Representative James Roosevelt from downtown Los Angeles tried to get amendments (akin to the earlier-mentioned Bass amendment) which would bring all commodity programs to a halt in 1963. Roosevelt's amendments failed, but the feeling against surplus-inducing programs erupted on an amendment by Representative Ralph Harding (D., Idaho) to end all supports on feed grains, which carried 101–62 in a division (standing) vote. Startled Republican and Democratic Committee leaders, who had agreed to brush aside all amendments to their compromise bill, immediately called for a teller vote on which they could watch members walk down the aisle and be counted, and so managed to defeat the Harding amendment. The bill itself passed the House by a wide margin.

Just what understanding had been reached between Committee Republicans and Democrats? Two agreements had already been carried out: the tabling of the Senate bill and the decision to bring voluntary programs to the House floor, which meant the Senate would have to repass the mandatory programs before they could even be considered in conference.

With respect to conference committee action Congressman Hoeven told the House:

I have every reason to believe that the conferees on the part of the House will sustain the position of the House if and when this bill is passed.

The conference committee would of course have a majority of Democrats—4 to 3 in the House and 3 to 2 from the Senate. Assuming Senator Ellender passed his mandatory programs and selected Senate Democrats who would support them in conference, the key voters would be the House Democratic conference committeemen. Chairman Cooley would name these. Cooley assured the House they would not be faced again with a mandatory feed-grains program. This was all that many of them needed to know, since the mandatory wheat program was much less controversial.[10] As to what they would do on wheat, Cooley stated only a general guideline: "We shall do the best we can to sustain the bill as it goes out of this House." [11]

Those unsatisfied by Cooley's assurance could hope that Senator Ellender and other Senate Agriculture committee members would continue to sulk in their tents because of the tabling of the Senate bill. But after the House passed its bill Ellender consented to take it. He still insisted that he would simply reimpose the mandatory programs (in which event the House might not even be willing to go to conference). Ellender further intimated that even if a conference did take place, he would not compromise on his mandatory program. So, the two Houses still appeared deadlocked.

Senate Reconsiderations

On Friday, the day after the House vote, the House bill got its first reading in the Senate, and a routine objection by Agriculture Re-

[10] *Congressional Record* (daily edition), July 19, 1962, p. 13187.
[11] *Ibid.*, p. 13217.

publicans made it lie over until Monday. On Monday, Ellender decided to bring up the bill for immediate debate and amendment, but Republicans insisted that it should first go to his committee. Ellender agreed, but with the stipulation that the bill must be reported out of his committee within seven days. Allowing for three additional days before debate, Ellender estimated that the bill would be back before the Senate by August 3rd, still in time to be implemented before the 1962 wheat referendum, which had been twice postponed and which now finally had to be held on August 30.

In the Senate committee, however, Ellender again failed to get approval of the mandatory programs. Instead, the Committee supported a Cooper amendment to substitute the bill originally reported from the Senate committee, similar to the House-passed voluntary bill though it included Freeman's new land-use schemes. Cooper then proposed to add the wheat-certificate program to go in effect after one more year under the voluntary program, and the administration Democrats supported this amendment.

The bill was in the Senate committee only two days, but was sidetracked for three weeks, nevertheless, by a six-day prolonged discussion designed to prevent a vote on a bill to permit private corporations to develop the communications-satellite system, and following that, by the threat of a retaliatory filibuster by several Republicans, and finally by another liberal talkathon.

Indeed, Republicans considered undertaking a filibuster after the farm bill finally came to the floor. But since the House of Representatives had planned to take a long weekend anyway (August 23–27), the bill could not possibly be enacted until after the wheat referendum of 1962 which, Republicans hoped, would show that wheat farmers were tired of controls.

Meanwhile the deadline for announcing the wheat program had arrived, so Secretary Freeman had been obliged to offer farmers the existing permanent program, hopeful that Congress would later give him voluntary tools to discourage overproduction in the coming year.

On August 20th, the Senate spent a first dilatory day on the farm bill. Meanwhile Chairman Ellender had been dissuaded from introducing his mandatory feed-grains amendment by the argument that, should the Senate and the conference committee accept the amendment, the conference bill would not pass the House. Instead, shortly after noon on the second day of debate, Ellender introduced the Bass amendment to repeal permanent feed-grain price supports, in an effort to force the hard choice in Congress in the next legislative year. Wayne Darrow's *Farmletter* referred to Ellender's action as a "scissors play" in which Freeman would push for the mandatory feed-grains program in 1963, while Ellender used the threat of 0–90 supports if Freeman's programs were not passed.[12] Senate Republicans charged he was "putting a shot-gun to the head of the farmer" (House Republicans had called it a blackjack).

Senator Cooper: A Timely Entrance

But at the moment Ellender introduced his amendment, many Republicans were attending their weekly Republican Policy Committee luncheon where they were planning strategy on the farm bill. Among the few Senators on the floor was Senator Aiken, the Republican watchdog for this bill, who was supposed to alert other Republicans of any surprise moves. But New Englander Aiken failed to shout the alarm.

Neither did many respond to Senator Ellender's perfunctory prevote quorum call. The call was rescinded to prevent having to adjourn the Senate when, as often happens, fewer than a quorum responded to the call. The presiding officer then asked for a voice vote on Ellender's amendment, and it carried.

After another amendment—by Senator Hart (D., Mich.) in behalf of cherry producers—also passed, Senator Cooper happened to wander onto the floor while still on his way, roundabout, to the Republican luncheon. When he quickly learned that Republicans had unknowingly lost a major battle that they were just now planning to fight, he rose to try to stall further proceedings until more

[12] *Washington Farmletter*, September 1, 1962.

Republicans could be summoned to deal with the crisis. Unprepared to speak, Cooper repeated a few observations again and again, and asked Senator Ellender questions several times over.

After votes on controversial amendments such as Ellender's, the sponsor and a cohort usually foreclose the possibility of reconsideration, by means of a little ritual in which one moves to reconsider the vote, and the other moves to table that motion, and the latter action is taken by a perfunctory voice vote.

Ellender had neglected to do this after his amendment had passed, but Cooper's presence spurred Senator Humphrey to correct the omission.

What followed was illustrative of the courtesies senators will extend to respected colleagues. When Humphrey made his motion to reconsider, and Ellender moved to lay it on the table, Cooper interjected, "Mr. President—," but was told that the tabling motion was not debatable. Yet in deference to Cooper, Ellender quickly withdrew the tabling motion, which would easily have carried. Humphrey then withdrew his motion to reconsider. Cooper was then able to discuss the amendment further, and explained he would like to reconsider it. To do so in this case required unanimous consent, but neither Humphrey nor Ellender objected. Once Cooper made the motion to reconsider, Humphrey moved to lay that motion on the table. Cooper asked for a quorum call, and this time senators came. Then Cooper asked Humphrey if he would withdraw his tabling motion so that there might be full discussion of the Ellender amendment before the vote. Humphrey withdrew it, thereby opening the floor for a Republican onslaught on the amendment. It still passed by a comfortable margin.

Though he failed to stop Ellender's amendment to repeal the permanent feed-grains supports, Cooper did secure an important amendment which guaranteed a price-support floor for wheat at 50% of parity in the event that wheat producers should reject the wheat-certificate program. Also passed was an amendment by Senator Fulbright which extended to "fish farmers" (who raise fish in shallow farm ponds) some benefits available to other farmers, and a Proxmire amendment to make government surplus feed stocks available to dairymen when radioactive fallout barred their pastures from use.

The Senate passed the amended House bill, 47–37, and President Kennedy hailed the action as "an opportunity to bring some sense and reason and control into an area which has been marked by excesses and chaos in recent years." All knew, however, that the bill had yet to be fully written. Though the mandatory feed-grains program was dead, the crucial decisions on most other controversial provisions would be made in the House-Senate conference committee.

A Rules Committee Detour

The bill did not go immediately to conference because a further obstacle developed when the House came back to work on August 27th. Republican Congressman Avery (R., Kans.) objected to a request (requiring unanimous consent) that the House name its conferees. His objection obliged the Rules committee to meet and propose a resolution which the House could then approve by majority vote. By this device—used only once or so each session—Republicans managed to delay the conference for three more days and to criticize the bill on the floor once again when the Rules committee resolution came up for an hour's debate. The farm bill's travails, for which the Republicans were mainly responsible, had already given them far more than ordinary opportunities to make political capital of a major issue, and they were observably gratified and self-congratulatory when a Gallup poll in early September showed that many farmers had lost confidence in the Kennedy administration.

In debate on the resolution, House Republicans pressed Cooley for a firmer stand in favor of the bill as passed by the House. Cooley insisted on remaining flexible.

On August 30th, the House approved the resolution permitting the bill to be sent to conference. As members of the committee Cooley named himself and Poage, skipped the lukewarm Grant in favor of the fourth man in seniority—Congressman Gathings (D., Ark.). And for the fourth Democratic member he jumped far down the seniority row to pick Floyd Breeding of Kansas, chairman of the subcommittee which had handled the wheat-certificate bill. Breeding favored the Senate's wheat-certificate provision, and would know most about it. For Republican conferees Hoeven chose himself, third man Page Belcher from a Northwest Oklahoma wheat district, and then dropped down to take Albert Quie, who was only fifth in seniority but articulate, forceful, and a spokesman for the more moderate Republican committee members.

In contrast, the five senior members of the Senate committee all asserted their prerogative to be on the conference committee, even though the two senior Democrats after Ellender—Johnston of South Carolina and Holland of Florida—had not taken as active a role in forming the legislation as had some lower ranked Committee Democrats. On the Republican side the two conferees were Aiken and Young.

Lessons of the 1962 Wheat Referendum

The conference committee held its first meeting on August 31st, the day after the wheat referendum in which the extended semi-voluntary wheat program barely passed. Perhaps because of Farm Bureau opposition in some states the percentage voting "yes" was 10% smaller than in the previous year. This omen was not lost on Senator Young of North Dakota, who had supported the wheat-certificate plan in each Senate vote, and now decided to oppose it, simply because he felt farmers would not approve it in 1963.

The slim wheat-referendum victory was viewed also as an indication that feed-grains producers would not accept mandatory controls. The administration was therefore urged by many of its friends to allow Freeman and the Democratic conferees to take steps toward a permanent feed-grains program with voluntary features.

During the summer, the voluntary route for feed grains had begun to look less costly and more workable, as new markets abroad had dwindled the surpluses despite increased production per acre. So the administration did open this avenue to new feed-grains solutions, and on this matter permitted even a Republican conferee to have a hand.

Meetings of the conference committee were held in an Appropriations subcommittee meeting room about half-way between the House and Senate Chambers, in the Capitol Building. The committee considered the competing versions of the program section-by-section, although they often backtracked to reconsider earlier decisions.

The first day the group agreed to retain the recreational and other land-use provisions which had carried through in the Senate bill, and to include some of the new authority asked by the administration for use in food-assistance programs.

After the Labor Day holiday week, the conference committee met again September 10th, 11th, and 12th, and then waited until September 14th for its final session, to permit Senator Ellender to wind up some business in his role as chairman of the Appropriations Subcommittee for Public Works.

Of the commodity programs, wheat was first to be considered. Two matters were involved—whether to retain the Senate-passed wheat-certificate program for 1964, and what to do to induce wheat farmers to further reduce their acreage for the current year, some of which had already been planted.

The certificate program was the critical one because it would be "permanent" legislation, and also because the administration's prestige was riding on it. If this program passed, Freeman could claim to have gotten an important part of the supply-management program he had asked Congress for. Since the conference committee's decision would presumably be the final one, interested groups buzzed around the conferees.

Pressures on the Conference

Farm Bureau representatives singled out conferees for earnest one-hour sessions before each meeting, and representatives of the

Wheat Growers tried again, unsuccessfully, to get adoption of a single wheat certificate with no set value.

The most interested party was the administration, which managed to control the conference decisions. Since bargaining was to be done between the two delegations after the group from each house had voted separately, opposition to the administration should have come from the House of Representative, which had once rejected the administration's bill. But this group was dominated by Congressman Cooley and his three selected Democratic colleagues, who had met secretly before the conference to decide they would insist on the mandatory wheat-certificate program. Congressman Breeding had gotten noticeably cold feet after viewing the referendum returns, but the USDA's persuasive Schnittker-Jaenke team was on hand—often in the committee sessions—to dispel doubts as to the technical and political soundness of the certificate program and, as they had done all along the way, to suggest small concessions in order to ward off big ones.

To hold down wheat acreage under the old program in the coming year, Schnittker and Jaenke introduced a scheme for compensatory payments— a direct government subsidy of 18 cents per bushel on top of the supported market price, to be given to those wheat farmers willing to cut back their acreage by an additional 10% below their regular allotment. This price subsidy, along with a payment to farmers of 50% of the average income from each diverted acre, seemed enough stimulus to keep the wheat surplus from building further in 1963.

However, these combined payments were more expensive and at the same time less effective in reducing surpluses than would have been a single large payment for each diverted acre, since the 18-cent compensatory payment would have to be made to the farmer based on the "normal" yield of all the acreage he was allowed to plant. Furthermore, many farmers did not like the compensatory (direct) payments. Freeman's feed-grains advisory committee had in fact rejected compensatory payments the previous December.

Also, the history of compensatory payments had made them controversial. In 1949 the Congress had voted down the Brannan Plan based in part on compensatory payments (called production payments) after a vicious battle between Truman, Secretary of Agriculture Charles Brannan, and the Farm Bureau's Allan Kline. There were many men on both sides who still honored the memory of this fight and viewed any proposal for direct payments on basic commodities as an invitation to resume the feud. Had compensatory payments been introduced earlier than 1962, they might well have been beaten down under a barrage of epithets from Republicans, the Farm Bureau, and from rural congressmen in general. Proponents of direct payments had assumed this, and had waited patiently in hopes they could slip them in at the tail end of the legislative process.

Why did the administration want them? Aside from the fact that they simplified the administration of voluntary programs, the administration may simply have wanted to set a strong contemporary precedent for the use of compensatory payments as a basis for a future cotton program. Cotton was in trouble due to an export subsidy which actually priced U.S. cotton much lower to foreign textile concerns than to domestic concerns. Many Southerners wanted to replace this export subsidy with a direct payment to domestic cotton producers and processors.

Other pressures in favor of putting compensatory payments in the 1963 feed-grains program came from the grain trade, which saw them as a means to keep government from interfering with the market price of feed grains. With its huge market sales both of grain taken in, and of some of its own surplus grain, the USDA's Commodity Credit Corporation had been controlling the market (some said the USDA was manipulating it). But if the USDA were to use a direct payment as an incentive for farmer participation instead of the artificially high price support, then it would not have to market any feed grain—once government surpluses had been removed—and the market could go its merry way.

Roy Hendrickson of the National Federation of Grain Cooperatives had argued this to Secretary Freeman as they flew together into a Midwestern snowstorm during the previous winter, but Freeman's mind at that time was on the mandatory programs. During the summer, representatives of Cargill Corporation, a private company dealing in feed grain and hybrid seed corn, had corresponded with the USDA where interest in the device picked up as hopes for the mandatory feed-grains program died.

A Cargill representative talked also to Republican Al Quie, who was ultimately the only spokesman on the conference committee for the younger, less dogmatic rural congressmen. Quie liked the idea despite its controversial past, and when it came time in conference to write a corn program for 1963, Quie suggested that the compensatory payment of 18 cents per bushel granted to wheat compliers should also be granted to corn compliers instead of larger per-acre diversion payments. Administration Democrats happily seconded his suggestion, and the deed was done.

The Farm Bureau roared angrily (and so did the Budget Bureau), so the decision was reconsidered on the last day of the conference. But Quie was insistent, and compensatory payments were kept for both temporary programs. Later in the year, Quie doubted the wisdom of compensatory payments, and the administration also had second thoughts. But it is accepted practice in Congress to write laws in the helter-skelter atmosphere of the conference committee, and often later to regret it.

Congressman Poage made an even bolder effort to bring in legislation through the backdoor of the conference committee. Though Poage still wanted a mandatory feed-grains program, he was barred by the earlier agreement with House Republicans from accepting one, even if the Senate had brought one in for bargaining. So Poage proposed in conference that feed-grains producers be required to accept acreage controls as a condition for getting subsidies under the 1963 program.

Technically, Poage was not asking for a mandatory program, since those who did not want subsidies or price supports were free to plant as much as they wished. But since the lower market price on corn would in effect serve as a penalty on noncompliers, the line between mandatory and voluntary had become very thin. The House Republican conferees felt they had been sold down the river, but they were saved by the House and Senate parliamentarians, who ruled that there was nothing in either bill which would suggest acreage controls for feed grains. So Poage's provision was ruled nongermane.

Senator Ellender's effort to repeal permanent feed-grains price supports ended in a compromise which allowed supports to drop to 50% of parity (the existing minimum was 65%) in the absence of a new program.

All of the minority conferees voted against the final conference bill and report. Congressman Hoeven had learned of the secret preconference meeting of House Democratic conferees and therefore had announced at the beginning that he would oppose the conference bill on the House floor. Other Republican conferees had begun as vigorous participants, and then had fallen silent as argument proved futile.

Quie participated effectively throughout, and Young of North Dakota gained some concessions on wheat. He subsequently advised his farmer constituents to vote in favor of the certificate program.

When the conference bill emerged on September 17th, Iowa's Senator Hickenlooper called it "one of the most ominous and dangerous measures for the over-all, long-range good of agriculture and a sound agricultural program that I have ever seen proposed." [13] It was also hit hard by a former Democratic Secretary of Agriculture, Senator Clinton Anderson of New Mexico. He said the bill was "probably the worst I have seen in my long experience." [14] Anderson had long favored moving to end price supports, controls, and government subsidies.

[13] *AFBF Newsletter*, October 1, 1962.
[14] *Ibid.*

The House Vote

The administration had decided to call the conference bill a major victory—if they could get the House to approve it. However, Freeman threatened a presidential veto if the House "bob-tailed" the bill by refusing to pass it intact. Votes on the conference bill could not but be anticlimactic. By this time all participants were tired. Nevertheless Farm Bureau lobbyists and Republican House leaders again went through all the effective motions of lining up and holding votes, while the administration forces put on virtually the same extensive campaign as in the first House decision which they had lost by ten votes.

The administration had reason for greater confidence this time. some Democrats from the Southwest had obliged their cattlemen by helping to defeat the mandatory feed-grains program. Two or more additional Midwestern Democrats would now switch over to favor the bill, though Democratic Congressman Mack of Illinois—whose initial support for the bill had proved a serious political mistake—would have to vote against it, and to ask an Illinois Democratic colleague to keep him company in the "no" column.

A scattering of other Democrats had been lost, for one personal reason or another, but these were compensated for by the Virginians who were now ready to vote for the bill.

The administration expected the vote to be close, though most observers predicted the bill would carry.

But when the roll was called, it did not! It lost this time by fourteen votes. Hurriedly, majority whip Hale Boggs (D., La.) began to roam the floor, buttonholing Democratic "no" voters, telling them, "Come on, you can vote for this. Go up and change your vote." While supporters of the bill gained time by asking the clerk repeatedly how their votes were recorded, a few new "yes" voters were hustled from their congressional offices.

Republicans managed to change one vote from "yes" to "no," but Boggs's last-minute effort carried the day. When the clerk was finally permitted to announce the tally, the bill had carried by five votes—202–197.

The Bill Becomes Law

Results in the Senate were never really in doubt. The final vote there, after a five-hour debate on September 27th, was 52–41 for the conference bill. (See Illustration 24.)

The President immediately signed the bill and read a prepared statement in which he expressed confidence that the new law would "sustain prosperity, reduce burdens of surplus, and maintain stable food prices." [15]

Standing among the tired but happy group which observed the signing was Secretary Freeman, who was given one of the pens used by the President. "This is one pen I really want," he said.[16] Freeman called the new law "an historic step."

As usual, reaction varied. Republicans denounced the wheat program as "regimentation or ruin," and in the forthcoming congressional election they did not let Midwestern voters forget that Republicans had saved feed-grains producers from a similar fate. The *Chicago Tribune* said the bill was another step toward making farmers dependent upon government instead of on the market. The *Des Moines Register* viewed the bill as a stopgap. The *St. Louis Post-Dispatch* liked the bill because it introduced the principle that supports should be accompanied by controls, though this newspaper regretted that the administration did not get its mandatory feed-grains program.

Just how much did the Administration fail to get? Below is an item-by-item summary of the differences between what the ABCD plan proposed, and what the Congress was finally disposed to grant:

1. *Recreational and land-use provisions:* Secretary Freeman got authority to contract with farmers to turn cropland into grassland or forest, or into such recreational uses as picnic and camping grounds, game reserves and fishing ponds, lakes for swimming and boating, restaurants, motels, swimming pools, hunting lodges and summer or winter resorts. For these purposes, the Secretary could make land-diversion payments to farmers, and provide some ma-

[15] *Wall Street Journal*, Sept. 28, 1962.

[16] *New York Times*, Sept. 28, 1962, p. 13.

terials for them. The Farmers Home Administration could loan money to build these recreational facilities. On the other hand, the Rural Electrification Administration which had asked for a new system to account for loans, got only a slap on the hand for some of its past activities.

The Secretary was not given power to take farm lands by eminent domain for use in recreational development. However, in cooperation with local governments, he could pay half the cost for building local public reservoirs for providing fish, wildlife, and recreational facilities in connection with them, though Congress decided to confine him to a few pilot projects in the first year. He could make loans to local and state agencies to shift land out of crops to other types of recreation and needed uses.

2. *Foreign food assistance.* There were provisions to finance more food-surplus sales with long-term dollar loans. The Secretary was given specific power, too, to set up nonprofit school-lunch programs abroad. The USDA was not authorized to distribute food through UN agencies or through multilateral arrangements, but USDA officials decided they already possessed this power anyway.

3. *The commodity programs.* Representative Johnson's "milk-toast" dairy provision was knocked out in the conference. Under the voluntary corn program to run for only a year, those who wished to go into the program got price supports at 65% of parity, to which was added an 18-cent compensatory payment. In return, a producer had to reduce his previous feed-grains production by 20%, to be paid an additional 50% of normal production on these diverted acres.

All government payments to the feed-grains producers could be made in kind, which meant in effect that the program could be

Illustration 24. THE HISTORY OF THE BILL. The next seven pages show records related to the history of Public Law 87–703, "Food and Agriculture Act of 1962." The first four pages are excerpts from the House of Representatives Legislative Calendar, Final Edition, 1962; these trace the history of the bill through the technical processes from introduction to passage and the President's signature. Some bills end short of passage: in defeat, or in other kinds of failure.

Docket No.	Date and by Whom Presented to the House	No. of Bill	Title	Report Requested	Action
444	Mr. Cooley Jan. 31, 1962.	H.R. 10010	To improve and protect farm income, to reduce costs of farm programs to the Federal Government, to reduce the Federal Government's excessive stocks of agricultural commodities, to maintain reasonable and stable prices of agricultural commodities and products to consumers, to provide adequate supplies of agricultural commodities for domestic and foreign needs, to conserve natural resources, and for other purposes. (Food and Agricultural Act of 1962.) (Title I: Land-Use Adjustment.) (Title II: Agricultural Trade Development.) (Title III: Marketing Orders.) (Title IV: A. Feed Grains. B. Wheat. C. Dairy.) (Title V: General—Amendments to FHA and REA Acts). HEARINGS: Serial AA, Pt. 1—Feb. 7, 1962.	----------	Executive communication 1639. Senate companion S. 2786. Hearings, full committee, open, Feb. 7, 19, 20, 21, 22, 27, 28, Mar. 1, 6, 7, 8, 9, and 15, 1962. Livestock and Feed Grains Subcommittee, executive on title IV(A), Mar. 20, 23; voted to report, amended to full committee, Mar. 23, 1962. Wheat Subcommittee, executive on title IV(B), Mar. 20, 21, 22, 26; voted to report, amended, to full committee, Mar. 26, 1962. Dairy and Poultry Subcommittee, executive on titles III and IV(C), Mar. 26, 30, Apr. 2; voted to report title III, amended, and title IV(C), amended, to full committee, Apr. 2, 1962. Foreign Agricultural Operations Subcommittee, executive, on title II, voted to report, amended, to full committee, Mar. 27, 1962. Conservation and Credit Sub-

			Serial AA, Pt. 2—Feb. 19, 20, 21, 22, 27, and 28; Mar. 1, 6, 7, 8, 9, and 15, 1962.		committee, executive on titles I and V, voted to report title I, amended, to full committee, Mar. 28, 1962. Executive, voted to report title V, amended, to full committee, Mar. 29, 1962. Full committee, executive, Apr. 3, 4, 5, 6, 9, 10, 11, 1962; approved title IV(B), amended, Apr. 5, 1962. Approved title IV(A), amended, Apr. 6, 1962. Approved titles I, II, and V, amended, Apr. 9, 1962. Approved title IV(C), amended, Apr. 11, 1962. Superseded by H.R. 11222, 12266, 12391. (Public Law 87–703.)
504	Mr. Cooley Apr. 11, 1962.	H.R. 11222	To improve and protect farm income, to reduce costs of farm programs to the Federal Government, to reduce the Federal Government's excessive stocks of agricultural commodities, to maintain reasonable and stable prices of agricultural commodities and products to consumers, to provide adequate supplies of agricultural commodities for domestic and foreign needs, to conserve natural resources, and for other purposes. ("Food and Agriculture Act of 1962.")	----------	Senate companion S. 3225. Supersedes H.R. 10010. (See hearings, SERIAL AA on H.R. 10010). Hearings, full committee, executive, Apr. 12 and 13; May 2, 7, 10, 1962; ordered reported, amended, to House, May 10, 1962. Reported to House, amended, May 16, 1962. H. Rept. 1691. Hearing, Rules Committee, June 5 and 6, 1962. Granted 6-hour open rule, June 6, 1962. H. Res. 678, H. Rept. 1786. Debate began June 19, 1962.

					Debate concluded, recommitted to committee by vote of 215 to 205, June 21, 1962. Superseded by H.R. 12266, 12391. (Public Law 87–703.)
554	Mr. Cooley June 22, 1962.	H.R. 12266	To improve and protect farm income, to reduce costs of farm programs to the Federal Government, to reduce the Federal Government's excessive stocks of agricultural commodities, to maintain reasonable and stable prices of agricultural commodities and products to consumers, to provide adequate supplies of agricultural commodities for domestic and foreign needs, to conserve natural resources, and for other purposes. (Food and Agriculture Act of 1962).		Senate companion, S. 3225. Supersedes H.R. 11222. (See hearings, **Serial AA** on H.R. 10010). Hearings, full committee, executive, June 25, 26, 27, 28, 1962. Executive voted to report, amended, to House (clean bill to be introduced), June 29, 1962. **Superseded by H.R. 12391.** (Public Law 87–703.)
565	Mr. Cooley July 2, 1962.	H.R. 12391	To improve and protect farm income, to reduce costs of farm programs to the Federal Government, to reduce the Federal Government's excessive stocks of agricultural commodities, to maintain reasonable and stable prices of agricultural commodities and products to consumers, to provide adequate supplies of agricultural commodities for domestic and foreign needs, to conserve natural resources, and for other purposes. (Food and Agriculture Act of 1962.)		Senate companion S. 3225. Supersedes H.R. 12266. (See hearings, **Serial AA**, on H.R. 10010.) Hearings, full committee, executive, July 10, 11, 12, 1962. Voted to report, amended, to House, July 12, 1962. Reported to House, amended, July 12, 1962. H. Rept. 1976. Hearing, Rules Committee, granted 2 hour, open rule, H. Res. 727, H. Rept. 1997. July 13, 1962. Passed House with committee amendments, by rollcall vote

			Title I: Land Use Adjustment. (a) Permanently extends and amends ACP program. (b) Amends Bankhead-Jones Farm Tenant Act. (c) Amends Watershed Protection and Flood Prevention Act (Public Law 566). Title II: Amendments to Public Law 480. (a) Amends long-term dollar sales program. Title III: Commodity Programs. (a) Amends and extends 1962 emergency feed grain program for 1 year. (b) Amends and extends 1962 emergency wheat program for 1 year. (c) Establishes a temporary dairy program expiring June 20, 1962. Title IV: FHA Amendments. (a) Expands loan activities to include recreational facilities.		(229–163) July 19, 1962. Referred to Senate Agriculture and Forestry Committee, July 23, 1962. Reported to Senate, amended, July 25, 1962. S. Rept. 1787. Debated in Senate, Aug. 20, 21, 22, 1962. Passed Senate by rollcall vote (47–37), amended, Aug. 22, 1962. Senate conferees appointed: Messrs. Ellender, Johnston, Holland, Aiken, and Young of North Dakota, Aug. 22, 1962. Objection raised in House to sending bill to conference, Aug. 27, 1962. Hearing, Rules Committee, granted 1-hour rule to send to conference H. Res. 772, H. Rept. 2283, Aug. 28, 1962. House adopted H. Res. 722 by voice vote and conferees appointed: Messrs. Cooley, Poage, Gathings, Breeding, Hoeven, Belcher, and Quie, Aug. 30, 1962. Conferees met Aug. 31, Sept. 10, 11, 12, 1962. Conferees met and agreed, Sept. 17, 1962. Conference report filed Sept. 17, 1962. H. Rept. 2385. House adopted conference report by rollcall vote (202–197) Sept. 20, 1962. Senate adopted conference report by rollcall vote (52–41) Sept. 25, 1962. Signed by the President, Sept. 27, 1962. Public Law 87–703.

COMMITTEE ON
AGRICULTURE AND FORESTRY
UNITED STATES SENATE

LEGISLATIVE CALENDAR

EIGHTY-SEVENTH CONGRESS

FINAL EDITION

DECEMBER 14, 1962

[No. 15]

85016 U.S. GOVERNMENT PRINTING OFFICE: 1962

Illustration 24. The cover of the Senate Legislative Calendar, and a page from the alphabetical listing. Note the numerous bills under the name of Senator Ellender.

	No. of Bill		Docket No.
E			
EASTLAND, MR.:			
Cotton acreage allotments	S.	1865	87
Enriched rice	S.	3152	151
Forest survey	S.	3064	148
Forestry programs	S. S.	2563 2638	120 123
Forestry research	S. S.	2403 3609	107 169
Hog cholera eradication	S.	1908	91
Refinancing, and disaster loans	S.	1243	66
ELLENDER, MR.:			
Administration of Department of Agriculture	S.	3430	163
Agricultural Act of 1961	S.	1643	82
Banks for cooperatives	S.	2788	130
Charges for inspection services	S.	665	31
Commodity Credit Corporation appropriation	S.	763	37
Commodity exchange regulation	S.	1980	95
Consolidated Farmers Home Administration Act of 1961	S.	764	38
Cooperative agricultural extension work	S.	2998	141
Crop insurance premiums	S.	762	36
Dairy price supports	S.	3655	170
Enriched rice	S.	3152	151
Extension of Public Law 480	S. S.	586 1027	26 52
Federal Land Bank loans	S.	1927	92
Feed grain program for 1961	S.	993	51
Food and Agriculture Act of 1962	S.	2786	129
Forest Service	S.	3235	153
Guam agricultural services	S.	2121	101
Honeybees, importation of	S.	2158	102
Import agreements	S.	3006	143
International wheat agreement	S.	3574	167
Livestock and poultry shipments	S.	3120	149
Meat inspection	S.	3513	166
Nematocide regulation	S.	1028	53
Road rights-of-way	S.	1151	61
Soil bank contract violations	S.	3446	164
State extension services	S.	2493	115
State participation in disaster programs	S.	761	35
Superior National Forest	S.	302	16
Watershed projects	S.	3402	162
Wheat acreage allotments	S.	3756	173
Wheat referendum	S.J.Res.	210	A-8

Public Law 87-703
87th Congress, H. R. 12391
September 27, 1962

An Act

To improve and protect farm income, to reduce costs of farm programs to the Federal Government, to reduce the Federal Government's excessive stocks of agricultural commodities, to maintain reasonable and stable prices of agricultural commodities and products to consumers, to provide adequate supplies of agricultural commodities for domestic and foreign needs, to conserve natural resources, and for other purposes.

Be it enacted by the Senate and House of Representatives of the United States of America in Congress assembled, That this Act may be cited as the "Food and Agriculture Act of 1962".

Food and Agriculture Act of 1962.

TITLE I—LAND-USE ADJUSTMENT

Sec. 101. The Soil Conservation and Domestic Allotment Act (49 Stat. 163), as amended, is further amended as follows:

Soil Conservation and Domestic allotment Act, amendments.

(1) by repealing subsections (b), (c), (d), (e), (f), and (g) of section 7;

49 Stat. 1148.
16 USC 590g.

(2) by repealing subsection (a) of section 8;

(3) by amending the first sentence of subsection (b) of section 8 of said Act, as amended, by striking out the language "Subject to the limitations provided in subsection (a) of this section, the" and inserting in lieu thereof the word "The"; and

76 STAT. 605.
76 STAT. 606.

(4) by adding a new subsection at the end of section 16 of said Act to read as follows:

49 Stat. 1151.
16 USC 590p.

"(e) (1) For the purpose of promoting the conservation and economic use of land, the Secretary, without regard to the foregoing provisions of this Act, except those relating to the use of the services of State and local committees, is authorized to enter into agreements, to be carried out during such period not to exceed ten years as he may determine, with farm and ranch owners and operators providing for changes in cropping systems and land uses and for practices or measures to be carried out primarily on any lands owned or operated by them and regularly used in the production of crops (including crops such as tame hay, alfalfa, and clovers, which do not require annual tillage, and including lands covered by conservation reserve contracts under subtitle B of the Soil Bank Act) for the purpose of conserving and developing soil, water, forest, wildlife, and recreation resources. Such agreements shall include such terms and conditions as the Secretary may deem desirable to effectuate the purposes of this subsection and may provide for payments, the furnishing of materials and services, and other assistance in amounts determined by the Secretary to be fair and reasonable, in consideration of the obligations undertaken by the farm and ranch owners and operators and the rights acquired by the Secretary: *Provided*, That agreements for the establishment of tree cover may not provide for annual payments with respect to such land for a period in excess of five years.

70 Stat. 191-195.
7 USC 1831-1837.

"(2) No agreement shall be entered into under this subsection covering land with respect to which the ownership has changed in the two year period preceding the first year of the contract period unless (a) the new ownership was acquired by will or succession as a result of the death of the previous owner, (b) the land becomes a part of an existing farm or ranch, or (c) the land is combined with other land as a farming or ranching enterprise which the Secretary determines will effectuate the purposes of the program: *Provided*, That this provision shall not prohibit the continuation of an agreement by a new owner after an agreement has once been entered into under this subsection.

Illustration 24. At last! The cover of Public Law 87–703, 87th Congress, H.R. 12391, approved September 27, 1962, 1:00 p.m., by President Kennedy's signature, after being voted in the House of Representatives and in the Senate.

partly financed by the sale of surplus stocks on the market. Unless Congress took action for the years after 1963, feed-grains producers could expect only a 50%-of-parity support, which meant cheap corn and no profit for most commercial farmers.

Under the new permanent wheat program which passed, the details of which were subsequently announced by the USDA, the 55-million-acre minimum national allotment had been abolished in favor of a much lower minimum necessary to produce at least one billion bushels of wheat. If two-thirds of the wheat farmers should be willing to vote for an additional 10% cut in their acreage (in a wheat referendum to be held the following spring) they would get certificates for their normal production equal to 70 cents per bushel so that the market price of wheat would drop to $1.30. Those using wheat for human consumption or for dollar exports would have to buy 70-cent certificates to go with each bushel of wheat. Those who produced 15 acres or less of wheat—who for years had been exempt from control—would be allowed to sign up and then to vote. These 15-acre men would have to accept the acreage cut if they wished to get the substantial price benefits under the program.

For the coming year, wheat production would be kept down by a temporary program (placed on top of the old inadequate mandatory wheat program) much like that passed in the first year of the New Frontier, except for the addition of the new 18-cent-per-bushel compensatory payment.

So except for the mandatory corn program, and the year's delay before the wheat-certificate program was to go into effect, Secretary Freeman achieved nearly what he had first sought—a miracle, some said, though the administration team no doubt felt they had earned their success several times over. By this time the administration had about decided not to push for a mandatory feed-grains program, and they were happy, too, that half-a-year remained in which to sell the certificate plan to wheat farmers. Experienced hands in USDA and Congress said they really needed three years or so in which to convince two-thirds of the farmers they should vote for it.

11. *The Wheat Referendum: Organized Opposition*

After the farm bill passed, administration people could bask for a few relaxed days in warm reflections on the past months, "the biggest year for rural laws since the 1930's," according to the respected *Kiplinger Agricultural Letter.*[1]

The once-ominous Billie Sol Estes scandal, though it had hurt USDA's public relations, had evaporated when investigators found no real corruption in Washington, nor any loss of federal funds. But it had turned Freeman's attention to the weaknesses of the vast farmer committee system which administered farm price programs and which was to play a central, controversial role in the forthcoming wheat referendum. After authorizing an immediate study by a citizen's committee of the ASCS farmer committee system,[2] Freeman followed its recommendations by reorganizing the Agricultural Stabilization and Conservation Service which ran the price support programs, and by reasserting his right to remove the ineffective hired or elected officials within the vast farmer committee system.

Freeman's new credit, recreational, and land use powers were expected to be made a part of the USDA's popular rural redevelopment efforts across the United States. Freeman did a little horn-blowing with respect to these provisions at another series of Land and People Conferences around the country. On October 15th,

[1] Sept. 29, 1962.

[2] Review of the Farmer Committee System," USDA, Nov. 28, 1962. Chairman—A. Lars Nelson, Master of the Washington State Grange; Staff Director—Joseph Hajda, political scientist, Kansas State University.

he told a New Orleans conference:

> The time is past when each program goes down a separate path. The time is here when local people can use as one the tools of credit, research, technical aid, electrification, educational services, marketing, and assistance in cooperative efforts.
>
> The time is past when land can be idled. Instead, land can be put to paying use for the production of grass, trees, and the establishment of factories and business enterprises to meet the needs of all Americans.
>
> And the time is past when it's even valid to ask, "Can rural America be revitalized?"
>
> Rural America is being revitalized now.[3]

Overshadowing practically all other problems of American agriculture was the threat that the new European Economic Community (EEC) would close the major regional market to U.S. farm products. Precedents for imposing trade walls were already being set, so President Kennedy gave Freeman, his emissary to the supranational government in Brussels, authority to speak plainly. Virtually all farm groups and interests rallied behind the Secretary in his effort to save American markets in Europe.

There was also the threat that autumn of war over Cuba. The President was relieved to learn that Freeman—a long-time civil-defense advocate—had been quietly developing plans for feeding America in the event of a nuclear war.

More crucial to the participants in the struggle over agricultural policies, however, were the fall elections, in which Democrats, Republicans, Freeman, and the Farm Bureau all hoped to be vindicated. As promised, Freeman took to the campaign trail in October, eliciting a largely indifferent response to his charges of Republican obstructionism. The Farm Bureau focused on the two races between incumbents whose farm districts had been consolidated, in each of which a Farm Bureau Republican was pitted against an administration Democrat. Republicans won both contests. At the same time, the Farm Bureau pointed out, all but two of the Demo-

[3] Speech keynoting regional Land and People Conference, Loyola University of New Orleans, Oct. 15, 1962.

crats who voted against the administration farm bill were reelected. However, eight House Republicans who voted against the farm bill were defeated, and the administration increased its farm bill majority in the Senate.

If the fall elections did not indicate what farmers thought about farm policy, they did dramatize that rural people were a declining minority. Nineteen rural House seats had been moved to the cities as a result of redistricting, and in countless other mixed (rural and urban) districts the urban population had quietly mushroomed into a position of dominance. For a more direct expression of farmer feeling, our urban nation would have to await results from the wheat referendum.

The Context of the Wheat Referendum

With few exceptions, past producer referendums had not been exciting or instructive. Farmers were originally allowed to vote on farm programs beginning in 1934 as a way to get them to meetings at which the programs were explained. Unless farmers understood and approved the programs, it was felt, they could not be administered.

Congress later required that farmers must approve quotas by a two-thirds vote in periodic referendums. Wheat referendums were held in 1941 and 1942 and in each year after 1952. Routine annual campaigns for a "yes" vote were conducted by the USDA's farmer committees and by the Farmers Union, and the few voters were overwhelmingly in favor of controls.

In 1961, however, the number of referendum voters increased sharply in Oklahoma, Kansas, and Nebraska, and the margin of victory was cut almost in half from the previous year. Some Washington observers immediately suggested that the two-thirds requirement be dropped in favor of a simple majority, but others felt that the tradition was too well established, and that programs would not work if many farmers were opposed to them. After considering this question in late 1961, Freeman decided to reaffirm the two-thirds requirement, and this decision was stated in the January 1962 President's message.

Eight months later the wheat program was nearly defeated, after Farm Bureaus in the Great Plains had run a small-scale opposition campaign.

Despite this recent downward trend in voting approval, the USDA apparently remained optimistic about the 1963 vote, though they felt that a vigorous campaign would have to be made to insure a "yes" vote.

The Fifteen-Acre Man—A New Element

A new element in the 1963 referendum was the wheat grower who grew fifteen acres of wheat or less, who had not previously been subject to mandatory controls. The "fifteen-acre exemption" (13½ acres for 1962) had been legislated in 1941 as a means to win Midwestern support for a wheat bill, and perhaps also out of a fear that small growers would defeat the program if allowed to vote. When surpluses grew, Plains wheat growers often traced them to the multitude of tiny wheat acreages in the Midwest and South (although regional proportions of total wheat production had not changed significantly).

At the insistence of the commercial wheat growers, controls were extended to fifteen-acre men in the 1962 law. Thereby the fifteen-acre men also gained the right to vote, and they outnumbered the commercial wheat producers two-to-one!

However, the program had not really been written for the fifteen-acre men. Although they were given several alternatives, one of which was to divert all their wheat acres in return for a payment of 50% of the normal gross returns from it (or they could also disregard controls and miss out on the 70-cents-per-bushel wheat certificates), these small producers would have to divide their tiny wheat plots in measurements of fractions of an acre if they wanted the full benefits of the program. Many of these men, especially in the Midwest, were unaccustomed to mandatory controls, nor did they fully appreciate that it was the government indirectly which kept prices high, since they had usually sold their wheat to nearby mills where they received more than the supported price per bushel.

From experience with the tobacco program, USDA people had at first thought that small growers everywhere favored mandatory-control programs. When they realized that the small growers did not, USDA officials began to hope that producers with small acreages would not be sufficiently interested to vote. Of those interested, the "no" voters might be further weeded out by the requirement—which seemed fair enough—that only those who signed up to participate in the program could vote. Indeed, there might have been only a few fifteen-acre voters if issues other than price and wheat acreage had not been raised in the campaign.

The Farm Bureau Campaign

Farm Bureau leaders decided to enter the wheat-referendum campaign in opposition to the program that they had tried earnestly to defeat in the Congress, because they were fairly certain they could win. From results of farm-organization activity in the previous referendum, from recent reports of their own people in the field, and from applying the politician's axiom that a considerable number of people can be roused to vote against any proposition, Farm Bureau leaders concluded they would have to sway only an additional small fraction of the voters in order to kill the program. To accomplish this, the Farm Bureau could mobilize its disciplined staff of public-relations men and organizers, and its grass-roots membership which could be found in most rural counties. They would get much help from the mass media in the wheat belt, which were mostly conservative, right down to the county newspapers. Local business, banking, and professional groups would also provide assistance.

There were risks involved, nevertheless. As an organization of proven influence in Congress and in state legislatures, the Farm Bureau had much to lose if it failed this unique new test of strength. But many Farm Bureau members were undoubtedly eager to make a fight for their principles, and many a Farm Bureau staff man was anxious to show what he could do. For example, the Farm Bureau's Secretary-Treasurer Roger Fleming had bypassed a career as an economist to help build an organization which shared his views. It was in excellent shape as described in his report to the National Farm Bureau Convention, December 13th, in Atlanta, Georgia. A successful fight, therefore, would leave the organization even more spirited than before, and sell more people on the political and economic principles the Farm Bureau advocated.

In deciding whether or not to campaign, national Farm Bureau leaders indicated they would be guided by decisions reached by wheat-state Farm Bureaus. All of them voted in late November to work for defeat of the program. So the national Farm Bureau convention in mid-December resolved to "organize and conduct an extensive information campaign with wheat growers in all commercial states to explain fully the provisions and implications of the alternative programs to be offered farmers in the 1963 wheat referendum."

The Main Farm Bureau Issue: "Freedom to Farm"

At this convention, President Shuman stated the Farm Bureau's referendum issue, which was not the same as that implied in the law. For the Farm Bureau this was to be more than simply a choice between two programs. It was to be a choice between regimentation and freedom. In words which were paraphrased in hundreds of thousands of pamphlets, President Shuman asked the Farm Bureau delegates:

"Who will run the farms of America? Will it be the farmers or the political bureaucrats?"

Freedom to farm, threatened by government! Following the convention, Farm Bureau leaders found many ways to state this theme. Farm Bureau economist Gene Hamilton defended it at the intellectual level before a group of philosophers, social scientists, and theologians in February, 1963.[4] Hamilton noted remarks by Dr. Bushrod Allin, a former president of the American Farm Eco-

[4] Conference on Goals and Values, Iowa State University. Printed in *Farm Goals in Conflict* (Ames, Iowa: Iowa State University Press, 1964) pp. 64–76.

nomic Association, that governmental restraints on individual action (perhaps including production controls) often increased the area of freedom rather than diminishing it, and remarks by Ted Schultz that freedom was not a legitimate issue in the farm controversy because "it is hard to see that our farm programs have endangered the civil rights of people."

In reply to Allin, Hamilton distinguished between restraints in the nature of "rules of the game" which applied equally to all citizens, and restraints which arbitrarily gave some citizens an economic advantage over others. To require that weights and measures be accurate might well enhance freedom of action, but to permit one section of the country to monopolize cotton production by law just because they could muster a majority of votes in Congress could not be justified.

Hamilton said Schultz was correct in a narrow sense that farm programs had not impaired civil rights. But "in a wider sense, programs which make people dependent upon the federal government impair their freedom to decide how they will use their right to vote."

To keep political and religious freedoms, Hamilton argued, we should maintain the economic freedoms of a free-market system, which was also the most efficient way to produce.

The Farm Bureau was always ready to meet its critics at the scholarly level. The organization placed high value on the scientific method and on adherence to proven facts, despite the signs of anti-intellectualism in its national and state programs.

Yet the tactics required in a referendum were not those of a scholar. Shuman had been outspoken against the producer referendum because it could be manipulated, and also because "it invites propaganda campaigns which tend to conceal facts and appeal to emotion and prejudice."[5] The Farm Bureau nevertheless played to win. Once they had decided to campaign, Farm Bureau leaders took full advantage of the loose rules of the game.

[5] *AFBF Newsletter*, Oct. 29, 1962.

Circumstances were in the Farm Bureau's favor in the endeavor to make farmers act out of a desire for freedom rather than on the basis of the ostensible referendum issues. The referendum was coming at the end of a three-year string of good crops in the commercial wheat area, so many farmers could afford the luxury of voting "no." It also followed eight straight years of acreage controls, during which many farmers had accumulated grievances against local administrators of the program, and all had been obliged to watch productive land lying idle, and to plow up beautiful green wheat acreages (used for pasture) just before the wheat began to bud.

To aggravate farmer frustration with controls, the Farm Bureau dubbed the new wheat program "the tightest, strictest, most complete control plan ever considered for a major farm commodity," a statement which other observers said was untrue. "That is extreme language and it is careless language," said an editorial in the respected *Des Moines Register*, which was reprinted by supporters of the program and distributed all across the country. Farm Bureau speakers, to prove their point, came up with eight new "controls," but the proponents replied by noting five new "flexibilities," and when Congress authorized the free interchange of wheat and feed-grains allotments in an expected though last-minute action, little basis remained for the Farm Bureau's strong words.

Central to the freedom issue was the theme that agriculture was at a "crossroads" (both Benson and Freeman had said so), the future course of which would be set by the vote in the wheat referendum. "If wheat farmers say no on May 21, they can change the whole course of the Freeman-Kennedy farm program. They can, in fact, blow it out of the water," said the *Des Moines Register's* Richard Wilson in an article that was reprinted widely by those favoring a "no" vote.

Controls on Other Products?

But if farmers vote "yes," said Farm Bureau's Shuman, "the door will be opened for the extension of similar controls and certificates

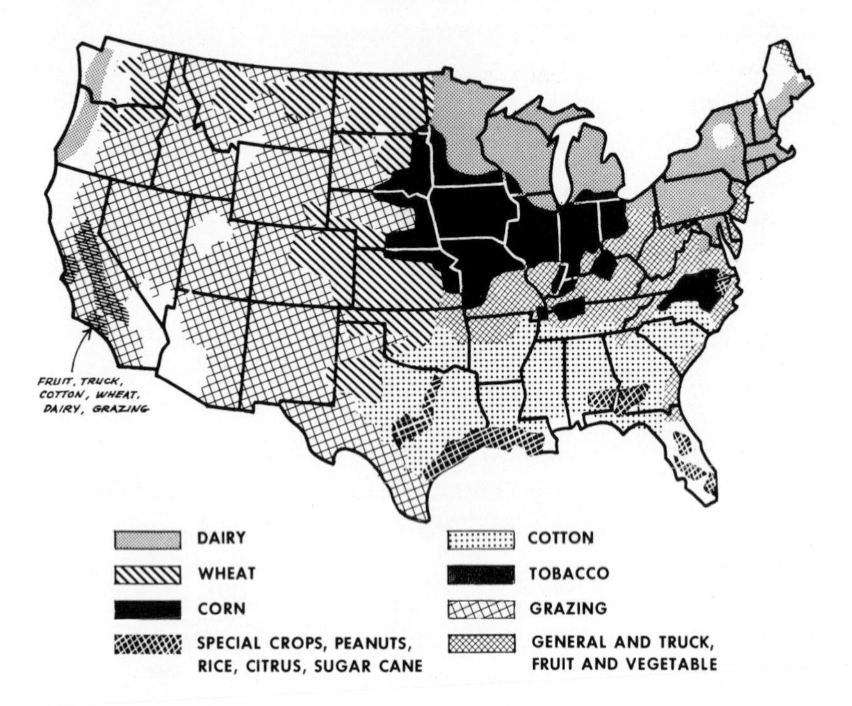

Illustration 25. MAJOR CROPS BY REGION. Reprinted by permission from *The Congressional Quarterly*.

or licenses to the producers of feed grain, livestock, poultry, dairy products, cotton, fruits, and vegetables."[6] (See Illustration 25.)

By shifting the contexts in which the phrase "supply management" was used, Farm Bureau leaders also made it easy for skittish feed-grains producers to conclude that Congress was about to pass mandatory feed-grains legislation, though it was actually preparing to renew the voluntary program for two more years. The *Farm Bureau Newsletter* printed testimonials by dairy, potato, and egg producers who disclaimed any financial interest in wheat but planned to vote "no" in the referendum to keep government from running their commodities.[7]

Mississippi Farm Bureau chairman Boswell Stevens held out hope that a "no" vote would help reduce Secretary Freeman's unhealthy

[6] *Nation's Agriculture*, March 1963, p. 4.

[7] *AFBF Newsletter*, March 18, 1963.

control over the cotton industry,[8] although the Kentucky Farm Bureau felt that a large "no" vote in tobacco areas would help solidify the popular, tightly controlled tobacco program.

In response to calls from desperate "yes-vote" leaders who could feel the freedom issue taking hold—especially among the feed-grains stockmen at the grass roots—Secretary Freeman stated and then reaffirmed that no new mandatory programs were planned. He even assured beef producers—who stiffened at the merest suggestion of controls—that the USDA would not submit to Congress any supply-management controls for livestock "now or in the future." But the Farm Bureau did not slacken its freedom blitz, noting that President Kennedy himself had said in April that the referendum "will show whether or not farmers want a national policy of farm supply and farm income stabilization." [9]

Stressing the Issue

Numerous devices were used to entrench the freedom issue. The Farm Bureau's Illinois organization illustrated talks at farmer meetings with slide-photographs of bayonets, nooses, bayonets and nooses together, and nooses wrapped around shocks of wheat. The Mississippi Farm Bureau president suggested to a television audience that the original farm price-support programs were Communist inspired. Posters in Texas pictured the next generation enmeshed in barbed wire. Some billboards on Kansas highways affirmed simply "FREEMAN OF FREE MEN."

After Secretary Freeman dedicated a new data-processing center in Kansas City which would be used, he said, to keep tab on surplus stocks, President Shuman reused some of Freeman's remarks in such a way as to conclude that "farmers will become faceless punch cards [and] will need only to know how to follow orders [from] a huge bureaucratic setup." Charles Bailey, in another widely heralded *Des Moines Register* story, took Shuman to task for misrepresenting Freeman's remarks and for misquoting him as well.

[8] *AFBF Newsletter*, April 1, 1963.
[9] *Kansas Farm Bureau News*, April 1963.

While emphasizing the freedom issue, the Farm Bureau did find time to play down the presumed economic benefits of the new program. Aside from disputing ASCS claims about the anticipated wheat price levels [10] Farm Bureau implied that subsidies for the first year were merely bait to trap farmers into future, less lucrative programs.

Another tactic was to tell each group of producers they were being discriminated against, and thus to strike the dissonant notes of regional and commodity antagonisms which the Congress had patched in order to enact the program. According to highly particularized Farm Bureau literature, each major group would suffer, to the advantage of others. Three examples:

1. Fifteen-acre producers were reminded they would not be able to expand their acreage, while big commercial farmers were reminded that part of the national allotment was being given to fifteen-acre producers.
2. Producers of most varieties of wheat were said to be taking unfair cuts, including soft red winter wheat (Midwest, South, Middle Atlantic), durum wheat (small group of producers in North Dakota and Montana), and white wheat (Michigan, Idaho, Oregon, and Washington—distributed abroad in foreign food assistance programs), because these varieties of wheat were not much in surplus. Yet producers of the surplus hard varieties (the Plains States) were told they would not be able to cash in on their higher quality products, and would lose traditional allotments to other states.
3. While big wheat men were being told they would lose allotments to the Midwest, Midwesterners were being told that wheat acres might slip back into overproducing feed grains, which would then have to be put under a mandatory program. Midwesterners were warned that the interchange provision might allow the Plains States to grow bountiful, competitive, feed-wheat crops on their otherwise unproductive feed-grains acreages, which would have been good news to farmers from Texas to North Dakota. Yet

[10] Discussed on pages 281-282.

Farm Bureau's Shuman would not concede that more wheat would thus be raised in the Plains, because Secretary Freeman might use his discretion—though given him by Congress to prevent inequities—to curtail feed-wheat production.[11]

A Better Program from Congress?

What would happen if the program were defeated?

Farm Bureau literature denied that a "no" vote indicated support for the alternative program with its much lower supports, though Farm Bureau leaders privately saw virtue in it as a step toward balancing wheat supply and demand. Instead, they said, a "no" vote was a mandate for Congress to pass a better program. President Shuman told the Extension Services that farmers should not "be led to ignore the virtual certainty that Congress will enact a sensible wheat program if the certificate plan is not approved. . . ." Opponents assumed that the Democrats would not dare to let the farm economy languish under the "no" program during the 1964 election year.

In fact there would be other pressures for remedial action which Freeman had stated in his confidential December report to the President: uncontrolled wheat production might mean flooding of international markets in violation of trade treaties, and use of wheat for feed might cause the collapse of feed grains, poultry, and meat markets.

Would Congress pass a "better" program? (See Illustration 26.) On this crucial question there occurred a battle of testimonials in which the administration supporters had the big guns. The Farm Bureau obtained a statement from freshman Senator Daniel Brewster (D., Md.) that "the Congress would still have both the power and the responsibility to deal with any problems that might arise, and Congress will not abdicate this responsibility." Similar statements were made by Congressman John Dent (D., Pa.) and freshman Senator John Tower (R., Tex.).

[11] *Hearings on the Feed Grain Act of 1963*, Senate Agr. Comm., pp. 187–88.

Illustration 26. A View of the Farm Bureau Campaign. The Farm Bureau received some press criticism for its campaign, as in the above *Denver Post* cartoon, by Conrad. Reprinted by permission.

On the administration side, Senator Ellender said "Congress cannot and should not take action" in the event of defeat, and House Democratic majority leader Albert affirmed they would await farmers' decision in a future referendum. Congressman Frank Thompson (D., N.J.) said urban legislators would not override a farmer veto of wheat price supports programs.

President Kennedy himself made a statement in late January,

and at the urging of proponents in the field who wanted the lid sealed on this question, the President reaffirmed his position in early April:

Had the Congress intended new legislation to be considered as an alternative to wheat marketing quotas, I believe it would have so provided. Instead, Congress provided a stopgap program. . . . It also provided an opportunity for the wheat farmer to vote again in 1964 after he had a chance to see what happened under the stopgap program. It is clear, then, that no new wheat legislation was intended or needed this year.[12]

To say that Congress would not act if farmers voted "no" was simply a tactic to scare farmers into voting "yes," the Farm Bureau asserted. Shuman implied that, once the referendum campaign was over, "the Administration, Secretary of Agriculture, and the members, the leaders in Congress, will look toward a constructive and better type of wheat legislation." [13]

The problem was apparently not that simple. Senator Humphrey recalled that "we had a hard fight last year, a close battle to get the farm legislation we now have. If we have to go through another battle, with members of Congress seeing a good program defeated in referendum, I doubt whether there will be any program at all or any action by Congress." [14] Dakota Republicans Mundt (S.D.) and Young (N.D.) concurred in that judgment and therefore asked their constituents to vote for the program they had earlier tried to defeat.

Farm Bureau Organization on the Wheat Referendum

Roger Fleming coordinated the referendum campaign from Washington, although the Chicago office was, as usual, the main communications artery to the state organizations. In Chicago, Gene Hamilton and his assistants churned out materials to help state and

[12] *Farmers Union Herald*, April 29, 1963.

[13] *Hearings on the Feed Grain Act of 1963*, Senate Agriculture Committee, p. 201.

[14] *Farmers Union Herald*, April 29, 1963.

field people exploit the effective issues. They tried to make certain that Farm Bureau positions and statements were never contrary to fact, and to be equally certain that the sundry interpretations in Farm Bureau literature were never embarrassingly at odds.

The two national offices cooperated in producing many of the arguments, the slogans, the press releases, the cartoons, and the statements used by the Farm Bureau and other opponents of the certificate plan, all of which were to provide a picture of the world which the Farm Bureau wanted voters to accept. These were used, in one or another form, in the Farm Bureau's weekly newsletter and monthly magazine, and in the various state Farm Bureau newspapers. They were rephrased for radio spot announcements, and to be used in public debates and in discussions. They were sent out as press releases for farm radio and television programs, and for regional and county newspapers.

In addition to their research and public relations work, the national Farm Bureau staff mimeographed tactical schemes for local action groups and published several pamphlets which were made available to state units at cost. (See Illustration 27.) Over four hundred thousand copies were printed of two principal campaign pamphlets, one of them for 15-acre farmers, and the other for commercial farmers. All national Farm Bureau activities were financed by the annual one-dollar dues paid by each of the 1.6 million members.

State and Local Farm Bureaus

The state and local organizations which received an average of $10 to $15 annually from each member, had staffs varying with the size of the total state membership. In the states with the largest potential wheat votes State Farm Bureaus had large memberships, good organizations (including 25 to 35 full-time staff men in each), and fairly enthusiastic leadership. After Kansas, these states were mostly in the Midwest (Ohio, Illinois, Missouri, Indiana, and Michigan). Farm Bureau problem states were Missouri, North Dakota, and South Dakota, where competitor farm groups were large, and

Illustration 27. "Freedom to Farm." One of two Farm Bureau pamphlets which proved its usefulness on Referendum Day.

in the South—especially the Southeast—where the Farm Bureau's grass roots favored controls and where state Farm Bureau leaders had little stomach for a campaign. Spotted throughout the state leaderships elsewhere and in scattered counties there were a minority of elected officials who did not think the Farm Bureau should be fighting the certificate program, and some local Farm Bureau leaders in the wheat belt no doubt wished Farm Bureau were on the other side.

To get maximum help from all state and local organizations, the national Farm Bureau leaders argued that personal opinions had to give way if necessary to save the life of the organization. This was a make-or-break struggle—the Farm Bureau's toughest battle. If certain state and county groups simply could not go along they were to say and do nothing—to "dead-head it," as one local Farm Bureau official put it.

Parts of the organization did sit out the campaign, though out of the 2,700 county and 50 state organizations only the tiny unit in Webster County, Nebraska, saw fit to publicly oppose the Farm Bureau's stand. Furthermore, the Farm Bureau's appointed officials were able to work around the numb spots in order to cultivate local members who agreed with the Farm Bureau's view. No doubt they had to scurry to put out a few brush fires during the campaign, but their lines were very straight by comparison with the organizations whose leadership favored the program.

At the state level the Farm Bureau's campaign organization was led by a coordinator selected from each state staff. These state coordinators met with Fleming at regional conferences held in the winter, and again in mid-campaign. Fleming, known by detractors as a steam-roller type, lectured these picked men in the same spirit and with the same terminology that he had once used as a coach of athletic teams. They were either to play hard or to get out of the game. Fleming urged them to pull out all the stops in this effort and yet to clear with him to avoid making serious mistakes. At these meetings the coordinators suggested ideas to each other, and economist Hamilton discussed the confusing and the controversial sections of the wheat program.

The coordinators remained in close contact with the national office, and when Fleming had his way they were given first priority in the use of state staff and facilities. In the Plains and in most Midwestern states, state staffs devoted themselves nearly full-time to the campaign during its closing weeks.

Kansas Farm Bureau Activity

In Kansas, for example, with the sixth largest membership and the largest wheat referendum vote, the coordinator—state Secretary-Treasurer J. D. Smerchek—was able to schedule Kansas President Walter Pierce for numerous public appearances, including a debate against the President of the Kansas Association of Wheat Growers, Anson Horning. Smerchek also scheduled other state Board members for appearances, organizational work, letters, and debates, and for financing of advertising. Two Kansas Farm Bureau (KFB) public relations men wrote radio and television spots, pamphlets, and press releases which were used both by KFB and by *ad hoc* groups.

Meanwhile, KFB's commodity marketing experts aroused and coordinated activities of the allied Kansas Livestock Association, the Kansas Feed Dealers, and dairy groups. A Farm Bureau ladies' auxiliary, in a fundamentalist spirit reminiscent of earlier prohibition campaigns, wrote letters to editors, served as babysitters, and conducted telephone campaigns across the country.

Farm Bureau men were organized at several area meetings within each intrastate district in which a full-time man was stationed. At the Kansas area meetings—attended by the area field men, three or four state staff members and officials of county Farm Bureaus—the state men reviewed the certificate plan and the special problems relating to the fifteen-acre producer, and with the local field man they discussed the plan for organizing the campaign.

County delegates were expected to implement the plan as follows:

1. Get the County Farm Bureau Board's approval for an all-out effort.
2. Appoint a campaign committee and chairman, all of whom were

to be in favor of defeating the referendum.

3. The committeeman in each community should select other workers to form a community committee.
4. Then the state field man would come in to orient these committees.
5. Each County Farm Bureau president was to appoint a special committee to work with allied groups such as bankers, Livestock Association, implement dealers, Medical Association, to encourage ads in the newspapers, radio, and television. Much advertising in the mass media was apparently financed by one or a combination of these allied groups, affiliated in local committees on the initiative of local Farm Bureau leaders. Relatively little advertising was actually paid for or sponsored by Farm Bureau organizations.
6. Each campaign worker was to be given a complete list of eligible voters, obtainable (often with great difficulty) from the ASC office. Each farmer and his wife were to be contacted, and given whatever assistance was necessary in order to vote.
7. The Campaign chairmen and committee were also to attend state Farm Bureau training meetings, conduct county training meetings, set up and conduct farmer information meetings, and provide poll watchers on election day, both in order to phone those who had not voted by late in the day, and to insure against dishonesty.

Performance obviously did not equal plans, especially in the Southeastern states where almost nothing was done, and in states with tiny Farm Bureau staffs, or few voters, where efforts were token.

But the Midwest and Plains states mounted an impressive campaign! In five Plains states, according to surveys of radio advertising alone, "no" campaigners bought approximately 235 20-second spots, 245 30-second spots, 475 60-second spots, and at least 31 hours of programming. (Nationally, "no" campaigners bested "yes" campaigners by about three to two in expenditures for radio and television advertising.) A poll of Ohio farmers just before the referendum revealed that 52% of them had been contacted by Farm Bureau, compared with only 13% at most who had been contacted by farm organizations favoring a "yes" vote.

Illustration 28. THE FARM BUREAU OBJECTS TO FREEMAN CAMPAIGNING. A cartoon streamer from the March 11, 1963, *AFBF Newsletter*. Reprinted by permission.

In Harvey County, Kansas, the local Farm Bureau had formally contacted 35% of those who voted and this county effort was just a little better than average, according to a prereferendum judgment by KFB officials. In Kansas alone, Farm Bureau distributed 14,585 copies of the pamphlet for 15-acre farmers, 27,410 copies of the pamphlet for commercial farmers, 51,635 copies of a handbill criticizing the opponents' issues and hundreds of copies of other circulars and posters. On referendum day, most voters in the Midwest and the Plains knew on which side of the issue Farm Bureau stood though the same could not be said for other major farm organizations.

Yet national Farm Bureau officials were not always sure that their efforts were adequate. A week and a half before the referendum only 15% of the 15-acre farmers in the Midwest had signed up to vote, so Fleming told those at a statewide meeting in Illinois (2,000 present) that they should do everything they intended to do and also register five additional voters on the following weekend, if they expected to win. Last-minute efforts were stepped up in other Midwestern states.

12. *The Wheat Referendum: Rephrasing the Issue*

FROM THE beginning, Farm Bureau President Shuman phrased the referendum as a contest between the bureaucrats and the farmers—between Freeman speaking for the administration, and the Farm Bureau (and two cattlemen's associations) speaking for farmers. In rejecting this view, supporters of a "yes" vote pointed out that a number of farm organizations had joined hands in support of the program. The fact remained that on one side was a large organization with considerable financial resources committed to the fight, and on the other was a loose coalition of smaller organizations (most of the big grain cooperatives were not really involved). (See Illustration 29.)

Furthermore, all proponent groups lacked enthusiasm for the Administration program. Some leaders of national farm organizations had backed it reluctantly as the best possible compromise, but at the lower levels in these organizations, many leaders remained unreconciled. In November of 1962, the Montana Wheat Growers were thinking of withdrawing from the National Association, and the Washington and Nebraska groups would not promise their support in the referendum until Secretary Freeman had responded to their demands relative to the amount of acreage cut, the percentage of diversion payments, the price at which certificated wheat would sell, and the way certificates would be administered.

After badgering the administration during the winter months to get the best possible terms, these "friendly" farm leaders had been

Regions	Farm Bureau [1]	Grange [2]	Farmers Union [3]	Wheat Growers [4]
NEW ENGLAND—*Totals*	*18,912*	*166,215*		
Maine	1,356	51,125		
New Hampshire	4,119	25,325		
Vermont	5,970	15,417		
Massachusetts	4,828	39,757		
Rhode Island	168	6,553		
Connecticut	2,471	28,038		
MIDDLE ATLANTIC—*Totals*	*31,244*	*201,652*		
New York	14,273	111,988		
New Jersey	6,102	17,163		
Pennsylvania	10,869	72,481		
SOUTH ATLANTIC—*Totals*	*193,208*	*22,480*		
Delaware	1,526	1,827		
Maryland	10,056	2,829		
West Virginia	4,576	1,518		
Virginia	22,503	1,376		
North Carolina	55,451	10,512		
South Carolina	22,676	4,418		
Georgia	43,284			
Florida	33,136			
NORTH CENTRAL (EAST)—*Totals*	*466,109*	*225,567*	*19,908*	
Ohio	50,345	183,661	2,047	
Indiana	129,343	4,628	3,537	
Illinois	193,766	7,634	3,605	
Michigan	69,073	27,280	1,251	
Wisconsin	23,582	2,364	9,468	
NORTH CENTRAL (WEST)—*Totals*	*287,484*	*29,553*	*119,096*	*60,200*
Minnesota	30,439	2,338	39,102	
North Dakota	16,129		41,965	
South Dakota	2,821	448	16,815	1,200
Iowa	110,442	2,115	2,673	
Missouri	34,228	2,248		
Nebraska	13,493	1,607	10,526	3,000
Kansas	79,932	20,797	8,015	56,000

Membership of the Missouri Farmers Organization, 1962: 158,000.
Membership of the National Farmers Organization is not revealed.

Illustration 29. MEMBERSHIP IN FOUR FARM ORGANIZATIONS BY STATES, CENSUS REGIONS, AND CENSUS DIVISIONS. This table on farm organization membership demonstrates the large, widespread backing of the American Farm Bureau Federation as compared with other groups.

Regions	Farm Bureau [1]	Grange [2]	Farmers Union [3]	Wheat Growers [4]
SOUTH CENTRAL (EAST)—				
Totals	*273,413*	*370*	*307*	
Kentucky	72,939		307	
Tennessee	64,515	370		
Mississippi	52,570			
Alabama	83,389			
SOUTH CENTRAL (WEST)—				
Totals	*197,062*	*3,724*	*67,423*	*10,664*
Arkansas	49,318	476	13,019	
Louisiana	21,700			
Oklahoma	41,202	1,225	50,201	9,700
Texas	84,842	2,023	4,203	964
MOUNTAIN—*Totals*	*60,428*	*21,731*	*33,302*	*3,878*
Montana	3,366	1,540	14,295	1,800
Idaho	11,705	10,722	768	639
Wyoming	7,754	838		166
Colorado	14,559	8,631	16,414 [5]	1,273
New Mexico	8,559			
Arizona	4,104			
Utah	8,852		1,825	
Nevada	1,529			
PACIFIC—*Totals*	*74,003*	*117,739*	*1,539*	*4,782*
Washington	3,855	48,150		3,282
Oregon	8,905	26,009	1,539 [6]	1,500
California	60,313	43,580		
Alaska				
Hawaii	930			
OTHER—*Total*	*5,642*			
Puerto Rico	5,642			
Total Membership	1,607,505	789,031	241,575	79,524

[1] American Farm Bureau Federation, November 30, 1962.

[2] National Grange, March 31, 1958, last publicized state-by-state figures. Grange membership is not comparable to the others because wives and older children are members as well as heads of households. Other groups enumerate only families, or heads of families.

[3] National Farmers Union, 1963.

[4] National Association of Wheat Growers, as reported by officers in 1962.

[5] Includes Rocky Mountain States.

[6] Includes State of Washington.

informed in late January that the administration would subsidize farmers for only 20% of normal income on the acres required to be diverted (they had asked 50%). Certificates would be issued on only 80% of production of wheat allotments, and these fixed-value certificates would keep the food wheat price at $2 per bushel (farm groups had hoped for $2.20 or even 100% of parity—$2.40). The administration did quiet their fears of an additional 30% acreage cut (the cut was to be only 10%) and it made one further concession after Carl Bruns of the Nebraska Wheat Growers had slammed doors at the USDA following threats to pull out of the campaign fight. He persuaded the administration to permit farmers to store wheat raised on surplus acres which might be sold later in event of a crop failure.

The unsatisfactory terms of the program were only one reason why the Washington State Wheat growers stuck by a November decision to take no sides (though national President Glen Bayne campaigned vigorously in his home state), and why a number of other state-level groups within the friendly organizations proved to be halfhearted campaigners. Some of these groups feared they would lose members by making a fight for the program. The local Granges, particularly, were not accustomed to taking a militant role on one side of a controversial issue. As a further embarrassment most Grangers—and many in the other groups—were Republicans who would have doubts about any program that had been passed by the Democrats over the opposition of virtually all Republicans.

Early in the campaign Freeman had unwittingly helped set a partisan tone as a result of his own initial eagerness to lead the fight. In December, he had told a Farmers Union Grain Terminal Association convention audience that "a campaign of calculated distortion has already been launched against the wheat program," but "together we can make sure that the farmer has all possible information so that his vote can be the result of fact, not fiction. . . ." Two days later, speaking to the Wheat Growers Convention in Denver, Freeman had called the certificate plan "your program," but he had again promised his audience "together we can make sure."

In off-the-cuff remarks Freeman charged that opponents of the program were linked with John Birch elements. Without doubt, national and local right-wing groups had committed their financial help, their access to Mountain and Plains states mass media, and their considerable local support in those regions to defeating the certificate plan. Yet some of Freeman's advisers thought it a mistake for him to become involved in such charges.

For two weeks thereafter, the Freeman advisers hotly argued whether he should actively campaign. But as opponents began using him and the Kennedy administration as effective targets, and when a GTA (Grain Terminal Association) poll of North-Central farmers revealed in early January that farmers resented advice from Washington politicians, Freeman was persuaded to sideline himself during the remaining months of the campaign, after an organizational speech in Omaha on January 10th.

The Grange Pamphlet

Recognizing that the program would not get a two-thirds vote if it were labeled as Freeman's, the Grange printed 500,000 copies of a pamphlet (see Illustration 30), distributed also by Wheat Growers and Farmers Union People, which asserted that the real father of the certificate program was the venerable, respected, rigorously nonpartisan Grange. The pamphlet stated that—except for slight changes needed to deal with surplus stocks—the wheat-certificate program was the "long advocated program developed by the Grange, later endorsed by the Wheat Growers Association and subsequently by the National Farmers Union and many other groups." The effort to keep the campaign on a nonpartisan plane was perhaps the Grange's principal contribution in the campaign. Besides contributing the pamphlet, Grange Master Herschel Newsom vigorously endorsed the certificate program in many articles, letters, speeches, and taped statements.

Illustration 30. THE NATIONAL GRANGE PAMPHLET. The National Grange printed half a million copies of the pamphlet whose text is shown here. An effort was made to take the wheat program out of politics and show it as part of the program long advocated and developed by the Grange.

HOW WILL YOU VOTE
in
The Wheat Referendum?

For twenty-five years the Grange has consistently sought expansion of the COMMODITY - BY - COMMODITY APPROACH to a domestic parity-type over-all farm program. For the past twelve years the Domestic Parity Wheat Certificate Program has been a part of the total GRANGE PROGRAM.

For the LAST TEN YEARS it has been increasingly apparent that we could no longer expect Government to maintain support prices at a satisfactory price level on ALL the wheat that American farmers can produce, even on the 55 million acres defined as the MINIMUM NATIONAL ALLOTMENT.

Between the demands for *higher level of price support* with lower acreage allotments on the one hand vs. NO acreage allotments on the other, with support levels *to reflect the relative feed value of wheat as compared to corn* (about $1.25 per bu.), the Grange has stood with its Domestic Parity Wheat Certificate Program, for these 10 or 12 years.

The Grange Wheat Certificate Program has been passed by the House and by the Senate, three times. It was actually sent to the President once—but then, it was a part of a total "omnibus bill" that was NOT acceptable.

Because of failure to otherwise make any appreciable modification in the Wheat Price Support Program, in these several years, the matter of acceptability of Marketing Quotas and PENALTIES for EXCESS PRODUCTION, has been submitted to the growers by referendum year after year. These referendums have carried by the required two-thirds majority.

The alternative available in the event the referendum HAD FAILED IN ANY ONE OF THESE YEARS would have been to *drop price supports to 50% of parity* and, even then, *only the growers who stayed within their acreage allotment* would have been eligible for price support. Failure of the referendum would have meant only, that there would have been *no penalties for excess marketings.* In fact, there would have been in that event, *no marketing quotas.* The only advantage to those who would have conformed to the acreage allotment would have been their eligibility for price support at the 50% of parity on all they could produce on their acreage allotment.

Rising Government storage of wheat, and constantly increasing costs of this old price support program, generated pressures in recent years *to eliminate,* or substantially modify the program, to be submitted for referendum. Meanwhile, because of the continually increasing stocks of wheat (and of OTHER FEED GRAINS), some measure of downward adjustment, even in connection with the Grange Wheat Certificate Program, was deemed by the Congress to be necessary. This brought on the "Emergency Wheat Program" of '61 and '62.

These *adjustment features,* as well as those in the proposed 1964 wheat program, would NOT have been necessary in our program as it passed the Congress in 1954 and again, even in 1958.

With this modification. the long advocated program DEVELOPED by the Grange, later ENDORSED by the Wheat Growers Association and subsequently by the National Farmers Union and many other groups, is now being offered to the wheat growers of the United States in the referendum this Spring. The law with respect to the program that will be in operation in the event the referendum fails to get the required 66-2/3rds "Yes" vote still provides the 50% support as outlined above.

With this introductory statement, we invite your attention to the *Facts* below.

FACT: . . . *With a favorable vote each grower will receive* certificates covering about 80% of the normal production of his allotted acres. Wheat covered by certificates will be supported at $2.00 per bu. (national average) non-certificated wheat from allotted acres will be supported at $1.30 per bu.

With an unfavorable vote acreage allotments will still be in effect and all wheat grown on allotted acres would be supported at 50% of parity or about $1.22 per bu. There would be no price supports for growers exceeding their allotment.

FACT: . . . *With a favorable vote* each grower's 1964 allotment will be 10% below that for 1963. A diversion payment will be made on this 10% reduction. This payment will be determined by multiplying normal yield by 30% of the support level. (Example: Assuming a 1963 allotment of 100 acres with a normal yield of 25 bu. . . . The payment would be 30% x $2.00 x 25 bu. x 10 acres or $150.00)

With an unfavorable vote there would be no diversion payment.

FACT: . . . *With a favorable vote* a grower may divert up to an additional 20% of his allotment. (In addition to the 10% already mentioned) payment on these additionally diverted acres will be determined by multiplying the number of acres so diverted by 50% of the support level. (Example: With a 25 bu. normal yield and an additional 18 acres diverted, this payment would be 50% x $2.00 x 25 bu. x 18 acres . . . or $450.00.)

With an unfavorable vote there would be no diversion payments.

FACT: . . . *With a favorable vote* Government-owned stocks of wheat will be reduced by about 150 million bu. per year. It is estimated that within four years the surplus would be down to 600 million bushels . . . the amount recognized as desirable as a "safe or strategic" reserve. Once this level is reached the number of certificates issued will be increased.

With an unfavorable vote wheat production would increase; Government-owned stocks, acquired at taxpayer expense, would continue to mount. Grange studies clearly indicate that (a) wheat acreage would increase to at least 65 million acres, (b) production would rise to about 1 billion 800 million bushels, (c) the market price of wheat will drop to about $1.00 per bu. and, (d) the surplus will continue to grow by about 600 million bu. annually.

FACT: . . . *A favorable vote* will greatly strengthen the U. S. position in International trade; negotiations can be continued without uncertainties created by unstable U. S. wheat prices.

An unfavorable vote would create serious international problems. U. S. wheat prices would, for the first time drop below the world market price . . . lower than the *minimum* called for by the International Wheat Agreement. Repercussions would be felt throughout the world. Fulfillment of trade commitments already made by U. S. would become increasingly difficult; it would point toward an expansion of the role of Government in the International wheat market.

FACT: . . . *With a favorable vote* the certificate program will provide a total producer income of about 2 billion 300 million dollars.

With an unfavorable vote producer income would drop to around 1 billion 600 million . . . a loss of $700 million despite an estimated harvest of 65 million acres.

(Bringing this to an individual farm level, it means that a farm which could produce an income of $2,300 under the certificate program would gross about $1,600 under the only other program offered in the referendum . . . a loss of $600 for the individual grower involved . . . and to the economy of his community.)

FACT: . . . *With a favorable vote* the miller's cost of wheat will remain about the same as for 1962 and 1963; thus, the certificate program *will not* provide the basis for an increase in bread price.

FACT: . . . Growers participating in the referendum will, for the first time, have an opportunity to vote for a "Wheat Certificate Program."

FACT: . . . Basic principles of the certificate program offered are those consistently recommended by the Grange since the early thirties.

FACT: . . . With a single exception, the wheat certificate program has been endorsed by all nationally recognized general farm organizations and by the National Association of Wheat Growers.

FACT: . . . Some promise that if the certificate program is turned down by growers, Congress will "bail us out" with passage of new and improved wheat legislation. To the Grange, this seems to be wishful thinking. This is the first basically new wheat program by Congress in 20 years; why then is it reasonable to expect the immediate passage of "something better" if the wheat program is not accepted by producers? Before Congress can act upon such new legislation it must be approved by Agricultural Committees of the Senate and House. Chairmen of both committees have said that no such action is contemplated. Also President Kennedy has said that new wheat legislation is neither necessary nor desirable.

FACT: . . . The certificate program will go into operation only if two-thirds of the growers participating in the referendum vote for it.

A "YES"! vote is a vote to continue to develop the Grange Domestic Parity Program —Commodity-by-Commodity.

A "NO" vote will resurrect the 10 or 12 years of *stalemate* through which we have passed.

NATIONAL GRANGE
1616 H Street, N.W.
Washington 6, D. C.

The Omaha Organizational Meeting

Freeman's Omaha speech was delivered to more than a hundred representatives from farm organizations favoring the certificate program. These men had gathered to form a National Wheat Committee through which they could coordinate their campaign efforts. Preparations for this organizational meeting had been made by M. W. Thatcher, whose giant GTA grain cooperative had helped finance earlier Farmers Union campaigns for a "yes" vote. The elderly but still ambitious and unpredictable Thatcher was expected to be a principal donor as well as the organizer in the 1963 nationwide campaign, and because of this he was named chairman of the new committee.

Yet Thatcher did not view the program as an unmixed blessing. As he noted, many of his cooperative grain-storage elevators would become empty if the surplus-reducing program passed. His more enthusiastic associate in the Farmers Union, President James Patton, pleaded in vain for a hard-hitting campaign. (See Illustration 31.)

Decisions in Omaha were taken in an informal meeting the evening before the formal sessions. The group decided to institute a coordinating committee as the action agency, to be run by Thatcher out of the St. Paul (Minnesota) headquarters of the GTA. Its principal task would be to institute state and county committees throughout the wheat belt. These committees composed of businessmen, bankers, and farmers, would schedule informational meetings, raise funds for advertising, distribute literature, and get voters out through personal contact. At middle level in the hierarchy would be a state organization or an outstanding individual, with primary responsibility for organizing certain states. Thus GTA was to take charge in Minnesota, North Dakota, Montana, and South Dakota. Farmers Union was to concentrate on Oklahoma, Colorado, Wyoming, Wisconsin, and Utah. The Grange was expected to make some kind of leadership effort in Ohio, New York, Washington, Michigan, Indiana, and California, where other groups had little or no organizations. The Wheat Growers were to organize Oregon, Idaho, Texas, and Kansas.

SPEAKING OF HYPOCRISY. Down South where the Farm Bureau is strong, controls were voted in overwhelmingly by peanut growers (96.9%), upland cotton growers (93.7%) and long staple cotton growers (81.9%), with the Farm Bureau's blessing. In the wheat area where Farm Bureau is weak and getting weaker, the organization is working tooth and nail against a similar program to help the wheat farmer.

Illustration 31. THE FARMERS UNION RAKES FARM BUREAU ACTION. In the above cartoon the *Farmers Union Newsletter*, February 15th, 1963, goes after the Farm Bureau for permitting its Southern members to support mandatory controls, while urging its Plains States members to vote against them. The comment that the Farm Bureau "is weak and getting weaker" in the wheat area is open to some question. (See Illustration 29.)

In Nebraska, State Commissioner of Agriculture Pearl Finnegan was to be in charge, and in Missouri it would be the local but powerful Missouri Farmers Association. In Illinois, Howard Mullins of the DeKalb Farm Policy Council and former Grange Master Dorsey Kirk would organize committees, and in Iowa, Fred Maywald of the Iowa Grain Dealers was to have responsibility.

At the Omaha meeting farm leaders made clear to the USDA people at the meeting that "friendly" farm organizations lacked the means to do very much. USDA people agreed that the burden of educating farmers would fall on the ASCS in the Department of Agriculture.

This predominant role intended for ASCS was given emphasis when Wheat Growers lobbyist Jim Dyess, who was expected to be a pillar in the farm groups' campaign, was hired as a regional director for ASCS. Dyess was to have directed a Washington committee which would publicize group statements, serve as a research arm for wheat-committee campaigners, and be in touch with the USDA effort. Lacking Dyess, the Washington Wheat Committee never came alive. Dyess' former secretary Jane Taylor handled affiairs for several weeks while the group looked for another director. They settled finally on an elderly Kansas Grange Master, Harry C. Coleglazier, who found he had no taste for Washington politics though he stayed until the referendum was over. To energize the Washington operation, the Missouri Farmers Association lent their highly regarded public-relations man, Jack Hackethorn, and GTA sent Jim Gilfillan, former editor of GTA's *Farmers Union Herald.*

Hackethorn and Gilfillan proved to be incompatible, so Coleglazier was obliged to send Hackethorn back to Missouri, while Gilfillan moved from the Wheat Growers' Office to the Farmers Union's office, where he released statements by farm leaders and rebuttals to Farm Bureau arguments. The mass media generally reported both sides in the debate, except for a number of Midwestern dailies which all but ignored "yes-vote" releases. Some research and writing disseminated by the Wheat Committee was done in the USDA, justified on the ground that such services leading to greater farmer understanding should be made available to any person or organization, including even the Farm Bureau had they asked for it. In practice the USDA was sometimes reluctant to cooperate with the Farm Bureau.

Notwithstanding Thatcher's obviously mixed views about the certificate program, his St. Paul headquarters for the National Wheat Committee directed an impressive organizational effort within the GTA and Farmers Union states. Farmers Union established state committees in North and South Dakota, Minnesota, and Montana, which included as many prominent farmers, businessmen, women, retired ASCS and extension people, and bankers as could be persuaded to join. These, like the county committees set up below them, were formally to explain the program, but actually worked in several ways for a "yes" vote. They answered farmer questions about the program, distributed bumper stickers and literature, organized informational meetings in cooperation with the local ASCS, and sought maximum coverage in newspapers.

These committees were to have been financed by local solicitations, after an initial subsidy from the national coordinating committee. The local committees were to sell $2 memberships in "2 for 1" clubs ($2 vs. $1 wheat, or 2 votes to 1 vote in the referendum).

Funds for the "yes-vote" campaign were everywhere insufficient to do what was planned. Even in North Dakota where businessmen and bankers more often favored the program, the State Wheat Committee was able to raise only $9,600, and had to borrow an additional $3,500 for a last minute effort to let farmers know that Congress had passed the 1963 feed-grains bill which permitted farmers to plant wheat on their feed-grains acres.

Outside the Farmers Union and GTA states and the MFA's Missouri, local organizational "yes-vote" campaigning was ragtailed and spotty. In the Midwest and Southern Plains the small, weak state organizations did what they could to awaken a yes-vote, particularly the militant—if skeletal—state Farmers Unions, and the young, aggressive National Farmers Organization.

From Kansas to Ohio the nonpartisan NFO-ers had access to neighbors in the traditional Republican farm areas, and their evangelism for higher prices in order to save the family farm matched the mood of the "no-vote" campaigners. But in many counties, the only organization supporting the program was the ASCS and the only real campaigners were the ASCS committeemen who—ex officio—distributed the national and state wheat committee literature, scheduled meetings and urged their neighbors to vote for the bill.

Farm groups played no real part in the vigorous campaign conducted by the ASCS and community groups in the Southeast. In the strong Grange counties in New York and Pennsylvania, state and local grangers were unresponsive to pleas by Coleglazier and Master Newsom to participate in the referendum campaigns as a way to increase local membership. Only the Washington state Grange, headed by Master Lars Nelson, was enthusiastic in its grass-roots work.

National Wheat Committee Chairman Thatcher, whose forces had spent about $18,000 campaigning for a "yes" vote in the previous wheat referendum, had expected that the 1963 campaign would cost the Coordinating Committee about $75,000. However, there was no way to assess the member farm organizations, even had they possessed the means to make large contributions. The participating groups did share among themselves the costs of the Washington Committee. But GTA paid the larger bill for the organization and materials which came out of the St. Paul Committee office, and GTA money turned up in other places, as in sponsorship of an ad by the Tuscola County, Michigan, "Wheat Growers." In this case of misrepresentation the GTA used a Michigan ASCS field man as their intermediary. (See Illustration 32.)

The USDA: Informing the Farmers

USDA people had anticipated—correctly—that opponents of the program would make the most of any indiscretions committed by USDA officials, or by the bureaucrats and farmer committeemen under USDA's Agricultural Conservation and Stabilization Service,

MR. WHEAT GROWER:

We Suggest You Vote Yes in the May 21 Wheat Referendum

BECAUSE:

1. This is a fair program. It offers you a fair price in return for your cooperation in bringing production in line with demand, and for helping to reduce costly surpluses;

2. It is a one-year program that applies only to the 1964 wheat crop. You will have another opportunity to vote again in 1964 on whether you want to continue the program in 1965;

3. This is the best—and undoubtedly the only—wheat program that will be offered farmers this year. Congress has provided that if farmers reject the 1964 program, a similar referendum will be held again next year.

4. Other government programs have failed. This program represents a new and practical approach to the problem. We think you should give it a fair trail by voting yes in the referendum.

5. With **YES VOTE,** wheat farmers can gain half billion dollars in income yearly.

Tuscola County Wheat Growers

Illustration 32. A CASE OF MISREPRESENTATION? A few days before the wheat referendum the above advertisement appeared in the *Tuscola County Advertiser* (Michigan). The signature "Tuscola County Wheat Growers" made it appear that the ad had been placed and paid for by a local organization.

Such was not the case. When Melvin L. Woell, of the Michigan Farm Bureau, wrote to J. R. Schantz of the Caro Farmer Cooperative Elevator Company, in Tuscola County, inquiring about the ad, Mr. Woell was told that the space was paid for by the Farmers Union Grain Terminal Association in St. Paul, Mr. Duane Andreas, assistant general manager of GTA, receiving the bill. Furthermore the ad had been placed by an ASCS man, Mike Hatles.

Victim of Fast-Play

An advertisement in last week's Advertiser, signed "Tuscola County Wheat Growers", which urged a "Yes" vote on the wheat referendum Tuesday of this week, has caused some little stir among some wheat growers.

A few have called this office, asking who was responsible for insertion of the ad, and saying they were mad because, while they grew wheat, they were not in favor of the proposition. These callers remarked also that they did not know of any organization called the "Tuscola County Wheat Growers."

We believe that those who are kicking about the ad have a very distinct point.

The signature on the ad was a patent attempt to make people believe that there was some sort of a Tuscola county organization which was sponsoring the ad when in fact that was not the case.

The Advertiser feels itself somewhat at fault for accepting an advertisement with such a vague signature, and in the interest of fair play tells the following story:

The advertisement came to us in the mail, with a Caro postmark. Attached to the copy for the ad was a small slip reading as follows: "Duane Andreas, G.T.A. North Snelling Drive, St. Paul, Minnesota. Under that were the instructions to "make bill out to him (Andreas), send bill to Mike Hatles, Owendale."

After receiving several telephone calls about the matter, we became curious ourselves and after some little effort we found that Duane Andreas is the assistant general manager of the Farmers' Union Grain Terminal Association, which operates a big business in Minnesota, North and South Dakota, Montana and others of the northern wheat-growing states. His address is Box 3597, St. Paul Minnesota.

Mike Hatles of Owendale is an area field man for the Agricultural Stabilization and Conservation section of the United States Department of Agriculture or more familiarly the "ASC". The area which he oversees is 10 counties in this section of Michigan.

For several weeks, perhaps even months, since this particular type of government control of farmers has been proposed, Secretary of Agriculture Orville Freeman has been charged by the American Farm Bureau Federation and other farm organizations with using federal funds to influence a favorable vote on the proposition with the taxpayers' money. This present situation in this one county, with an employe of the ASC helping to pass on our bill to the G.T.A. would seem to give some idea that the charges are true.

Nobody who has called, or The Advertiser, questions the right of any group to promote in a legitimate way, such as open advertising, any proposition they favor.

But we, with the maddened wheat farmers here, feel that by a half-true signature on the ad we printed, we have been the victims of an attempted fast play.

We don't like it, and this little incident will make us much more careful in the future!

Mr. Woell then wrote Roger Fleming, Farm Bureau secretary-treasurer, in Washington, D.C. The point was made that government money was probably not used to pay for the advertising space, but that the ASCS man had knowingly participated in a plan to make readers of the *Tuscola Advertiser* think that a local organization was backing the wheat-referendum "yes" vote.

When the case was brought to the attention of the *Tuscola Advertiser*, the editor took a dim view of the procedure, and said as much in the above editorial. He wrote, "But we, with the maddened wheat farmers here, feel that by a half-true signature on the ad we printed, we have been the victims of an attempted fast play."

(Prints supplied by the Tuscola County Advertiser.)

on whom friendly farm groups were depending to get the facts to the voters. This year the ASCS would be criticized even for its ordinary referendum activities. Yet, with a new program, with three times as many voters, and with the opposition, in the opinion of the ASCS, misrepresenting the program to farmers, the ASCS effort would have to be immense.

So one problem was how to mount such an information drive without letting opponents make a campaign issue out of the government effort. Another task was to activate the 90,000 farmer committeemen one-fourth of whom—according to Freeman's study committee survey—were opposed to the program.

In late November of 1963, Freeman named staff economist John Schnittker to head up the USDA information effort. Schnittker was picked, rather than an ASCS official, partly because he had performed well with the Congress and in other capacities, but perhaps also because the Billie Sol Estes case had shaken Freeman's confidence in the ASCS leaders.

Schnittker's first official act was to direct USDA economists to make an analysis of the economic effects of a "yes" vote as compared with the effects of a "no" vote—of the certificate program versus the alternative of no mandatory controls and price supports at 50% of parity, but only for those farmers who voluntarily complied with the new, tighter acreage limits. To give the study an authoritative basis, he invited six distinguished agricultural economists from land-grant universities to help outline it. When it was completed they were to testify regarding its accuracy. Published in early January, the USDA study entitled "Wheat, the Program for 1964: an Economic Analysis," contained a prefatory letter by the six outside economists which stated in part:

> We, as consultants, believe the interpretation of the law and the historical data [in the study] to be accurate. The assumptions and quantitative estimates appear to be reasonable. . . . While we offered suggestions and criticisms of the text, the final wording is the choice of the authors.

The study made clear that wheat farmers would make more money under the certificate program than under the alternative.

Although it did project other bad consequences from a "no" vote, such as violation of international trade agreements, it emphasized that gross income from wheat would be a third lower under the "no" alternative, and that "annual average prices would be as low as $0.90 to $1.10 per bushel on U.S. farms, while in the event of a 'yes' vote the guaranteed price for compliers would be about $2 per bushel for 80% of the production on allotted acres, and the rest of the crop would sell at about $1.30 per bushel." The USDA built its informational program around this authoritative analysis of short-range economic consequences, which opponents found difficult to criticize.

The $1–$2 Issue

How should such an analysis be presented to farmers? Should it be in careful, technical language—or should it be written for maximum effect on farmers? It was decided that these economic issues must be presented in commanding terms if farmers were to make an economic decision rather than be governed by their frustrations or by their ideological bias. The USDA therefore phrased the issue, as it was first heralded by Secretary Freeman at the GTA and Wheat Growers conventions in early December, as a contest between $1 and $2 wheat. This was the "gut issue," to be repeated in the local ASCS offices and by ASCS committeemen in visits with farmers, in the hundreds of newsletters prepared in state and local offices with their pseudotechnical diagrams featuring two black lines out to the right, one to the "no" and $1 wheat, the other to the "yes" and $2 wheat. As stated in the principal USDA pamphlet —a small, red-inked, folded-page, printed in 2,330,000 copies—

> Wheat growers will choose between: (1) marketing quotas with price support at $2 a bushel on 80 per cent of the normal production of acreage allotments and with diversion payments for acreage taken out of production, (2) unlimited acreage with market prices of around $1 a bushel. (See Illustration 33.)

Farm Bureau's Shuman said the $1–$2 issue was "phony" because it was based on an oversimplification. Farm Bureau pointed out that the $2 price was only for 80% of normal production on allotted acres, so that if a farmer should raise a bumper crop which was 150% of normal he would average only $1.67 per bushel. And with differing freight costs and qualities of wheat, some farmers would not get as much as $2 per bushel for any of their wheat. Furthermore, in future years the Secretary might lower the certificate price and reduce the percentage of wheat covered by certificates.

In disputing the lower price which might result from a "no" vote, the Farm Bureau emphasized that price supports of $1.25 per bushel would still be in effect for those who complied with acreage allotments, and Farm Bureau statements continuously inferred (though without presenting any evidence or discussion) that the market price would in fact be $1.25 or better.

But the principal counterattack was to label the $1–$2 issue a scare tactic—to accuse Freeman of blackmailing farmers into voting for the program. In effect, Farm Bureau charged, the government of the United States was telling farmers that if they did not vote "yes" the administration would let them go broke.

On this issue, Wheat Committee Chairman Thatcher thought the Farm Bureau had a good argument. Thatcher had warned Schnittker and other USDA strategists that farmers would not be bullied, and that they were too realistic in any case to accept the simplistic $1–$2 interpretation. As Thatcher anticipated, wheat-state Farm Bureaus printed thousands of handbills entitled "The $2.00 Promise—the $1.00 Threat" and in other ways used the issue more effectively than anything else to discredit the ASCS informational effort.

On every hand, it seemed, there were dilemmas for the USDA.

Illustration 33. THE $1–$2 ISSUE. Departments of the U.S. Government have the right and the duty to prepare pamphlets, books, and other materials to inform citizens on laws, on issues where votes are required, and on other matters. Few questioned the right of the USDA to present the facts on the wheat referendum. When the writers of the principal USDA pamphlet, however, simplified the issue to the effect that a "yes" vote equals $2 a bushel for wheat, while a "no" vote knocks down the price to $1 a bushel, opponents of the government wheat program, as well as those friendly to the administration, felt the turning point against the government was reached. The Farm Bureau renamed the issue "The $2.00 Promise–the $1.00 Threat."

THE REFERENDUM
on the 1964 Wheat Program
Tuesday, May 21, 1963

Marketing quotas for the 1964 wheat crop have been proclaimed and May 21, 1963, has been set as the date of the referendum.

The referendum is on the program for one year only—1964.

The proclamation and a referendum are required by law whenever wheat supplies are excessive. The law gives the guidelines as to what are excessive supplies. In the absence of marketing quotas, the supply of wheat for the marketing year beginning July 1, 1964, is estimated at 2.8 billion bushels. This would be more than twice as much as estimated domestic disappearance and exports.

Wheat growers will choose between: (1) marketing quotas with price support at $2 a bushel on 80 percent of the normal production of acreage allotments and with diversion payments for acreage taken out of production, (2) unlimited acreage with market prices of around $1 a bushel.

If at least two-thirds of the producers voting in the referendum favor quotas, the quotas will be in effect on the 1964 crop. Price support levels, payments and market prices depend on the outcome of the vote on quotas.

The Program with Quotas in Effect

Here is the program for 1964 authorized in a new act of Congress if marketing quotas are approved:

1. Price support to cooperators. $2 a bushel, national average, for wheat with certificates; $1.30, national average, for noncertificated wheat.

Certificates will be issued for 80 percent of the normal yield of the acreage allotment—but not more than the normal yield of the **planted** acres. The usual differentials for location, premiums and discounts will apply.

You can get the benefit of price support through loans and purchase agreements as usual, but for the first time you will have two levels of support—the higher support for certificated wheat and the lower for noncertificated wheat.

U. S. DEPARTMENT OF AGRICULTURE

After planting within your allotment and meeting diverted acreage requirements you will receive a marketing card that shows you are entitled to market wheat penalty-free. It will also show the number of bushels you are entitled to sell or put under loan or purchase agreement at the higher support rate.

As before, the market price for wheat should be at or near the support price. For wheat with certificates, this would be a national average of $2 a bushel with premiums and discounts for grade and quality. Likewise, wheat without certificates should sell for prices that reflect a national average of $1.30 with premiums and discounts for grade and quality. Loans and purchase agreements are available to protect you against any drop in market price.

When you sell wheat with certificates, the buyer will show on your card that he paid for certificated wheat and the number of bushels purchased.

If you have more certificates than you need to market your wheat–perhaps because your crop is short or you use it on the farm, you may redeem your unneeded certificates at the county ASC office at the rate of 70 cents per bushel. This is important income insurance.

2. Marketing quota and acreage allotment. Your marketing quota will be the full production of your acreage allotment.

The national acreage allotment of 49.5 million acres is down 10 percent from the former legal minimum of 55 million acres. Farmers who help make this reduction in wheat acreage will earn payments. They can do this by planting within their acreage allotments and putting the diverted acres to soil conserving uses.

The number of acres on which you earn a diversion payment in this way is computed by taking 11.11 percent of your acreage allotment. (The reason for using this percentage is this: 11.11 percent of the national allotment of 49.5 million acres is 5.5 million acres, the amount of the reduction from the former legal minimum of 55 million acres.) Payment may also be earned for voluntary diversion from the allotment to conservation uses.

3. Payments. There are two rates.

(A) For planting within the acreage allotment, and putting the diverted acres to soil conserving use, the diversion payment is 30 percent of the county support price for wheat on the normal production of the acreage diverted (computed on 11.11 percent of the allotment).

(B) For voluntary added diversion to conserving uses, the payment is computed by using 50 percent instead of 30 percent of the county support price. The top limit on voluntary diversion is 20 percent of the allotment **or,** if this is larger, the number of acres that will make the total diversion 15 acres on the farm.

The 50 percent rate also applies where the wheat allotment is 13.5 acres or less, and the producer diverts his entire wheat acreage to conservation.

Advance payments of half the total for diversion of acreage will be available on request.

The acres diverted to conserving uses in this program are to be in addition to the acreage on the farm normally devoted to conservation, left idle, or diverted through other programs.

4. Grazing of diverted acres. Land diverted from wheat production to conserving uses may be grazed during the winter, early spring and late fall without affecting payments or eligibility for price support. The dates for such grazing will be established by State ASC committees. The diverted wheat acres may be grazed during the summer grazing season, but this will reduce the diversion payment by half.

5. Small farmers with 1964 wheat allotments of less than 15 acres have a choice of two alternatives:

A. The operator on the farm may elect for the farm to be an allotment farm for 1964, and be eligible to qualify for price support, certificates, and diversion payments. All producers on such a farm are eligible to vote in the referendum. This choice offers the grower an opportunity to divert all his wheat acreage (up to 15 acres) to conservation uses at the higher diversion rate of 50 percent of the county support price. The operator makes his choice by signing his allotment notice (MQ-24) and taking or sending it to the county office not later than May 13, 1963.

B. If the operator does not make this election, he may produce without penalty an acreage of wheat equal to the larger of his farm allotment or the small farm base. However, no price support, no certificates, and no diversion payments are available for the farm. The producers on the farm will not be eligible to vote in the referendum. Any producer on a small farm who desires to vote and participate in the 1964 Wheat Program should see that the operator signs and delivers the MQ-24 in time for the farm to be an allotment farm.

6. Penalties. When marketing quotas are in effect, the wheat produced on acres in excess of the farm allotment is subject to a marketing quota penalty of about $1.65 per bushel.

Under some circumstances, a land use penalty may be assessed on acreage not meeting the requirements for conservation use of diverted acres or the maintenance of the normal conserving acreage. This penalty may not be assessed on an acreage in excess of 11.11 percent of the allotment at the rate of about $1.65 a bushel for the normal yield.

Who Can Vote?

All wheat growers who have an interest in the wheat production on a farm with a 1964 wheat acreage allotment of 15 acres or more are eligible to vote in the 1964 wheat marketing quota referendum.

The operator of a farm with an allotment of less than 15 acres has until May 13 to decide whether he wants to participate as an allotment grower in 1964. If he elects to participate, he and other producers with an interest in that farm's wheat crop will be eligible to vote.

Individuals who have questions concerning their eligibility to vote should consult the ASC county office not later than May 13.

Polling places will be designated and announced by the ASC county committee well in advance of the referendum.

If Quotas Are Not Approved

The law provides the following if quotas are not approved by at least two-thirds of the producers voting in the referendum:

1. The farm wheat acreage allotments determined before the referendum would remain in effect.

2. Price support at 50 percent of parity—about $1.25 a bushel, national average, would be available to those producers who stay within their allotments.

Reliable economists, both within and outside the Department of Agriculture, predict that the market price for wheat would drop to about $1 per bushel and that wheat income would decline about $700 million. They also point out that this would have a serious adverse impact on prices for feed grain, livestock and livestock products.

3. No certificates would be issued.

4. No diversion payments would be made.

In the spring of 1964, if the supply situation required proclamation of a marketing quota for the 1965 crop, a referendum would be held and producers would again decide whether to approve or reject quotas.

This is a general description of the 1964 Wheat Program. For information on how it applies to your farm, see your county ASC committee.

PA-565 GPO 828547 April 1963

Organizing the ASCS Campaign

Even more dilemmas were involved in organizing the USDA campaign. In early December, Schnittker called together officials from all major USDA agencies to discuss the wheat-referendum campaign. He advised agencies not directly connected with the price programs—such as the Farmers Home Administration, REA, the Farm Credit Administration, and the Soil Conservation Service—to do as much as seemed appropriate to inform farmers of the issues, though admittedly their thousands of employees across the country would hesitate to become much involved.

Other agencies were given jobs. The Office of Information—traditionally a service agency—was to help with public relations under a new politically oriented director. The congressional-liaison people would solicit statements from friendly congressmen, and also ask them to put favorable articles and speeches in the *Congressional Record*. The Economics Research Service was already at work on the wheat-program analysis, and would also be asked to do another publication which provided background facts about wheat production and wheat programs. The Federal Extension Service would write up pamphlets and other materials for the State Extension Services to use.

The big job, however, would fall to the ASCS, whose local committeemen had helped round up "yes" votes throughout past years of quiet referendums, but which was now expected to be more discreet than ever before and yet to put forth a larger campaign.

Much had to be done at all echelons to ready the ASCS for the campaign. As a first step, Schnittker scheduled a series of regional wheat workshops. These were to be conducted jointly by the ASCS, the Economics Research Service and Freeman's staff, and were to be attended by the state ASCS committees, their chief employees, and the several ASCS traveling field men in each state, along with State Extension advisers and representatives of the mass media. At these meetings held in late January and early February in Kansas City, Chicago, Portland, Fargo, Denver, Columbus, and

Amarillo, the details of the program and the economic implications of the "yes" and "no" votes were thoroughly explained. The Washington teams also introduced a budget technique later used in all local ASCS offices, in which each farmer was asked to "use your pencil for your own farm." A variation of this—showing how much income each county and state would "lose" if the program did not carry—was also used widely by the friendly farm groups.

The ASCS operation did not get under way immediately after these meetings, despite Schnittker's urging, because ASCS officials wanted to wait until farmers finished signing up for the feed-grains program, and because they hoped to catch the crest of a reaction against Farm Bureau's early campaigning. When the feed-grains sign-up had been wrapped up, secret regional meetings were held by ASCS leaders in early March, where final terms of the program were announced and administrative relationships were tightened up. As with the Farm Bureau, national leaders told state leaders that the chips were down. Their agency's fortunes and their own might well be at stake in this campaign. On the one hand—driven by a Washington whiplash if necessary—state leaders were expected to mount an extensive, pervasive, and ultimately victorious campaign. Yet it was to retain the image of an informational program rather than a campaign for a favorable vote. Absolutely no indiscretions would be tolerated, even in personal affairs. ASCS regional directors were to spend much time assisting in the field but also assuring that every ASCS person walked the tightrope.

Criticism of the ASCS Activities

Few expected as good a performance from ASCS as occurred. The rules for campaigning differed somewhat by area. In Midwestern states efforts were restrained because a large majority of the ASCS committeemen were Farm Bureau members, while in the cotton, peanut, and rice areas traditional support for production controls allowed ASCS people to go beyond the rules enforced in other areas.

In fact, the case against ASCS activities rested mainly on criticisms of the USDA guidelines rather than on evidence that the guidelines were violated. Five charges—as catalogued by the Farm Bureau, and by Senator Bourke Hickenlooper (R., Iowa) at congressional hearings in early May—referred mainly to the framework of the educational program:

1. While ASCS did not openly advocate a "yes" vote, they compared alternatives in such a way as to make farmers conclude they should vote "yes." To this charge Freeman replied that "when you present both sides . . . the results are so overwhelmingly affirmative in favor of the benefit of the wheat farmer to vote yes, that those people who philosophically oppose the program then feel that there is a campaign on rather than a presentation of the honest facts." Had ASCS gone on to discuss the differences of philosophy which opponents emphasized, Freeman said, the ASCS would certainly have been judged guilty of impropriety.

Shuman also noted that a pamphlet sent to 1,337,039 15-acre growers did not inform them that they could vote "no" if they wished, which is what most ultimately did.

2. The ASCS oversimplified the alternatives, particularly in the case of $1–$2 slogan, in order to frighten farmers. To this, ASCS replied that the complex alternatives had to be framed so as to get the widest possible understanding. According to the weight of expert opinion, ASCS said, the slogan was basically accurate.

3. The government spent too much money in the campaign. Most such charges were framed as unspecific sweeping statements such as "the massive amounts of your money and mine being used . . . to get you to vote 'yes'." [1] Senator Hickenlooper, however, wondered how much the Department might be paying local committeemen per day for referendum activities. The USDA would not give him a figure or even an estimate of per diem and mileage expenses, but said, "State ASCS committees have been advised that budgetary limitations would not permit payment of

[1] *Hearings on the Feed Grain Act of 1963*, Senate Agriculture Committee, p. 76.

Illustration 34. FOUR CAMPAIGN CARTOONS. As referendum day approached cartoonists on both sides employed their skills with mounting fervor. The above appeared April 15th in the *AFBF Newsletter.*

community committeemen to make down-the-road contacts. . . . Any such effort would be at their own expense." [2]

Hickenlooper also asked for a list of expense-paid speaking trips by Freeman and members of his department in connection with the wheat referendum. The department reported a total of 15 speeches made over a 5-month period.[3]

[2] *Ibid.*, p. 77.
[3] *Ibid.*, p. 78.

Illustration 34. The *Chicago Tribune* characterizes the choice in the wheat referendum in a Parrish cartoon. Reprinted by permission.

Hickenlooper acknowledged that Freeman's group had a right to speak in support of their programs. But he sensed many improprieties, as when Undersecretary Murphy criticized the Farm Bureau and then predicted that if the certificate program failed farmers might haul their $1 wheat to market in trucks labeled as "Shuman wagons."

Point was also made of the quantity of literature mailed to farmers by state and local ASCS offices. One Kansas farmer claimed to have received thirty pieces of literature from ASCS during the campaign. The only explanation, said ASCS, was that his name must

Illustration 34. Another *AFBF Newsletter* comment.

have been recorded more than once in the machine which addresses mail. ASCS estimated farmers received a maximum of four or five communications from them relative to wheat during the campaign period.

4. Program experts in the USDA were obliged to go to the field to "explain" the program, under circumstances which these career employees regarded as somewhat improper. This procedure was necessary, the USDA said, because only they could give authoritative explanations of this new, complicated program.

Illustration 34. From the *Farmers Union Herald.*

Well-discussed at the grass roots was the "loyalty pledge" for ASCS county committeemen which the Freeman study committee had recommended as a means of assuring that programs would be administered by men who supported them. Though Freeman insisted that the pledge was not intended to prevent committeemen from opposing a program in the referendum, the pledge was strongly criticized and never implemented. Freeman was also criticized for reasserting his right to fire committeemen and local office managers for misconduct in office.

5. The ASCS tried to commandeer free television and radio time. During the campaign, attention was called to a directive from the Kentucky ASCS office telling local committees not to hesitate to ask for free time, since stations "have the general obligation to provide listeners with information on public programs of interest to them." Following the referendum, however, it was learned that the national ASCS had told all state and local committeemen to remind radio and television stations that their licenses could be suspended after three years if they did not give adequate time for public-service programs. Representative Findley called this pressure on radio and television "an example of brainwashing unknown west of the iron curtain."

Apparently, any pressure brought to bear on radio and television stations was largely unsuccessful. Some ASCS people felt they got even less free time than had been granted them in years when the program was not controversial.

No doubt the ASCS wanted more free time partly out of a sincere desire to counter "misrepresentation" by opponents who bought much time on television and radio. Both sides were convinced their cause was righteous.

The State Extension Services

In this heated environment the State Extension Services also undertook to explain the "facts" to farmers. Extension, which was pioneered more than fifty years ago as a means to persuade farmers to accept new, more efficient ways, had headquartered in the land-grant colleges and universities and for many years had made its farmer contacts through the college-trained county agents, aided by groups of progressive local farmers known as farm bureaus. These latter farmer groups had joined together along both state and national lines, and the resulting new Farm Bureau had gone into politics. Even after it had become a farm organization the

Farm Bureau continued to rely on the county agents to recruit new members.

In the period after World War II, formal ties were broken between Extension and its then-healthy offspring, though their kindred personnel, similar emphasis on farmer efficiency, and habits of cooperation lingered on in some states. However, Extension began to reflect a sensitiveness to social and economic problems which Farm Bureau leaders did not always share, and Extension also marked out a broader role for itself than merely teaching better farming methods to increasingly self-reliant commercial farmers.

Beginning with home-economics-training and rural-youth programs, many State Extension Services moved toward an interest in the whole rural community. They helped rural people understand the effects of the agricultural revolution (in which Extension had played a big part); and they helped communities plan for the future. By the time of the 1963 wheat referendum, Extension's economists, sociologists, and field men and women were caught up in many aspects of public policy, with the blessing and encouragement of the USDA, whose grants-in-aid helped support these state agencies.

In addition to telling farmers about social and economic trends, Freeman wanted Extension to help farmers understand farm programs. Assistant Secretary John Duncan, who supervised the Federal Extension Service, directed Extension to help explain the 1963 wheat-certificate program.

But as the campaign approached, national and local Farm Bureau leaders pressured the State Extension Services to stay out of it to avoid being "exploited" by supporters of the plan. As the Farm Bureau had feared, Federal Extension materials compared the short-range economic results of the alternative plans, which admittedly made the wheat certificate plan look good. Shuman told State Extension Directors in a February letter that to follow this line "will do a great disservice to farmers and could seriously impair [Extension's] further usefulness."

Extension in most states decided not to sidestep the issue. In Ohio, for instance, Extension distributed 10,000 copies of a USDA publication, held ten multicounty meetings for lay leaders, prepared news releases, radio tapes, and magazine articles, held three television programs, and sponsored 119 farmer meetings in 51 counties.

Rather than relying on USDA materials, most State Extension Services prepared their own elaborate materials which roving Extension economists and county agents used to describe the referendum choices. Although the state ASCS and all interested farm organizations were usually invited to comment on these materials before they were used, most Extension Services apparently viewed the referendum as an occasion to declare their independence from political and other ties, and to demonstrate that they could handle controversial issues in an objective manner. Their vested interest in being objective was in sharp contrast to the interests that often motivated farm organizations, the mass media, and the ASCS.

Yet the different Extension Services varied considerably in the way they approached the task, and what they said. The Kansas Extension explained only the provisions of the law. Most other Extensions went on to predict the economic consequences. On this matter, though, the Washington State Extension told farmers the wheat price would not drop as much under a "no" vote as most other Extensions were assuming in the budget forms they prepared for farmers.

Indiana, Ohio, and Michigan went even further to speculate on programs that Congress might pass if the certificate program failed. Extension Associate Director Carroll Bottum of Indiana advanced six alternative programs, including his own land-retirement program, which would give the average farmer more income than under the certificate plan offered in the referendum. In these three Midwestern states, Extension activities pleased the Farm Bureau and dismayed Freeman's group. Elsewhere, Extension was generally given encouragement by supporters of the certificate program (though Extension kept them at a discreet distance) and was often criticized by local Farm Bureaus, which found the means to sideline many county Extension agents.

Involvement in the hot campaign very likely prepared the Extension Services for a larger role in discussing future public policy questions. Except in the Midwest it demonstrated Extension was no longer a ward of the Farm Bureau or a mouthpiece for other state and federal agencies. Extension people gained in self-respect.

The Struggle for a New Feed Grains Act

A sideshow to the referendum campaign, but much related to it, was the Administration's effort to pass a feed-grains bill before the wheat referendum, and the effort by opponents of the wheat-certificate plan to prevent this. The bill would permit farmers to grow wheat on their feed-grains acres—and vice versa—and thus make the certificate plan more attractive to many farmers. Freeman said farmers ought to be assured that they could substitute one for the other before they voted in the referendum. Opponents wanted to wait so as to enact different feed-grains legislation and to tag on a new bill for wheat as well, in event the referendum failed.

Republicans again demonstrated their artistry in delay tactics. When the bill finally passed the House April 25th, Republicans frustrated Senator Ellender's effort to have it reported from his committee without hearings. Senator Hickenlooper used the hearings to stall the feed-grains bill as well as to review the case against ASCS conduct in the campaign.

Senate Democrats prevented any of the 16 Republican amendments from being adopted, and this success avoided the need for a conference committee for further House action once the Senate passed the bill.

Republican leaders decided not to filibuster the bill, though several senators were willing to do so. It passed on May 16th, five days before the referendum. However, the House had adjourned for a long weekend on that day—Thursday—without authorizing their Speaker to sign bills.

So by Monday morning, May 20th, congressional clerks had already enrolled the bill. Pages and chauffeurs were waiting to race it from the Senate to the House Chambers, and then to the President. Local ASCS offices at all levels were poised to release the news as soon as the President signed the bill (some of them released it by mistake a day early), and the friendly farm organizations gave last-minute publicity to a bill that they thought would considerably increase the "yes" vote.

The President used the signing as an opportunity to put himself on record again as favoring a "yes" vote in the wheat referendum:

> Tomorrow is the day of decision for the wheat farmers of our nation. The issues are clear. And I think it is important that the wheat farmers of this country understand them. It is our best judgment, the Federal Government's best judgment, that a negative vote will permit high production and increased wheat surpluses. . . . that the price of wheat will decline to about $1.10 a bushel, if there is a negative vote.

13. *Referendum Day: May 21st, 1963*

THE LARGE turnout of voters was the first surprise of referendum day— 1,222,856 people took action in the process of governmental decision.

These included farmers in New England—dairymen, growers of potatoes and green peas, many who sold entire crops to food processors; farmers in the Southeast, many of whom had grown no wheat the preceding year, many whose red clay earth was more compatible to other crops in any case; farmers in the Middle Atlantic states, again dairymen, vegetable growers, truck gardeners, in a rich-soil territory which had been under cultivation since the seventeenth century; and farmers in the Midwest—producing hogs, small fruits, truck, dairy products, corn—many of whom raised a patch of wheat just for the wheat straw to be used as bedding in hog houses and chicken nests.

Among these million-odd farmers were those from the Rocky Mountain cattle area, the wheat states of the Northwest, and the great fruit and truck areas of the Pacific coast.

In South Dakota the farmers around Aberdeen had been amused and bemused by Max Cooper's column in the *South Dakota American*.

"The real issue," he wrote, "is not more government control or freedom, as the Farm Bureau claims. This would be an easy choice . . . Everybody but Khrushchev prefers freedom. And he can't vote because he doesn't even have a decent wheat farm in all Russia." He continued:

Nor do the ordinary run-of-the-farm pessimists see the issue correctly. These sad birds say if you vote "no" you won't get anything for the

The American Wheat Farmer

IN WHOSE HANDS RESTS THE DECISION OF A DECADE ON TUESDAY, MAY 21

Illustration 35. THE MAN AND THE CROP. One of man's most ancient crops, a persistent U.S. problem. The *North Dakota Union Farmer* emphasizes the occasion on the eve of referendum day.

wheat you sell. And if you vote "yes" the government will cut you down to a piddly little wheat patch that would make any Dakota farmer hang his head in shame.

We superpessimists, who like to believe the worst, have read enough to know that a "no" vote is a vote for depression, disaster and big farmers. Then we read the Farm Bureau information and we learned that a "yes" vote is a vote for slavery, bureaucrats and big government.

Nobody wants to vote for any of those things.

. . . Every red-blooded American boy is brought up to despise some classes of people. And the classes that are despised the most thoroughly are bureaucrats, big farmers and newspapermen.

. . . It wouldn't be so bad if [the farmer] had only himself to worry about. But the fate of the whole country rides on his decision.

If he votes "yes" he'll start the whole country down the road to slavery, one side worries. One little "yes" vote too many could throw the Constitution out the window, overturn the Supreme Court and make Congress useless. If he votes "no" he'll put us on the toboggan slide to a horrible depression, the other side frets. And if we ever get into another depression, a dictator will take over, they warn.

I'm thankful, I'm not a wheat farmer. I couldn't stand all that responsibility. I believe I'd chicken out and not vote either "yes" or "no." I'd just write "maybe" on the ballot and let the ASCS make what it could of that.

Also included in the voter group was the desperate, diminishing breed of small commercial farmers everywhere, whose expenses had increased as their acreage allotments had decreased; farm wives, most of whom knew little or nothing about the program, but who voted as their husbands did; and the farmers of the Plains states—where nearly three-quarters of the national allotment of wheat was grown—often "big" in terms of the number of acres they farmed, but not necessarily "big" in terms of what they owned, or in their income; and among the voters were the landlords.

Kearny County

In Kearny county, Western Kansas, for example, the average farm was about 1,700 acres, but only a third of it was planted to wheat —because the climate is so dry west of the 100-degree meridian, which cuts the center of Kansas, that most land must lie fallow every other year to build up moisture enough to raise a crop.[1] The acreage allotments cut further into the half available to be planted.

Most of the land was actually owned by outsiders, in parcels of a half section or quarter section (a section is 640 acres). Much of

[1] These statistics and descriptive data of the Kearny county area were gathered by Don Hadwiger during the week preceding the wheat referendum in that area.

it was bought before World War II at $3 to $50 an acre. A good amount of the land was in the estates of deceased persons, whose beneficiaries often had never seen the land or the people who farmed it.

The average farmer in Kearny county was a local big renter who farmed for over a dozen absentee landlords, or for estates of former landlords, each of whom had title to a quarter or a half of one section, and so the farmer had to plant much of his wheat in fifty-acre patches. Virtually every farmer could easily farm more land than he had, but little land changed hands. Farmer tenants often did "undercut" one another by writing letters to another's landlord in a bid for the land, though without causing any apparent hard feelings. Because of the land hunger, some local residents thought the biggest farmers might vote "no" in order to break the wheat price and force off the less solvent farmers, or in order to sell their "hot" wheat (produced in previous years on acres outside the allotment) which had been stored in farm granaries.

On the point of size, these "far country" men were less than happy about their fifteen-acre brethren in the Midwest.

"Talk about poor representation in the legislature," one man said, "isn't it worse to give those little fellows in Iowa and Indiana the votes to kill this program?"

One Farm Bureau man felt the small-acreage man was a reason to vote against the program. "Give us $1.25 wheat for a couple of years, and we'll get rid of the fifteen-acre fellows. Then we won't have too much wheat."

In the Kearny county area, wheat is the only crop that 70% of the cultivated land will grow. The remaining 65,000 acres of cropland are irrigated from wells, and will go into grain sorghum if the wheat price falls. Grain sorghum may fatten cattle cheaper than Midwestern corn, and Kearny county agent Merwin Lines pointed to big new packing plants in nearby Garden City as proof of a trend.

Few who lived many years in Kearny county wanted to leave this flat land where highway signs warn motorists of wind currents. Lakin, the only real town (1,432) in a county of 3,000 people, did not look tired and neither did the farmers who drove as far as thirty miles to the nearest store, and several miles to their nearest neighbor. They had learned to live with distance, weather, and undercutting neighbors, in somewhat good humor. Whether they could live very long with $1.25 wheat was a question, one which they were prepared to gamble on when they voted on referendum day.

The county ASCS manager, Tod Vincent, had set up only one polling place—in Lakin. The three-farmer referendum committee opened shop in the American Legion building at 8 a.m. on May 21st.

They had a hint, from the absentee ballots, that there would be more than the usual 200 voters. Despite a light drizzle, voters immediately arrived in carloads—sometimes in caravans of two to six families. These voted quickly and left quietly, whereas farmers who voted later in the day often stayed to talk.

The county Republican chairman joshed voters, as they arrived, about the "Kennedy farm program." The national secretary of the Wheat Growers Association, who happened to live in the county, talked about the economic long run to a transitory group outside the voting room. Neither the Wheat Growers nor the Farm Bureau had campaigned as local organizations, though some individual members had donated money or had gotten neighbors to the polls.

Kearny county voters were "high-risk" farmers, often blanked several years in a row by some combination of high wind, winter kill, drought, and heavy hail. They were expecting a poor crop in 1963, and a second poor crop in 1964 due to lack of moisture, after having had four consecutive good crops. Though used to gambling, they obviously attached importance to their vote and complained about being upstaged by the more numerous "fifteen-acre fellows" in the Midwest and South.

Their radios and lofty television aerials had brought in the "propaganda" from distant Hutchinson, as had the farm magazines which most farmers had read, and the regional papers.

A large share had talked with ASCS manager Vincent. He had explained to them that they could raise more wheat (due to the clause permitting "substitution for feed-grains acres") and make more money under the new plan than under the existing program, and that they would get insurance in the form of 70-cent certificates on 80% of normal production on their allotments, even if their crop failed. The plan seemed so right for these dry-land farmers that Vincent predicted a 70% "yes" vote. The USDA, in fact, expected a very favorable vote in this area, as compared with the low 50% approval in Kearny county in 1962.

The Second Surprise of the Day

When the polls closed at 8:00 p.m., the committee began to stack the ballots in four piles—the "yes," the "no," the challenged ballots, and absentees. The "yes" and "no" piles grew evenly. Vincent's face fell as the count ended in an almost perfect split. Four hundred twenty-two farmers had voted. The young farmer on the referendum committee who had decided only late in the day to vote "yes" suddenly said, "this is going to separate the men from us boys," and he repeated this several times as they concluded the official tallying.

Indeed, a call to Kansas ASCS headquarters revealed that the certificate program had lost nationally by an astounding margin. Over a million farmers and their wives had voted, five times as many as in the preceding year. Only 48% of them had voted for the program. (See Illustration 36.)

The crushing defeat of the program was unexpected. In Ireland, delegates to a meeting of the International Federation of Agricultural Producers had expressed fear that America might flood the international grain markets if the controls program should be rejected. IFPA President Herschel Newsom (of the Grange) had assured them the night before the referendum that the program would pass.

Illustration 36. THE WHEAT REFERENDUM VOTE. The statistics, state by state, showed that six states had voted the necessary two-thirds approval: Maine, Georgia, Kentucky, North Carolina, South Carolina, Tennessee. Three states, Alaska, Hawaii, and New Hampshire cast no votes. States marked with an asterisk have less than .05 of the acreage allotment. Figures are tabulated on the following pages.

Region and State	*% of Nat'l allotment 1963*	*Eligible voters*	*For*	*Against*	*Total*	*% Yes*
MIDWEST AND NORTHEAST						
Maine	*	35	24	8	32	75.0
Connecticut	*	45	8	22	30	26.7
Delaware	.1	1,507	403	427	830	48.6
Illinois	2.6	128,995	21,262	49,783	71,045	29.9
Indiana	2.0	144,189	20,269	59,015	79,284	25.6
Iowa	.2	17,399	5,709	3,255	8,964	63.7
Massachusetts	*	25	4	18	22	18.2
Michigan	1.7	143,020	15,871	61,987	77,858	20.4
Missouri	2.4	224,310	57,184	30,928	88,112	64.9
New Jersey	.1	2,724	559	1,181	1,740	32.1
New York	.5	38,534	7,005	15,239	22,244	31.5
Ohio	2.7	180,840	20,169	68,722	88,891	22.7
Pennsylvania	.9	51,564	7,345	26,031	33,376	22.0
Rhode Island	*	10	2	6	8	25.0
Vermont	*	54	5	38	43	11.6
West Virginia	.1	3,510	1,384	1,482	2,866	48.3
Wisconsin	.1	10,153	3,519	2,827	6,346	55.5
	13.4	946,914	160,722	320,969	481,691	33.4

50.9% of eligibles voted; 39.4% of U.S. vote; ⅔ plurality minus 160,405; simple majority minus 80,124

Region and State	*% of Nat'l allotment 1963*	*Eligible voters*	*For*	*Against*	*Total*	*% Yes*
SOUTH						
Alabama	.1	5,736	1,719	1,243	2,962	58.0
Arkansas	.1	12,066	1,914	3,697	5,611	34.1
Florida	*	1,116	270	654	924	29.2
Georgia	.2	18,387	13,143	1,985	15,128	86.9
Kentucky	.4	40,506	22,875	3,803	26,678	85.7
Louisiana	*	1,682	159	784	943	16.9
Maryland	.3	8,529	963	4,802	5,765	16.7
Mississippi	.1	2,543	428	1,415	1,843	23.2
North Carolina	.5	107,858	64,756	15,250	80,006	80.9
South Carolina	.3	30,157	16,664	3,350	20,014	83.3
Virginia	.4	29,604	7,429	11,767	19,196	38.7
Tennessee	.3	42,229	20,367	6,332	26,699	76.3
	2.7	300,413	150,687	55,082	205,769	73.2

68.5% of eligibles voted; 16.8% of U.S. vote; ⅔ plurality plus 13,507; simple majority plus 47,802

Region and State	*% of Nat'l allotment 1963*	*Eligible voters*	*For*	*Against*	*Total*	*% Yes*
WEST						
Arizona	.1	1,631	177	544	733	24.2
California	.8	5,703	878	2,268	3,146	27.9
Idaho	2.2	52,036	7,756	18,725	26,481	29.3
Nevada	*	653	87	276	363	24.0
Oregon	1.5	24,501	4,992	5,191	10,183	49.0
Utah	.5	8,687	1,307	3,233	4,540	28.8
Washington	3.7	37,863	7,673	8,576	16,249	47.2
	8.8	131,074	22,870	38,823	61,693	37.7

47% of eligibles voted; 5.0% of U.S. vote; ⅔ plurality minus 18,259; simple majority minus 7,977

Region and State	*% of Nat'l allotment 1963*	*Eligible voters*	*For*	*Against*	*Total*	*% Yes*
NORTH PLAINS						
Minnesota	1.3	83,648	32,310	16,850	49,160	65.7
Montana	7.3	42,022	13,296	12,446	25,742	51.7
North Dakota	13.7	123,380	54,632	28,387	83,019	65.8
South Dakota	5.0	69,080	22,634	12,028	34,662	65.3
Wyoming	.5	4,450	1,212	1,721	2,933	41.3
	27.8	322,580	124,084	71,432	195,516	63.4

60.6% of eligibles voted; 16.0% of U.S. vote; ⅔ plurality minus 6,260; simple majority plus 26,326

Region and State	*% of Nat'l allotment 1963*	*Eligible voters*	*For*	*Against*	*Total*	*% Yes*
SOUTH PLAINS						
Colorado	4.8	31,159	7,916	8,280	16,196	48.9
Kansas	19.6	221,534	48,404	65,131	113,535	42.6
Nebraska	5.7	106,232	27,542	22,993	50,535	54.5
New Mexico	.9	4,847	1,087	1,457	2,544	42.7
Oklahoma	9.0	86,250	18,488	26,838	45,326	40.8
Texas	7.3	79,001	22,484	27,567	50,051	44.9
	47.3	529,023	125,921	152,266	278,187	45.3

52.6% of eligibles voted; 22.7% of U.S. vote; ⅔ plurality minus 59,537; simple majority minus 13,173

Near the close of working hours on referendum day, John Schnittker had dictated a memorandum to Secretary Freeman, in which he reviewed the hard-fought campaign, and concluded that if the program did not pass it was not because farmers lacked information about it. Schnittker then went home for a leisurely dinner. Later in the evening it was his job to phone the results to Secretary Freeman at his home.

Farm Bureau President Shuman and some of his staff had left their Chicago office at the close of the work day while others remained to receive returns from the states. These were relayed to the Washington office, where two visiting state Farm Bureau presidents sat through the evening. There were no formal Farm Bureau celebrations.

Impact on the Participants

For Farm Bureau officials the next day was a busy one, with television cameras stalking the halls beneath a foot-high banner "We Won" in the Chicago office, while in Washington Farm Bureau lobbyists immediately began an offensive to obtain new legislation.

Election-night emotions were strongest on the losing side. For the Freeman group, passage of the wheat-certificate program was to have been the capstone of two vigorous years, during which they had not contemplated that the big obstacle would be farmer voters rather than the Congress. On election night, many of them had gathered in a large improvised press room where runners from the ASCS field offices elsewhere in the USDA's complex of offices brought results to four men operating calculators and adding machines. These men posted the refined figures on a huge blackboard at the front of the press room. From this room, grim USDA officials and Democratic congressional assistants adjourned in knots to the ASCS office suites, especially after returns from the East and Midwest made clear the stunning defeat. Others sat weirdly fascinated by the returns until the press room was closed at 3:00 a.m. or they listened to older career employees philosophically compare this defeat to the Supreme Court decision which invalidated the first Agricultural Adjustment Act in 1936. A few assisted in preparing policy statements for leading Democratic politicians. Later, a number of Freeman's people said they had become semi-numb and had remained so for weeks thereafter.

Farmers Union's head lobbyist Reuben Johnson had invited his staff to his home to listen to the election-night returns. After the guests had left at 1 a.m., shaken by their overwhelming defeat, Johnson phoned the results to President Jim Patton in Ireland. Patton, ever the optimist, consoled Johnson, "Don't worry, Reuben. The Farmers Union will live to fight another battle."

Reflections on the Referendum Defeat

There were undoubtedly many causes for the stunning upset vote. First, tremendous regional differences showed up as the votes were analyzed. Almost three-fourths of the voters in the South and Border states supported the program, while two-thirds of the Midwestern and Northeastern voters opposed it. A phenomenal 69% of the eligibles voted in the South, and 51% voted in the Midwest-Northeast, though few farmers in either section had much direct economic interest in the vote.

However, the Southern margin of 13,507 votes did not compare with the Midwestern-Northeastern deficit of more than 160,000. In the Plains states, with 75.1% of the national wheat acreage allotment, the vote was close, and the "yes" votes outnumbered the "no's" by 26,307. But this majority was far too slight to overcome the Midwestern-Northeastern deficit. (See Illustration 37.)

The vote was clearly related to the type of farm production. In Kansas, where areas of feed-grains production for beef shaded into wheat areas and where dairy, sorghum, and cattle country could also be found, there was a significant correlation between the change in the "yes" vote percentage between 1962 and 1963, and the percentage of total farm land from which wheat was harvested within each county in 1959. This relationship appeared also in North Dakota. In the areas where wheat production was concentrated there was a tendency to cast more "yes" votes.

Region	% of Nat'l allot-ment 1963	% of Total U.S. ref-endum Vote 1963	% of Eligi-bles who Voted	No. of eligible voters	No. of yes voters	No. of no voters	Total voting	Divergence from ⅔ plurality	Divergence from simple majority
Midwest and Northeast	13.4	39.4	50.9	946,914	160,722	320,969	481,691	−160,405	−80,124
South	2.7	16.8	68.5	300,413	150,687	55,082	205,769	+13,507	+47,802
West	8.8	5.0	47.0	131,074	22,870	38,823	61,693	−18,259	−7,977
Plains	75.1	38.7	55.6	851,603	250,005	223,698	473,703	−65,797	+13,154
North Plains	*27.8*	*16.0*	*60.6*	*322,580*	*124,084*	*71,432*	*195,516*	*−6,260*	*+26,326*
South Plains	*47.3*	*22.7*	*52.6*	*529,023*	*125,921*	*152,266*	*278,187*	*−59,537*	*−13,173*
Total	100.0	99.9	54.8	2,230,004	584,284	638,572	1,222,856		

Source: Column 1 is from Table 13 in *Wheat: The Program for 1964,* USDA (January 1963). Other columns are derived from totals in the official county-by-county summaries submitted by ASCS Committees in each state.

Illustration 37. WHEAT REFERENDUM STATISTICS BY REGION. More than half the wheat farmers in the big-acreage states—the eleven states with 75.1 percent of the national acreage allotment—wanted the Kennedy farm program. They didn't get it. The fifteen-acre men combined with the bare minority of the big-acreage men to send the program to overwhelming defeat.

Party Differences

There was also evidence from polls of referendum voters taken in two Kansas counties, one North Dakota county, and one Ohio county, that political party or other political loyalties were important.[2] Republicans constituted 78% of the "no" voters in a central Kansas county, but only 32% of the "yes" voters. Another study of all Ohio voters conducted just before the referendum by Professor John Bottum of Ohio State University,[3] revealed that Democrats were 56%–44% against the bill in Ohio while Republicans were 83%–17% against.

The Impact of the Campaign

What had been the impact of the campaign by the ASCS and the farm organizations? This question opened a Pandora's box.

In the South, ASCS personnel had worked vigorously to encourage a large voter turnout. They indeed deserved much credit for the large Southern vote in the absence of farm-group campaigning and especially where there was the typically low economic interest in wheat prices. Similarly, the Farm Bureau deserved considerable credit for organizing the Midwestern vote.

But the campaign apparently had a different effect in the big-acreage wheat country. ASCS efforts there became a very effective issue for program opponents. And some reaction against Farm Bureau activities could be noted. In fact, in Kansas counties where local ASCS groups campaigned hardest, the percentage of "no" votes increased most; and where Farm Bureaus worked hardest, the percentage of "no" votes increased least.

While local groups did not successfully persuade farmers to vote with them, the Farm Bureau and ASCS did much to motivate farmers to vote. They made it clear that there was a contest, and

[2] The polls were taken by Don Hadwiger and his associates for a study of the wheat referendum, using county-by-county data as well as surveys in the counties referred to above. Surveys of referendum participants were also made.

[3] John S. Bottum, "Wheat Referendum: The 1963 Ohio Vote and Farm Policy Implications, AE345 (Wooster, Ohio: Ohio Agricultural Experiment Station), June, 1963.

the sound of the conflict drew community attention to the referendum. The campaigners made the vote seem so relevant that farmers could not in good conscience refuse to participate. These groups also verbalized the issues in such a way as to get a strong farmer response. In the big-acreage wheat states—such as Kansas—a disproportionate majority of the new voters voted "no."

Confusion about the Economic Issues

Aside from having increased the size of the referendum vote, the hard-fought campaign had one other principal result: it confused the voters.

Farmer voters had read a good deal about the program. Well over 85% of the county-survey respondents had read both county newspaper and farm magazine articles dealing with the program, and most had consulted the ASCS office. Many had visited with their neighbors about the program. Obviously farmers did not lack information about the program. On the whole they were aware that the issues were complex, and that uncertainties attended either alternative.

The "No" Vote as a Protest Vote

Economic issues were, of course, not the only ones. The opposition had suggested that farmers use the referendum mainly as a vehicle for protest. Opponents had urged producers to vote against centralized government, against the Kennedy administration, against favoritism allowed to other regions or to other kinds of wheat, and against acreage restrictions. Right-wing organizations had said the referendum was a chance to vote against socialism—even against Khrushchev.

In the Plains, the dynamic factor which produced a "no" vote was the protest against the inconvenience and economic sacrifice involved in the long-suffered production controls. In contrast, other voters who were not primarily wheat producers—and they were the majority—used the vote mainly to protest against confusing restrictions on their relatively insignificant wheat acreages, and also to protest against efforts to put mandatory controls on their principal product, whether it was meat, milk, or feed grains. "Freedom to farm" was a very appealing slogan, except in the South where producers of cotton, tobacco, and peanuts saw fit to cast another vote of confidence for mandatory programs.

For commercial wheat producers, the decision to protest against controls was not easy. It is true that grievances had accumulated during nine years of controls. Also, rising costs had made it increasingly difficult for many small and medium-sized wheat farmers to idle further acres, or indeed to make ends meet much longer in accord with existing restrictions. For those who felt they needed increased gross income in order to maintain an adequate net income, the "no" vote appeared to offer some hope: there was a chance that the price of wheat would somehow stay up, even as the producers managed to increase their total production by harvesting formerly idled acres.

Banking on New "Better" Program

Most commercial wheat producers who voted "no" were clearly gambling that Congress would pass a new "better" program if the mandatory certificate program failed.

Kansas farmers wanted a change in the direction of fewer or no controls, less regimentation and less centralization. They also wanted a less complicated program. Some "yes" voters in all counties objected that the certificate program was too complicated. Despite the presumed popularity of the two-price program, the various groups polled—including ASCS committee chairmen—seemed to feel that the two-price certificate program was not popular with farmers.

But if Congress did not enact a new program following defeat of the certificate program, those whose income depended on wheat sales would be big losers. Perhaps because the stakes were so great and also because commercial wheat farmers were better acquainted with the program provisions, voters in the Plains counties with the highest concentrations of wheat were more reluctant to cast a protest vote—despite their long-standing frustration with controls—than were farmers with small wheat acreages who had little to lose.

Just what were the odds—in farmers' minds—that Congress would pass a new program? Key congressional and administration Democrats had said Congress would not be likely to pass another program in 1963 if the referendum failed. In that event farmers would probably have to live with the undesirable alternative program. However, Farm Bureau spokesmen had promised they would work for a new program, and so had many congressmen from the Republican districts where a majority of referendum voters lived. A poll of congressmen from districts with many eligible wheat voters had revealed that 94% of the Republican congressmen felt the program should not pass, and two-thirds of them had so informed their constituents. Slightly under half of the Republicans believed that Congress would certainly pass a new program in the event that the referendum failed, and the remainder of the Republicans polled felt that Congress would likely pass a new program.

In the county polls, about half of the western Kansans knew how their U.S. Representative, Robert Dole, stood. However, a small fraction of "yes" voters were misinformed about his stand, as were a small fraction of central Kansas voters about the position of Senator Frank Carlson of Kansas. (Both were opposed.) The great majority of the voters in Grand Forks County (N.D.) knew how both of their U.S. senators stood with regard to the referendum issue. (They favored the program.)

About two-thirds of the "no" voters surveyed in two Western and Central Kansas counties and in a North Dakota county believed that Congress would pass another program in 1963 if the mandatory certificate program failed. On the other hand, most of the respondents who voted "yes" felt Congress would not pass a new program.

The Politics of Rejection

The referendum vote was, in a sense, the sequel to a series of votes against candidates in office that farmers had cast in congressional and presidential elections in recent years, apparently always in the expectation that they would be offered better alternatives. Secretary Orville Freeman had stressed that farmers would finally have to make a choice between a program which effectively controlled production or one in which government abdicated responsibility for maintaining high market prices. But nearly 49% of the major commercial wheat farmers had rejected his supply-management program in the expectation that Congress would pass a program more to their liking.

With the defeat of the wheat-certificate plan, there would be pressure on wheat growers to seek a new legislative charter, and pressure on an urban-oriented national government to devise a plan which divided farmer interests would be unable to reject.

The Summing Up

An editorial headed "A 'No' that Sparkles," in the *Manhattan* (Kansas) *Mercury* of Wednesday, May 22, 1963, sums up some of the issues from an approval-of-the-outcome viewpoint. In part it reads:

> There's a breath of freshness and brightness to this beautiful spring morning that even improves on nature. It was added by the American farmer yesterday by his vote in the wheat referendum.
>
> Perhaps this is a bit too lyrical a way to describe a reaction to how the wheat farmers did vote but their unmistakable indication that they've had it clear up to here with too much government meddling in agriculture is remarkably akin to a clean breath of spring.
>
> To even suggest that the world of agriculture and the lives of farmers have been transformed into one big, beautiful world of no worries and no sweat is, of course, silly. The negative vote, as a matter of fact, may well have caused more problems for the moment than it eased. . . . In passing comment one cannot help but congratulate and admire the American Farm Bureau Federation and its state organizations such as the Kansas Farm Bureau in this effort. The Farm Bureau had a tremendous amount at stake in this referendum. Had the vote been "yes" it would have been a blow from which it would have been difficult to recover. . . . The Farm Bureau of all the organizations had more to gain and more to lose than any others . . . That its feelings did prevail so overwhelmingly puts it in a powerful position with Congress.

14. *A Voluntary Program Goes Into Effect*

THE "NO" vote may have sparkled in Kansas but it was cyclone black in Washington, D.C. Democratic leaders hardly disguised their resentment at the verdict.

Chairman Ellender said, "Democracy has spoken and wheat farmers have voted themselves out of a program. I wish them well."

House Democratic majority leader Carl Albert agreed: "The farmers have made their choice."

President Kennedy said:

> Yesterday the producers of wheat . . . participated in an election without parallel in the world. . . . Wheat farmers in this instance voted for the right to produce whatever the market will pay, rather than for high prices and limited production.
>
> We accept this judgment and it is my sincere hope that this will prove to be a wise choice for wheat farmers and for the country.

Secretary Freeman observed: "The point of view which prevailed in the referendum is entitled to a full and fair trial." The USDA took steps to assure that the world market would not be flooded with U.S. surplus wheat, and then sat tight.

But jubilant opponents of the certificate program immediately presented legislative proposals. Three Republicans on the House Agriculture Committee—Quie of Minnesota, Dole of Kansas and Short of North Dakota—introduced a voluntary acreage-diversion plan for wheat similar to that in effect for feed grains. The Farm Bureau, after considerable effort, persuaded 19 Representatives and 16 Senators—mostly Republicans—to reintroduce their cropland-retirement bill. Neither the three House Agriculture Republicans nor the Farm Bureau liked the other group's plan. In fact, when rural House Republicans held a strategy meeting, they found themselves in deep disagreement over alternative programs, though most did agree that a program was needed. Advocacy for abolishing all programs had come mostly from urban Republicans.

Urban Democrats, most of whom had cast a reluctant vote for the program which the farmers had rejected, vowed they would vote for no more farm bills. A city Democratic spokesman, Representative Frank Thompson of New Jersey, said, "The farmers have made their choice. I warned them. The President warned them and all the national farm organizations except the Farm Bureau warned them."

Opponents who had promised a better program if farmers defeated the certificate plan relied on the administration to assert leadership once again. House Republican farm leader Charles Hoeven predicted hopefully that Democratic leaders would "fall all over themselves to enact new legislation. They couldn't do anything else."

A New Plan

Certainly most legislators from wheat states believed themselves under pressure to get new legislation, although it seemed that the relatively low volume of post-referendum mail came from farmers who wanted an end to all farm programs, or from disgruntled "yes" voters who wanted prices kept low to teach a lesson to those who had voted "no."

It appeared most farmers were still amazed by the force of their decision at the polls, and yet puzzled like others as to its meaning. Their initial amazement and inaction might well give way—when the price consequences began to be felt next year—to strong farmer resentment against both Republican and Democratic incumbents.

As if in response to the plight of the Plains legislators up for reelection in 1964, an attractive, feasible plan did emerge. It was a plan which could draw bipartisan support. It involved relatively little change in existing legislation. It was unbelievably simple. Indeed it seemed so good that when introduced to it, wheat politicians often responded in exasperation, "Why didn't we think of that before?"

The new program could be implemented without a referendum, because farmers would not be required by law to participate. In most other respects it was the same program which farmers had just rejected. The mandatory features of the certificate plan could be dropped, it was calculated, because an estimated 70% to 80% of the commercial producers would voluntarily submit to controls in order to obtain the valuable wheat certificates and the acreage-diversion payments, and to avoid an annual reduction in their valuable "wheat acreage base" which to a certain extent had become capitalized into the value of their land.

Though it seemed the new program would cost somewhat more or reward the farmers somewhat less than the mandatory program rejected in the referendum, the new idea met two criteria imposed on all immediate proposals by the thumping referendum defeat: (1) Farmers would not have to vote on it, and (2) Technically it was voluntary. Farmers who valued "freedom" more than the program benefits could plant wheat on the whole of their farms.

The idea for the new program originated with a Freeman staff member but had to be smuggled out of the USDA because Freeman had placed a moratorium on staff work on any new proposals following the referendum. Neither Freeman nor most of his staff could immediately overcome their deep bitterness which was a reaction to the stinging defeat. Even had they been willing to "bail out the farmers," they faced the predicament in strategy that Farm Bureau had predicted for them: If they did not act, opponents would accuse them of being vindictive. But on the other hand the administration could hardly suggest an alternative, voluntary plan on the morn of defeat without seeming to concede that "no" voters were right in anticipating a new "better" program. Thus, to offer a new program would be to throw open to question the honesty, the good judgment, and inevitably the prestige of the ASCS, the USDA, the Democratic congressmen, and friendly farm organizations, and even of the administration itself since it had told farmers there would likely be no new program in 1963.

In any case chances were dim that Congress would be persuaded to pass any program. Southern and urban Democrats were in a sour mood. With farmers themselves confused and divided, some rural congressmen would hesitate to favor any plan.

So the USDA took the firm even if tentative line: "Farmers have made their choice—let experience test its wisdom." This became the strategic policy of the National Farmers Union, which assumed farmers would shortly see their mistake and return to the mandatory programs. Even the Wheat Growers Association, also smarting from defeat, took the no-action line of the administration. Officials of these friendly organizations scheduled long vacations, just as Secretary Freeman himself was planning an extended trip to study agriculture in the Soviet satellite countries.

This strategy did not serve the interests or the inclinations of the few rural Democratic legislators from Midwestern and Plains States. Having heroically backed the mandatory plan which their farmer voters had now rejected, these incumbent legislators wanted to move quickly to get a program which would maintain farm income in 1964.

The New Plan Becomes a Bill

The new certificate idea was first given to Ben Stong, who had long served congressional liberals as a sounding board and clearing house for farm-policy ideas. Stong, a staff member of the Senate Interior and Insular Affairs Committee, also acted as assistant to Senator George McGovern (D., S.D.), who had resigned as President Kennedy's "Food-for-Peace" administrator to win the seat vacated by the death of South Dakota's Senator Francis Case.

Stong discussed the new voluntary plan with legislative reference specialist Walter Wilcox, the old critic of the administration's mandatory programs. Wilcox worked out the economic basis for a program he was confident would work. It remained for these two veteran staff members to decide how to introduce this new measure to the world.

Stong wanted to do it in a way which would benefit Senator McGovern. But since they—and presumably McGovern—were intent on getting it passed in 1963, they wanted to get support from the beginning both from some Republican wheat legislators and from some of the Southerners on the Agriculture Committees. They also hoped to secure the backing of Democratic congressional leaders, and to get at least the acquiescence of the administration.

In early July the new plan was put into a bill (consisting mainly of deletions of the mandatory provisions in the 1962 law), and this was circulated—with an accompanying explanation—to Republican and Democratic wheat leaders. The replies were all either favorable or neutral. The GTA's Bill Thatcher apparently urged Hubert Humphrey, the Senate farm-policy dean, to support the bill (though the National Farmers Union continued to hold out for another referendum on the mandatory program). But opposition from the USDA caused McGovern to delay introducing the bill until July 29th. He submitted it then at the urging of Senate Democratic leaders, with Democratic cosponsors Burdick (N.D.), McCarthy (Minn.), McGee (Wyo.) and Nelson (Wisc.), and Republican Young of North Dakota. (See Illustration 38.)

Senator Hubert Humphrey gave McGovern strong support: "I say to the administration, as one of its loyal supporters, that we cannot content ourselves with doing nothing. Let that be clear. Nor can we content ourselves with blaming somebody else if things go wrong. As senators, we have a responsibility regardless of political party."

McGovern admitted Congress was unlikely to pass legislation introduced so late in the session "though the need is great." He hoped the administration and Southern Democrats would be

---

Illustration 38. THE SALVAGE STARTS. Two months after R-day, Senator McGovern (D., S.D.) introduced new wheat legislation. Co-introducers were Senators Burdick (D., N.D.), Young (R., N.D.), McCarthy (D., Minn.), Nelson (D., Wisc.), and McGee (D., Wyo.). The proposed voluntary wheat-certificate program was presented as an urgent and minimum measure to give wheat growers some assurance of $2 wheat in 1964. The opening portion of the McGovern speech is from the *Congressional Record*, daily edition, July 29th, 1963.

CONGRESSIONAL RECORD — SENATE

Mr. McGOVERN. Mr. President, I introduce, for appropriate reference, for myself and Senators BURDICK, MCCARTHY, MCGEE, NELSON, and YOUNG of North Dakota, a voluntary wheat-crop adjustment and price support bill, and I ask unanimous consent that the bill lie on the table 5 legislative days.

Mr. McGOVERN. Mr. President, the bill would make the wheat certificate plan in the Food and Agriculture Act of 1962 an entirely voluntary program, to become effective with the 1964 wheat crop, by repealing the compulsory features, which were the principal target of the opposition in the wheat referendum in May. Otherwise it would make little change in the program which our Agriculture Committees considered very carefully, and the Congress enacted about a year ago.

I have submitted this proposal to agricultural analysts in the Legislative Reference Service and had it studied and discussed unofficially with experts at the Department of Agriculture. Without any exception, the experts who have been consulted have agreed that the voluntary wheat certificate plan, with the penalty provisions for overplanting wheat acreage allotments removed, would achieve very desirable results.

First. They report that it would permit farm income to go to a more favorable level than any other voluntary program which has been proposed. If the compulsory wheat certificate plan had been adopted, wheat producers in 1964 would have received 70 cents per bushel certificates on 950 million bushels of food and export wheat, enhancing their income $665 million. They could, by voluntary action, get certificates up to this full amount under the proposal now being introduced.

Second. The proposal would permit continued orderly reduction in Government stocks of wheat. The analysts believe that 70 to 80 percent of producers, and a like amount of the total wheat crop, would be in voluntary compliance to become eligible for certificates, thereby reducing production sufficiently to allow sale of some wheat from CCC stocks.

Third. The proposal would reduce Government costs.

Fourth. The proposal would avoid any increase in the price of food since the price of wheat for food use would remain stable.

I feel very strongly that Congress should take early action to avert overproduction and a deep cut in the income of wheat farmers in 1964. Consequently, I think that this proposal, or the proposal to extend for another year or two the old voluntary acreage reduction program effective on this year's crop, or any other constructive suggestion, should have early consideration by Congress.

It is true that wheat farmers rejected a compulsory certificate plan in May by a majority of "No" votes. It is true that the Food and Agriculture Act of 1962 provided an alternative in such an event: 50 percent of parity price supports for those producers of wheat who stay within their share of a national acreage allotment. This is support at about $1.25 per bushel compared to an average support of $1.81 per bushel on the 1963 crop.

It is also true that there is little demand for enactment of a new wheat program coming to Members of Congress from the country. A wheat crop is now being harvested which will bring producers prices based on food value. The effect of the May referendum will not be felt directly for another year. The effect will be evident July, 1964, after another wheat harvest has started, and after it is too late to do anything about controlling the size of the crop or preventing a price break. Then farmers will find that their wheat is bringing only $1.25 per bushel or less and then the full effects of the May referendum will be felt.

In my opinion, it is our obligation, as the elected representatives of the citizens of the Nation, to be foresighted and to avoid just such serious developments, whether there is demand from the country or not. We do not postpone the military defense of our country until we are attacked and our citizens are crying for help. Neither should we delay now in taking steps to safeguard our agricultural economy against an otherwise certain disaster a year hence.

Unless something is done before winter wheat planting gets well underway in the Southern wheat-producing States in late August and September—within 60 days from now—we can expect a 1964 wheat crop of several hundred million bushels more than our needs, and an unnecessary drop in farm income of a half billion dollars or more.

obliged to accept his bill as a condition for gaining support from him and other Plains states legislators for forthcoming cotton legislation.

But as the summer progressed, the heated integration battle stalled cotton legislation. Meanwhile crop failures within the Soviet bloc raised the prospect for a painless reduction in surplus wheat stocks through sales of wheat to Communist countries. On October 10th President Kennedy gave U.S. approval for an initial sale to the Soviet Union, backed by the U.S. Chamber of Commerce and most farm leaders but opposed by major Republican spokesmen who promised to make this an issue in future election campaigns. Initial bargaining was for about 150 million bushels in the anticipation that the Soviets might enter one-year purchase agreements for as much as 500 million of the more than one billion bushels in the U.S. wheat surplus. At the same time it was noted that if America decided to drop the barriers against trade with the agriculturally backward Soviet bloc, America's farm abundance might ultimately become a far greater source of economic strength in international affairs, and the supply-management policies such as proposed by Willard Cochrane and vetoed by farmers would be largely a thing of the past. This was as yet but a fond hope.

McGovern's voluntary-certificate plan continued to pick up support, especially from the Democratic side, while the USDA began an agonizing reappraisal of the mandatory programs for supply management.

Then an assassin's bullet struck down President Kennedy.

The Transition

As President Kennedy had done, President Johnson chose to make a fight for new legislation. The resulting battle, in the spring of 1964, was in many respects similar to the one in 1962: use of extraordinary procedures by Republicans to delay action beyond the deadline for a 1964 wheat program, and by Democrats to shortcut ordinary processes; bitter, partisan struggles in committee and on the floor; a regional, rural-urban Democratic coalition put together by the administration and Democratic congressional leaders (who—

it will be recalled—had told wheat farmers there would likely be no new legislation before the next crop in the event of a referendum defeat); and—making every effort to defeat the bill—a coalition of conservative Democrats and most Republicans led by the Farm Bureau, which had earlier promised farmers Congress would pass new legislation before the next crop in the event that farmers voted down the mandatory wheat program.

In some respects the fight was different. The wheat bill—the voluntary version of the 1962 wheat certificate program—was now regarded as a congressional product even though the administration had supported it and perfected it. Furthermore, it was not to be a permanent program: a two-year authorization was as much as wheat producers could hope to win.

In 1964, too, the wheat provision had different legislative companions. A cotton bill had passed the House a few days after President Kennedy's death, providing a subsidy which would permit U.S. textile firms to buy domestic cotton at the same price it commanded abroad. The Senate passed this cotton bill March 6th, in a revised form favored by Southerners, and attached to it the voluntary wheat-certificate bill.

With just one month remaining in which to act on legislation for the 1964 wheat crop, House Democratic leaders sought a rule for debate which would prevent amendments to the Senate-passed bill and thus prevent the need for a conference committee or other further action following House passage. (To blunt the criticism that the wheat bill had not been properly considered in the House, the Agriculture Committee reported out a bill containing the voluntary wheat certificate program.)

Another companion to the 1964 wheat program was a food-stamp program, which a number of urban Democrats had demanded as the price for their crucial votes on the wheat-cotton bill. Assisted by heavy pressure from the administration which arranged this link-up among food stamps, wheat, and cotton, Chairman Cooley pried a food-stamp bill out of his reluctant House Agriculture Committee. After stalling for precious days, Representative Howard Smith's House Rules Committee provided the procedural arrangements desired by Democratic leaders, with the result that both the commodity and the food-stamp bills were passed in a long stormy House session which concluded at midnight, April 8th. President Johnson signed the wheat-cotton bill April 11th.

As in 1962, the bill passed by the barest margin—211–203, and only after severe pressure had been brought by the administration, after a grass-roots campaign by the National Farmers Organization, and after an expensive, widespread advertising campaign conducted by the Farmers Union GTA.

The Farm Bureau had again put forth a vigorous effort to defeat the bill, overriding protests of Southern members who supported the cotton provision. President Shuman explained—

> I'm sure that if wheat farmers were given a chance to vote on the Administration's proposed wheat program, they would vote it down. It's basically the same scheme they rejected in 1963 and gives the Secretary of Agriculture tremendous authority to determine wheat prices and allocate the use of wheat.[1]

Shuman looked forward to battling the certificate program again in 1965. Supporters of the certificate program looked to the future apprehensively, because they would need to fashion a new coalition. The Farm Bureau took comfort from the fact that only a third of the nation's wheat producers decided to participate in the new program, and the USDA took its comfort from the fact that over three-fourths of the total wheat allotment was nevertheless enrolled, which indicated that a large proportion of the commercial wheat producers were participating.

The administration turned to other pressing agriculture problems: a dairy program was needed, and it was also decided to reopen the question as to whether taxpayers could afford the $1.3-billion annual expenditure for the voluntary feed-grains program. Willard Cochrane—who had predicted that the voluntary program would prove too expensive—returned to his teaching post at the University of Minnesota. John Schnittker became Freeman's principal economic adviser.

[1] *AFBF Newsletter*, April 6, 1964.

Epilogue: *The Legacy of the Kennedy Administration*

THE KENNEDY administration left an impressive list of initiatives and accomplishments in rural development, new land use, food distribution, and new legislation to deal with feed grains, wheat, and cotton. The administration made a good start on the reduction of farm surpluses.

The USDA, under President Kennedy's leadership, gained a wealth of experience in considering new legislative procedures, and in testing what Congress and farmers would accept—or reject.

The day the farmers said "no" was likely to be well remembered in policy planning. The USDA was on notice that farm organizations would campaign—and campaign vigorously—at the grass roots, for and against government programs.

New leaders, new programs, old problems will continue to meet. Issues concerning food and fiber are never resolved; they are only temporarily accommodated. New decisions for accommodation will need new case studies.

Index